THE
RYDER
CUP

Foreword

Golf has been my passion since I can remember and turning professional in 1962 was a very proud moment for me. It was the culmination of years of dedication, laced with a lot of fun along the way. The game has taken me all over the world and I have been lucky to play in all the great tournaments against some of the finest golfers of all time.

I took part in my first Major – The Open – in 1963. Just standing on the first tee was such a thrill – with over a century of history behind it, being involved in that kind of competition was exactly what I had always dreamed of. That dream then turned into beautiful reality in 1969 when I had the pleasure of lifting the Claret Jug myself. The following year was just as special when I had the honour of winning the US Open.

As well as the competitive side of golf, the game has a set of principles that have always meant a lot to me. Its good grace, sportsmanship and integrity have made it a beacon among sports. Nowhere is this epitomized more than in the Ryder Cup, as I personally experienced in 1969 when Jack Nicklaus famously conceded my final putt, which resulted in the tournament being tied. Samuel Ryder, the Englishman who started this unique competition back in 1927, was very keen that the Cup that bears his name should be contested in the right spirit. That moment in 1969 would have made him proud.

But this does not mean that the Ryder Cup is a friendly exhibition match – far from it. It has always been played with an intense competitiveness that has captured the imagination of players and fans alike, who turn up in their tens of thousands to see the best players from both sides of the Atlantic go head-to-head. But at the end of the competition, win or lose, the players should always be able to raise a glass or two together.

I'm proud to say that I've been a player on what is now the European Ryder Cup team on seven occasions. The tension, drama and atmosphere of each of those Cups will live with me forever but my time as captain stands out. It was my great privilege to be the four-time captain who broke the American stranglehold on the competition in the mid-1980s. As if the European win in 1985 – its first since 1957 – wasn't momentous enough, the 1987 event was even more special as Europe won the Cup on US soil for the first time ever. I'm delighted to say that those wins, plus retaining the Cup in 1989, contributed to reigniting the Ryder Cup as a hotly contested event, one that is obviously still fiercely fought over today.

So I hope you enjoy reading about all the Ryder Cups in this book – the stories, titanic tussles and endless talking points make this a fascinating read.

Tony Jacklin CBE

OPPOSITE: *Tony Jacklin, captain of the European team, celebrates winning the 27th Ryder Cup in September 1987 at Muirfield Village, Ohio, USA.*

Introduction

There's something unique about the Ryder Cup, something that lifts it above other sporting occasions, that almost defies explanation. Maybe it's the unique team-play format. Or maybe it's the "us-versus-them" aspect of a game more usually associated with individual play that resonates so loudly over three tense, action-packed days. But whatever the reason, the end result is something truly special.

IT'S NOT EASY TO SUM UP what the Ryder Cup means to those who follow it avidly or to explain why the competition resonates so profoundly with the players themselves but over the next seven chapters, in which the story of golf's greatest team competition from its earliest beginnings in England to the high-octane drama of the current era will be recounted, the essence of one of the world's most remarkable sporting battles will surely start to embrace anyone who comes into contact with it, too.

   Of course, every golf fan has his or her own theory about what makes the Ryder Cup so unique. Perhaps it's the fact that in this modern, materialistic world, the competition generates such

immense passion and drama, even though there is nothing more than a golden trophy at stake – the players, teams and PGAs receive no revenue whatsoever for lifting it. Maybe it's because it combines individual head-to-head battles so easily with team play and team spirit or could it be the interaction of the crowd, who get closer to both the action and their heroes than in almost any other sporting event? But whatever the reason the Ryder Cup can justly claim to be right up there with the most iconic sporting trophies in the world.

   When the world's greatest golfers step out onto the 1st tee on the first day of each Ryder Cup, chills run down the spines of each

and every one of them – even superstars such as Bubba Watson or Rory McIlroy, who have been there and done it many times before. Those involved in future Ryder Cups will be following in the footsteps of some of the finest golfers ever seen, men like Arnold Palmer, Nick Faldo, Jack Nicklaus, Seve Ballesteros, Tom Watson, Colin Montgomerie, Tiger Woods, Tony Jacklin… the list reads like a Who's Who of golfing legends.

But the modern superstars already have an aura of their own; stars such as Europe's Ian Poulter and José María Olazábal, the player turned captain, who helped inspire the remarkable comeback win now known as the Miracle at Medinah in 2012.

America's Phil Mickleson was a key man at Medinah too, before playing a record tenth consecutive Ryder Cup when the teams met at Gleneagles in 2014. Englishman Justin Rose was the highest scorer with four points at Gleneagles and Northern Irishman McIlroy is now seen by many as the new Tiger. He has a challenger in the USA's own upstart Rickie Fowler who was just 21 when he played so well at Celtic Manor in 2010. The raw talents of Americans Jordan Spieth and Patrick Reed look to have long Ryder Cup careers ahead too.

There was a time in the post-war period that the USA was so dominant against Great Britain (almost always winning the trophy, often by large margins) that the future of the event as a properly competitive match was in jeopardy, but this is no longer the case.

Since the Great Britain team first opened up to include players from the Irish Republic, then players from all over continental Europe in 1979, matches have become increasingly competitive and passionate. That newfound competitiveness has its roots in a pulsating history that includes so many iconic tussles – for example, the "War on the Shore" at Kiawah Island in 1991, when controversy reigned on the back of Gulf War symbolism; the Battle of Brookline in 1999 when the USA came from 16-10 down to win on the final day in controversial but dramatic fashion. But the true spirit of the Ryder Cup is still the cornerstone of the whole event, shown most clearly of all by "The Concession" of 1969, when Jack Nicklaus conceded a putt to Tony Jacklin that saw the Cup tied.

These are just some of the moments that have built the Ryder Cup and today it ranks among the greatest, and most eagerly anticipated, sporting contests in the world. Not bad for a tournament that began in the mid-1920s with a round of golf and sandwiches at the Wentworth course in England. This book tells the whole story of every Ryder Cup – a story that gets richer and more compelling with every tournament.

BELOW (left to right): *Ryder Cup legends: Abe Mitchell and Samuel Ryder; Jack Nicklaus and Tom Watson (crouching); José María Olazábal and Severiano Ballesteros; Phil Mickelson and Tiger Woods.*

CHAPTER ONE
FROM HUMBLE BEGINNINGS

The Great Britain and USA teams pose with the Ryder Cup in 1929. Samuel Ryder (front centre, with moustache) is flanked by Britain's George Duncan (left, with the Cup) and the USA's Walter Hagen (right, arms folded).

The Ryder Cup is one of the most highly anticipated and intensely hyped sporting events on earth, but it hasn't always been this way. The story begins more than 90 years ago with a gentle exhibition match, the brainchild of an English businessman who was determined to see his idea take root.

A New Competition

The two key facts that any fan of the Ryder Cup often knows are that English merchant Samuel Ryder founded the competition and the very first one was staged in 1927. But what if both those assumptions were wrong or told only half the story? For golf historians, the debate surrounding the origins of one of sport's most iconic competitions still lives on.

ENGLISH BUSINESSMAN, BENEFACTOR and social riser Samuel Ryder, who donated the trophy and worked tirelessly to see the competition introduced, has become synonymous with the most prestigious team tournament in golf and one of the world's biggest sporting occasions. Indeed, his name still adorns the trophy and is recognized by golf fans across the globe – even though he himself was never a professional golfer and only came to the game late in life at the age of 50 at the suggestion of his church minister, after giving up cricket.

It's down to Ryder that the competition still exists in largely the same format as it began and maybe this too generates the kind of friendly rivalry and bonhomie between players that makes golf so different from other sports. In fact, to this day you'll hear players and commentators talk about "honouring the spirit of Sam Ryder" whenever putts are conceded or fair play is adhered to. In short, there's no doubt that Ryder is the Cup's founding father and without his investment, enthusiasm and support, this celebrated event would never have taken off. But was it necessarily his vision that created the competition in the first place? After all, for several years there had been talk of a Great Britain v USA tournament before Samuel Ryder took up his new interest and at least two other characters can claim to have played a part in the origins of the format.

In America, Ohio businessman Sylvanus P. Jermain encouraged English professionals Harry Vardon and Edward Ray to compete in the 1920 US Open at his home course of Inverness, and many regard him as the man who sparked the competition to life. Jermain believed in the worldwide appeal of golf and in an annual play-off between British and American professionals; reports suggest Walter Ross, president of the Nickel Plate Railroad Company in Cleveland, offered to pay for a trophy to kick-start the competition. So, if events had turned out differently, we might have been looking forward to the Ross Cup or the Jermain Trophy at the Medinah Country Club in Illinois, 2012.

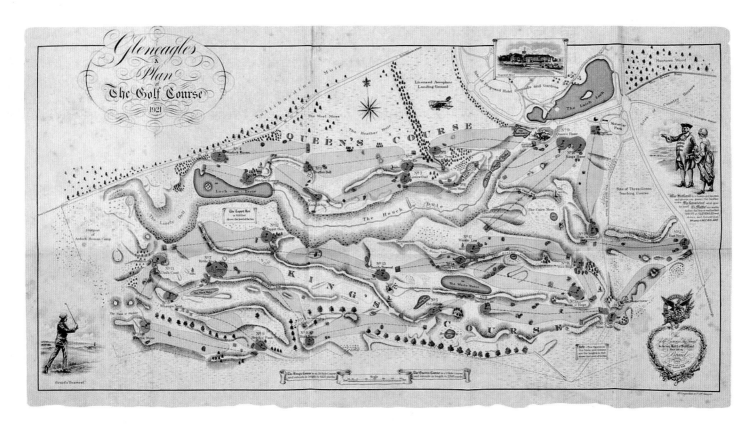

ABOVE: *A map outlining the design of the newly opened King's Course at Gleneagles, designed by James Braid, that staged the first Great Britain v USA match in 1921.*

It could just as easily have been the Harnett Cup, too, because the circulation manager of *Golf Illustrated* magazine, James Harnett, played a major role in making the Ryder Cup what it is today. Encouraged by support from Walter Hagen, possibly the greatest American golfer of his time and a player who would later win the British Open, Harnett began raising the finance to send a representative team of US golfers across the Atlantic to compete in a challenge match. In the end he couldn't quite achieve his goal, but the resulting publicity generated by the venture was crucial in opening up future possibilities for the expansion of the game. It proved there was an appetite for the venture among the golfing public and when the Professional Golfers' Association discussed the prospect, it proposed to advance Harnett enough money to finally make it happen.

At this stage, the only barrier was the opposition of PGA president John Mackie who, rightly with hindsight, disapproved of plans to fill the team with British professionals working in America in a bid to make the tournament more competitive (the suggestion being at this early stage in the game's history, US professionals were unlikely to make an impact). Mackie approved the motion only after a rule change was agreed, requiring players to have lived in the USA for at least five years before they could qualify for the American team. An important decision in the history of the Ryder Cup, it underlined an intention to create not just an exhibition match but also a serious and passionate competition between rival countries. And anyone lucky enough to have attended a Ryder Cup in the modern era – there were 35,000 fans on course at Celtic Manor in 2010 to witness Europe's narrow victory – will testify patriotic fervour only adds to the spectacle and importance of the occasion.

The first Britain v USA match was scheduled for June 6, 1921 on the King's Course at Gleneagles, Scotland. Suddenly the early seeds of the Ryder Cup were being sown, even though it would be another six years before the event really came to fruition. At this stage no one could have predicted the format would become so successful, so important, nor indeed, so loved, but on both sides of the Atlantic, a vision was now in place and was about to be realized.

RIGHT: *Sylvanus P. Jermain (right) was first to promote a Great Britain v USA match. Left is US golfer Bobby Jones.*

THE GLORY GAME

It may be some 86 years since its inception but the Ryder Cup has stayed true to its early values and one feature makes the competition stand out from almost every other major sporting event in the twenty-first century: no financial reward is offered. Indeed, profits from the tournament are split between the relevant PGAs, with much of it spent on development or charity projects. But the match itself is for glory only and there is no prize fund.

Crossing the Atlantic

When a team of American golfers – you could even call them the first Ryder Cup combatants, even if at this stage there was still no Cup to play for – arrived in Southampton, in 1921, there must have been a real sense of expectation and excitement. They would have little idea just what pioneers they would prove to be, especially when not everything went to plan. Having crossed the Atlantic by boat, America's top golfers faced the long trek to Scotland by sleeper train and one can only imagine just how tired they must have been after finally ending up in Perthshire. These days, of course, the Ryder Cup is regarded as glamorous and prestigious – the very pinnacle of sport. But the Americans arrived in Scotland to find that they were to sleep in five converted train carriages shunted into the sidings of a local train station. The sight of the US golfing greats fetching and carrying their own water would no doubt leave some of today's professionals wincing, but this is where it all began: six years before the first Ryder Cup officially took place.

The British team that day was filled with talent, including six-time Open champion Harry Vardon, James Braid, Ted Ray and Abe Mitchell. With Josh Taylor, James Ockendon, James Sherlock, Arthur Havers and George Duncan also selected, the home side were strong favourites for a match that strangely seemed to generate little enthusiasm, just weeks after Britain had lost 9-3 to the USA in an amateur competition at Royal Liverpool. It was also played 24 hours after the end of the prestigious *Glasgow Herald* 1000 Guineas, won by George Duncan, and therefore took place in front of a sparse crowd, who would have had no idea they were watching history in the making. Compare this to the scenes at Celtic Manor in Wales (2010), when a weekly total of 244,000 enthusiastic fans paid to watch Europe's memorable victory over a US team that included some of the legends of modern golf, among them Tiger Woods and Phil Mickelson.

POOR SHOW

American golfer Walter Hagen may have played a major role in the birth of the Ryder Cup, but professional golfers were not always treated so well in England. At the British Open of 1920, Hagen was forced to hire a Pierce-Arrow motor car to serve as his personal dressing room after being refused entry to the clubhouse dressing room.

LEFT: *Stylish American golfer Walter Hagen, a big character and a big influence on the growth of the Ryder Cup.*

RIGHT: *The British team that faced the USA at Gleneagles in 1921.*

The Americans of 1921 were not quite so well known and certainly not in Britain, where even two-times US Open winner Hagen was not yet a household name, although the crowd would have at least recognized Scottish exiles, Jock Hutchinson and Fred McLeod. Captained by Emmett French, the team also included virtual unknowns Clarence Hackney and Bill Mehlhorn – a real character who wore cowboy hats on course and was naturally nicknamed "Wild Bill". Wild Bill went on to play in the first Ryder Cup in 1927 and became a real favourite with the galleries long before Thomas Brent "Boo" Weekley famously "rode" down the fairway using his golf club as a horse during the 2008 Ryder Cup. At this stage he was hardly a legend with fans in Scotland and it came as no surprise to see the British trounce their visitors 9-3 in what proved to be a somewhat unheralded sideshow.

The players were presented with gold medals, courtesy of the *Herald*, but the match turned out to be such a walkover that even the home newspaper was scarcely filled with pieces calling for the competition to become a regular event. Stories of the US Ambassador driving up from London for the presentations only to make a hasty exit after learning his team had been trounced suggest no political will for the format, either. To their frustration, Harnett and Hagen's great vision of a regular Britain v USA tournament appeared doomed for hardly anyone had turned up to watch, the players barely socialized together and the British press seemed to have taken an instant dislike to the notion. But looking back, it's almost as if the Ryder Cup was destined to survive for over the next few years the competition between British and American golfers increased steadily, while the debate over which country's players were the stronger grew ever more intense.

Hagen certainly played a part, returning to Britain to win The Open in 1922 and 1924, with Britain's Arthur Havers securing the title in between after George Duncan won in 1920. Suddenly golf's greatest prize was being shared between two nations and all the fans wanted to know was: who would win in a play-off?

Ryder Cup legends
Samuel **RYDER**

In early twentieth-century England, Samuel Ryder was an enormously successful businessman. He was well thought of in civic circles and a generous benefactor in his local community, but his life – and the lives of so many others – was changed from the moment a friend suggested he should take up golf.

Most people have heard of the Ryder Cup, but how many of them would be able to tell you who it was that the competition is named after? In fact, the man whose name graces the coveted trophy was an English entrepreneur and businessman, who made his fortune selling packets of "penny" seeds. Generous though he undoubtedly was, and successful as he became, the memory of Samuel would surely not have endured until today, had a friend not handed him a piece of casual advice in 1908.

Having gone through a period of illness and injury, Ryder had given up his favourite sport of cricket and therefore needed an alternative pastime. His friend Frank Wheeler, preacher at Trinity Congregational Church in St Albans, suggested that he should try golf as a way to get more fresh air. Ryder duly hired a local golfer to give him personal lessons at his Hertfordshire mansion and practised relentlessly until he was good enough to join his local club, Verulam. Within two years, he had risen to the role of captain and national golfing promoter in three. Of course, the rest is history.

An incredible turn of events was set in place the day Wheeler made his suggestion. Maybe he knew Ryder would take his words to heart, because whether it was supporting city charities for the poor or helping the elderly, or even staging high-profile fund-raising events at his home, Marlborough House (including garden fêtes and concerts), Ryder was always involved in some kind of project. Very soon, golf – and in particular, promoting golfing events – became his all-consuming project. By June 1924, he had already placed an article in the *Herts Advertiser* stating his firm, Heath & Heather, "were contemplating challenging the Americans to a match".

Born in Walton-le-Dale (a village outside Preston in Lancashire, England) on March 24, 1858, Samuel Ryder was one of eight children of Samuel (a professional gardener) and Elizabeth (a dressmaker), and his early experience of poverty in northern England made him all the more determined to provide employment for others in the future. Having started work in his father's business, he eventually made his fortune as a seed merchant, selling penny packets of seed via mail order just as the British homemaker's interest in gardening took off. After moving to St Albans, where he set up a new company with his brother James, selling herbal remedies, Samuel's life really took off.

Whether at church (Samuel was a Methodist), in business, working for charities or carrying out civic duties (later, he became mayor of St Albans, as well as a magistrate and alderman), it seems Ryder threw himself into these roles with equal vigour – just as he did in golf. Within two years of starting lessons, he was a big name at Verulam and his love affair with golf was to have huge knock-on benefits for the sport, enriching the lives of so many for almost 100 years. Samuel made large donations to the club, where he was appointed captain in 1911, 1926 and 1927. He swiftly brought his handicap down to single figures, too, which gives an insight into the determination of the man.

As a promoter he first tinkered with the prospect of staging team matches in 1923 when Heath & Heather attracted the cream of British golf (including six Open champions) to play a challenge match. It was the first time that every player who turned up for such a match was paid expenses for appearing – and so the world of golf sat up and took notice. Ryder's growing friendship with British star Abe Mitchell also had a major impact on his status, especially when he took on his newfound partner as a personal coach, paying him an annual salary. The plan was to give Mitchell the time to practise and progress his own career. Sadly, he didn't achieve his great dream of winning the British Open, but it is Mitchell's likeness that graces the golden Ryder Cup trophy, earning him a place in history all the same.

It was Ryder who made the greatest contribution towards the moulding of the solid gold trophy produced by London jeweller Mappin & Webb and presented for the first time at Worcester Country Club, Massachusetts in 1927. Two years later, he himself presented the Cup in the first home match at Moortown, handing it to British captain George Duncan. In that moment a personal dream came true and a golfing phenomenon began.

Samuel Ryder died, aged 77, in 1936 and was fittingly buried at Hatfield Road Cemetery in St Albans with his favourite five-iron.

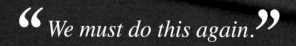

" *We must do this again.* **"**

Samuel Ryder addresses players after a Great Britain vs. USA challenge match in 1926

12 U.S. GOLF PROS TO INVADE ENGLAND

Hagen Will Captain Team That Will Meet Force Headed by George Duncan.

CONTINGENT SAILS MAY 26

Matches Between American and British Stars Will Be Played at Wentworth, Near London.

PINEHURST, N. C., April 4.—The strongest golf team ever to represent the United States, composed of twelve American professionals, will meet the British pros at team play in Great Britain this coming Summer, according to Walter Hagen.

Hagen has been working on plans for the matches during the past month and has decided to ask more pros than the original four for whom he was allowed $1,000. The professionals, eager to play, have waived all rights to a guarantee of $250 each and are willing to split the $1,000 among the whole team.

Hagen will name a committee of four or five leading players to pick the team. It is up to the British, according to Hagen, to name as many players as they like. If more than twelve are named it is likely the British will call on some of their famous old-timers, including Harry Vardon, J. H. Taylor, James Braid, and Sandy Herd.

George Duncan is captain of the British team and some of his team-mates are Abe Mitchell, Archie Compston, Arthur Havers, the Whitcomb brothers, Jimmy Ockenden, Ted Ray, Sid Wingate, George Gadd, Len Holland and Jimmy Ellis. Several younger players who may be added include Jolly, Boomer and Murray.

The First Competition

The seeds of the Ryder Cup had clearly been sown by this stage, not just by merchant Sam Ryder, but by others, too, and so the next question to look at is when was the very first competition played? The history books all state 1927, no questions asked and no arguments. In fact, a competition played a year earlier in England might have been the starting point, even if the PGA doesn't recognize the fact.

With interest in the rivalry between British and American golfers growing by the day, the public's appetite for a team competition to compare and contrast the great stars of the game had become increasingly obvious by 1926. And the first chance to test the depth of interest came at Wentworth that very year in what some have described as the "lost Ryder Cup". Certainly, it was here that the name Samuel Ryder first became important, and his part in turning the dream into a reality is unquestionable.

Over the last few years, the successful merchant – who came up with the concept of selling seeds to amateur gardeners in "penny packets" and lived in St Albans, Hertfordshire (just north of London) – had become the main talking point of many a fairway after ploughing funds into his new love. However, he only took up golf at the age of 50 because he could no longer play cricket and was advised by his local Methodist minister to try something new. Following this, he spent a fortune on lessons – first from his local club pro, John Hill, and then English legend, Abe Mitchell. Within a year, Ryder had joined his local club – Verulam – and 12 months later, had already been elected club captain. By 1923, his interest in the sport was all-consuming and so he began, along with his brother James and their new company, Heath & Heather (herbal remedies), to sponsor professional tournaments at Verulam. All competitors were paid an appearance fee of £5 (approximately $25 at the time), while the winner was awarded £50 ($250). These were astronomical sums (that year, the winner of The Open received just £75 ($375)) and so Ryder's event attracted some of

THE BIRTH OF AN IDEA

The "Eureka" moment that put the Ryder Cup in motion took place, according to Ryder's daughter, Marjorie (who produced a booklet about her father in 1979), at Came Down Golf Club in Dorset during a holiday game with club professional Ernest Whitcombe. Ernest casually remarked to his opponent: "The Americans come over here smartly dressed and backed by wealthy supporters, the Britisher has a poor chance compared to that." His comment clearly struck a nerve and in that moment Ryder vowed to do something about it.

LEFT: *A local newspaper reports the birth of the Ryder Cup as a team of American golfers heads to England in 1926 in a forerunner of the competition.*

ABOVE: *Samuel Ryder (right) greets friend and inspiration Abe Mitchell, the golfer whose likeness would adorn the Ryder Cup trophy.*

British golf's biggest names, from Harry Vardon to James Braid, George Duncan to Open champion, Arthur Havers.

Ryder's subsequent friendship with Abe Mitchell saw him pay the Englishman £500 ($2,500) a year to be his personal coach. Reportedly, his primary concern was not his own tuition, but to give Mitchell the time and funds to further his own career and achieve his dream of winning the British Open. Sadly, Mitchell was never able to do this but it wasn't long before golf's newest benefactor made his own considerable impact as he woke up to the excitement of team golf. In 1926, he pitted Harry Vardon and J.H. Taylor against James Braid and Alex Herd in an England v Scotland match at Verulam, noting the enthusiasm with which the event was received. Then, a few months later, came the beginnings of the Ryder Cup.

On April 26, 1926, Samuel Ryder announced in the Press that he had presented a trophy for an annual competition between British and American golfers to be played at Wentworth prior to The Open. His decision was perhaps sparked by the news that The Open – to be played at Royal Lytham & St Annes – was oversubscribed and the Royal and Ancient had therefore opted to stage three regional pre-qualifying tournaments. Naturally, the Americans arriving by boat in Southampton were allocated to the southern event at Sunningdale, giving Ryder the perfect excuse: everything, including a squad of 12 US golfers, was already in place.

> **❝***I trust that the effect of this match will be to influence a cordial, friendly and peaceful feeling throughout the whole civilized world. I look upon the Royal and Ancient game as being a powerful force that influences the best things in humanity.***❞**

Samuel Ryder's vision for the Ryder Cup

US captain Walter Hagen tees off at Wentworth in 1926, when Great Britain beat a much-weakened American team, 13.5-1.5.

The First Cup

With Ted Ray captaining the British team and Walter Hagen leading the American challenge, Wentworth hosted a moment in history on June 4 and June 5, 1926, when Samuel Ryder's vision became reality. As a contest it was destined to be scrubbed from the record books but its importance should never be overlooked.

Like its predecessor of 1921, the "lost" Ryder Cup match proved something of a walkover, with a strong British team trouncing their rivals, 13.5 to 1.5, but this time the interest was far greater as an enthusiastic crowd followed the players around the West Course. The British team, which included former Open champions Ted Ray, George Duncan and Arthur Havers, as well as Abe Mitchell, Archie Compston, Fred Robson, Ernest Whitcombe, Herbert Jolly, Aubrey Bloomer and George Gadd, was far too good to suffer serious setbacks, winning all five Foursomes on the opening Friday.

In the nine singles matches scheduled for the next day, highlights included a remarkable 6 and 5 victory for Duncan against Hagen – who had all-too readily accepted an invitation to play in his second Britain v USA clash. Mitchell, watched by his friend Ryder, thrashed Jim Barnes, 8 and 7 – although this time the match and the post-match presentations were much more convivial than in Scotland five years earlier, with Ryder in particular revelling in the camaraderie.

In fairness to the Americans, they were unable to field their strongest side after the Great Strike of May that year complicated travel arrangements – meaning the US team included guests such as Scotland's Fred McLeod and Tommy Armour, England's Jim Barnes and Joe Stain, plus Australian Joe Kirkwood. Players of the calibre of Gene Sarazen, who would go on to become a Ryder Cup legend, were unable to make it – and the United States PGA was understandably reluctant to recognize it as an official result. Even so, in many ways, this was the first Ryder Cup and the main reason why it is not included in the record books is because the trophy itself was never presented.

A report from Harnett's *Golf Illustrated* of June 11, 1926 provides the ultimate explanation, which even appeared under the headline "Ryder Cup".

BELOW: *US captain Walter Hagen (left) greets opposite number Ted Ray prior to playing Great Britain at Wentworth in 1926.*

RIGHT: *Scottish professional Tommy Armour lines up a shot at Wentworth in 1926 – but he was playing for the USA, not Great Britain.*

COMMISSIONING THE TROPHY

Much debate reigns over the sequence of events that led to the Ryder Cup trophy being commissioned. An alternative view may be found on the Cup's official website, where it is suggested Samuel Ryder took tea with British team members, George Duncan and Abe Mitchell, and the American Emmett French, after the match in 1926. It was Duncan who ventured the suggestion that Ryder might provide a trophy, to which he immediately agreed. Of course, we may never know for certain which version of events is true.

It read:

Owing to the uncertainty of the situation following the Strike in which it was not known until a few days ago how many American professionals would be visiting Great Britain, Mr J Ryder decided to withhold the cup, which he has offered for annual competition between the professionals of Great Britain and America. Under these circumstances the Wentworth Club provided the British players with gold medals to mark the inauguration of this great international match.

The success of the event, although never made official, further encouraged Samuel Ryder in his belief that the idea of an annual challenge match was now feasible and his trophy would not be wasted. In fact, he had already paid £100 ($500) towards its making, with *Golf Illustrated* adding another £100 ($500) and the Royal and Ancient Golf Club of St Andrews £50 ($250). It was initially unveiled a year later when the first true Ryder Cup took place in Worcester, Massachusetts.

By that time the trophy, which included a likeness of Ryder's great friend, Abe Mitchell, had been hallmarked 1927, so one must wonder whether it had ever been ready to present at Wentworth at all, even if the Americans had arrived at Southampton with a full team on board. Whatever the reasons for the "lost" Ryder Cup of 1926, a year later the most famous trophy in team golf was about to be presented. It would create a dynasty even its founding father could never have imagined.

> *❝I will give £5 ($25) to each of the winning players, and give a party afterwards, with champagne and chicken sandwiches.❞*

Samuel Ryder introduces his new competition

1927
USA 9.5
Great Britain 2.5

Worcester CC, Massachusetts

June 3-4

THE COURSE

Worcester Country Club
Location: Worcester,
Massachusetts, USA
Par: 72
Yards: 6,422

Designed by Donald Ross in 1913, Worcester Country Club had just staged the US Open in 1925 and is the only course to have staged the US Open, Ryder Cup and the US Women's Open. US captain Walter Hagen already had happy memories – two years earlier, he had scored his first hole-in-one there.

Worcester Country Club in Massachusetts holds a special place in Ryder Cup history because it was here, on June 3, 1927, that Samuel Ryder's great dream finally came to fruition. Unfortunately Ryder himself wasn't able to be there to see it, and the United States put down a marker for the future by scoring an emphatic victory against their rivals from across the Atlantic.

THE SIGHT OF US CAPTAIN Walter Hagen lifting the golden trophy for the first time must have sent a shiver down the spines of the men who had worked so hard to make it happen. But it would be wrong to give the impression that the event had been all plain sailing and had not taken a huge amount of effort – and money – to get it off the ground. Just getting the British team to America was no mean feat, given the distances and costs of the travel involved, and it took time and effort for the necessary finance to be raised. In fact, an appeal launched by George Philpot, editor of *Golf Weekly* for £3,000 ($15,000 at mid-1920s prices), fell on deaf ears, much to the chagrin of the magazine as it ran an editorial criticizing the "indifferences or selfishness" of golfers and golf clubs who opted not to pay.

Only 216 out of the 1,750 clubs that were contacted replied with a donation and even after a £500 ($2,500) contribution from Sam Ryder himself, there was a significant shortfall. It was eventually made up by Philpot, who contributed £500 ($2,500) of his own money to the project and was subsequently named team manager. His problems were then exacerbated by the news that Abe Mitchell, Ryder's friend, confidant and inspiration, had been struck down with appendicitis just as the team was due to leave London. It was a major blow for this was the man earmarked as captain for the first Ryder Cup, whose very likeness adorned the trophy.

Herbert Jolly was added to the squad and the experienced Ted Ray chosen as new captain. The Jersey-born golfer had learned his trade at the same course as the legendary Harry Vardon and

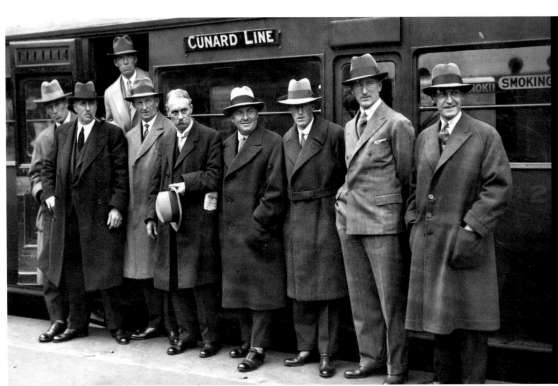

LEFT: *Samuel Ryder joins the British Ryder Cup team as they prepare to leave London en route to Massachusetts.*

OPPOSITE: *Late call-up Herbert Jolly practises his swing on the deck of a ship as he rushes to join the British team in America.*

was beloved by fans for his daring play and genial character. He was, by any stretch of the imagination, past his prime at 50, but considering he had won the US Open aged 43, it was decided his vast experience would serve the team well.

The next hurdle to clear was simply making it to America. After a particularly rough six-day crossing on the RMS *Aquitania*, the team arrived, tired and ill. And once they landed in New York, they were rushed to a glitzy reception organized by American captain Hagen. Limousines flanked by police officers whisked them off on a hectic schedule of sightseeing that included a gala at the Westchester Biltmore Country Club and an evening spent watching the New York Yankees.

By the time Ray's team got to practise they were in a whirl, but alert enough to turn down a last-minute request from their hosts to change the format to include Fourballs instead of Foursomes (known as "Scotch Foursomes" in the USA and rarely played); for two points instead of one to be awarded for a Fourballs' victory; and for matches level after 36 holes to be continued until there was a clear winner. Indeed, the only concession made by British team manager Philpot was to allow both teams to substitute a player in the second day's singles, if required, and he was secretly furious at having to make any late changes at all.

It was clear gamesmanship from the Americans, but they were to prove pretty adept at "Scotch Foursomes" as they won the opening session 3-1, with a side much changed from the one beaten so easily a year earlier at Wentworth. Having chosen a team of native-born Americans (with the exception of Eastern European immigrant Jimmy Golden), only Walter Hagen, Bill Mehlhorn and Al Watrous were retained. But Hagen teamed up with Golden to win the first match of the day, 2 and 1 against Ray and Fred Robson, before Johnny Farrell and Joe Turnesa completely demolished George Duncan and Archie Compston, 8 and 6, to put the USA two points ahead. The only British win came from Aubrey Boomer and Charles Whitcombe - a face-saving 7 and 5 win that prevented a whitewash. But with Gene Sarazen and Al Watrous comfortable winners against Arthur Havers and Jolly, clearly the British team were not adapting to new conditions as well as they hoped.

> **❝** *Let us hope our team can win, but it is the play without the Prince of Denmark.* **❞**
>
> Samuel Ryder on Abe Mitchell's withdrawal
> from the British Ryder Cup team

DAY ONE

CAPTAINS

USA: Walter Hagen   **Great Britain:** Ted Ray

FRIDAY FOURSOMES

Hagen/Golden *beat* **Ray/Robson**, *2 and 1*

Farrell/Turnesa *beat* **Duncan/Compston**, *8 and 6*

Sarazen/Watrous *beat* **Havers/Jolly**, *3 and 2*

Diegel/Mehlhorn *lost to* **Boomer/C. Whitcombe**, *7 and 5*

Session Score: 3-1

Overall Score: USA 3, Great Britain 1

" The Ryder Cup has done so much to foster that great spirit of international rivalry that makes the present-day sport the great thing that it is."

Golf Illustrated magazine

By the time the singles arrived, it was clear that the British team were mentally and physically washed out. By contrast, the Americans were vibrant and confident. Backed by surprisingly large crowds, they were in no mood to make allowances either. The victories rolled in one after the other and although the opening match was tight, with "Wild Bill" Mehlhorn beating Archie Compston by just one hole, most were not. Golden lived up to his name with an 8 and 7 victory over Jolly, while veteran Ray succumbed to Leo Diegel, 7 and 5. Hagen led by example with a 2 and 1 win against Arthur Havers.

For Great Britain, the only bright spots were Whitcombe's hard-earned half against Gene Sarazen and a welcome win for George Duncan in the last match, sneaking past Joe Turnesa at the last. But with Al Watrous also adding a point for the USA against Fred Robson, the singles were won 6.5-1.5 and the match 9.5-2.5 - a hugely convincing victory. As early as the first day, British captain Ray identified the problem, noting his side were competitive to the greens but regularly beaten once they arrived there, saying: "One of the chief reasons for our failure was the superior putting of the American team - they holed out much better than we did." However, if there was a feeling of huge disappointment and weariness for Britain as the first Ryder Cup matches came to a close, it was soon replaced by a pride in what had been achieved to set up the competition in the first place.

The final day's play received little coverage back home, no doubt primarily because of the result, but the Ryder Cup had been well received in the USA and there was a feeling on both sides that the format had a future. Philpot certainly remained enthusiastic, writing in *Golf Illustrated*: "If our young players profit by the experience, we can reasonably hope for a happier fate in the next match for the Ryder Cup."

He was soon to be proved right, and already a great sporting rivalry had begun.

DAY TWO

SATURDAY SINGLES

Bill Mehlhorn *beat* **Archie Compston** *by one hole*

Johnny Farrell *beat* **Aubrey Boomer,** *5 and 4*

Johnny Golden *beat* **Herbert Jolly,** *8 and 7*

Leo Diegel *beat* **Ted Ray,** *7 and 5*

Gene Sarazen *halved with* **Charles Whitcombe**

Walter Hagen *beat* **Arthur Havers,** *2 and 1*

Al Watrous *beat* **Fred Robson,** *3 and 2*

Joe Turnesa *lost to* **George Duncan** *by one hole*

Session Score: 6.5-1.5

Overall Score: USA 9.5, Great Britain 2.5

THE FIRST RYDER CUP TEAMS

USA

Walter Hagen (captain), 35: The swashbuckling figurehead of American golf professionals had already won two US Opens and two British Opens, and was destined to win in Britain, too (1928 and 1929).

Johnny Farrell, 26: Went on to win the US Open the following year.

Gene Sarazen, 25: Already a US Open champion, he went on to become a US golfing and Ryder Cup legend and is one of only five players to win a career Grand Slam of Majors.

Leo Diegel, 28: Went on to win the PGA Championship in 1928 and 1929.

Johnny Golden, 31: Not long a professional, he died aged just 39.

Joe Turnesa, 26: Only turned pro in 1925; five of his six brothers were also golfers.

Al Watrous, 26: Runner-up at the British Open in 1926. Remained club pro at Oakland Hills for 37 years.

Bill Mehlhorn, 28: Nicknamed "Wild Bill" for his love of wearing cowboy hats on course. He never won a Major but was runner-up at the PGA in 1926.

GREAT BRITAIN

Ted Ray (captain), 50: Won the US Open at the ripe old age of 43 (1920) and famously lost a play-off against winner Francis Ouimet and Harry Vardon at the same tournament in 1913 – a story Disney later turned into a movie called *The Greatest Game Ever Played* (2005).

George Duncan, 43: The Scottish golfer won the British Open in 1920 after one of the greatest comebacks in history, from 13 shots down to win.

Arthur Havers, 29: English golfer, who won the British Open in 1923.

Aubrey Boomer, 30: Brought up in Jersey, Boomer was to be runner-up to Bobby Jones in the British Open just months after the Ryder Cup. Won four French Opens during his career.

Fred Robson, 42: Never won a Major but finished in the top 10 of the British Open four times.

Archie Compston, 34: A renowned matchplay golfer, he famously went on to beat Walter Hagen in a challenge match in 1928.

Herbert Jolly, 42: Last-minute replacement for Abe Mitchell, he had been placed eighth at the British Open in 1923.

Charles Whitcombe, 33: The second of three famous golfing brothers, he went on to become a Ryder Cup captain.

George Gadd, 37: Malvern-born player, who won the British PGA Match Play Championship in 1922 (runner-up in 1924 and 1925).

OPPOSITE: *America's Leo Diegel in action on the 2nd tee against Ted Ray as the USA wins the Ryder Cup in Massachusetts.*

BELOW: *US captain Walter Hagen, surrounded by his victorious team-mates, picks up the Ryder Cup trophy after beating Great Britain.*

The Ryder Cup's founder Samuel Ryder (left) presents the trophy he donated to winning captain George Duncan of Great Britain in 1929.

1931

USA 9
Great Britain 3

Scioto Country Club, Ohio

June 26-27

From a windswept and rainy Leeds, the Ryder Cup transferred to 100-degree sunshine in Ohio, 1931. The USA turned up the heat on their new rivals with a thoroughly ruthless and convincing six-point victory at the Scioto Country Club that left British captain Charles Whitcombe facing intense criticism.

OVER THE YEARS, controversy and media outrage has almost become a regular part of the Ryder Cup, adding to the drama and intensity of the tournament. For Britain, it began in 1931 with a strange decision over team selection.

The PGA decided to bring in a new rule insisting players selected for the Ryder Cup not only were born in Britain but also continued to live there – meaning those players who intended to stay in America after the matches in Columbus to play lucrative exhibition matches would have to return home with the team. It was a particularly tough call for Henry Cotton, who had a professional post in Belgium – especially when he was informed that if he accepted a 'free ride' to America, he would be required to share his exhibition match fees with the rest of the team. In a row that continued for months, Cotton even offered to pay his own fare to the States but was refused... and was subsequently de-selected from the team.

So, instead of playing in the Ryder Cup, Britain's best player organized an "unofficial" private tour of America with Percy Alliss and Aubrey Boomer. Even when an olive branch was offered, he refused to change his mind – leaving the British team seriously weakened and without three of its better players. It seemed an unnecessary row over a residency rule that was primarily aimed at ensuring the USA didn't pick British players based in the States for their Ryder Cup team and had never been designed to punish those players who were keen to play abroad. Samuel Ryder tried to clarify the situation by assuring the PGA that if they wanted to change the competition rules, it was possible.

Whatever the rights and wrongs of the situation it hardly did Britain any favours. Nor did the intense heat in Ohio, which topped 37.7°C (100°F), or a decision to overlook George Duncan, who had lifted the trophy in 1929, as captain in favour of Charles Whitcombe – who proved less than inspirational.

The US team, led once again by Walter Hagen and featuring a blend of youth and experience, were more than a match for their rivals. In-form players

> ## " *The Cup is the sole property of the PGA and they can alter the terms in any way they think fit at the time.* "
>
> *Founder Samuel Ryder clarifies the rules over team selection*

ABOVE: *The victorious US players in 1931 (from left): Burke, Sarazen, Wood, Hagen (with the trophy), Farrell, Shute, Espinosa, Diegel and Smith.*

OPPOSITE: *Great Britain's Duncan and Havers (both left) line up with the USA's Shute and Hagen at the Scioto Country Club.*

DAYS ONE AND TWO

CAPTAINS

USA: Walter Hagen   **Great Britain:** Charles Whitcombe

FRIDAY FOURSOMES

Sarazen/Farrell *beat* **Compston/Davies**, *8 and 7*

Hagen/Shute *beat* **Duncan/Havers**, *10 and 9*

Diegel/Espinosa *lost to* **Mitchell/Robson**, *3 and 1*

Burke/Cox *beat* **Easterbrook/E. Whitcombe**, *3 and 2*

Session Score: 3-1

SATURDAY SINGLES

Billy Burke *beat* **Archie Compston**, *7 and 6*

Gene Sarazen *beat* **Fred Robson**, *7 and 6*

Johnny Farrell *lost to* **William Davies**, *4 and 3*

Wiffy Cox *beat* **Abe Mitchell**, *3 and 1*

Walter Hagen *beat* **Charles Whitcombe**, *4 and 2*

Denny Shute *beat* **Bert Hodson**, *8 and 6*

Al Espinosa *beat* **Ernest Whitcombe**, *2 and 1*

Craig Wood *lost to* **Arthur Havers**, *4 and 3*

Session Score: 6-2

Overall Score: USA 9, Great Britain 3

such as Craig Wood, Wiffy Cox, Denny Shute and Billy Burke (who had only earned selection a few weeks before the tournament began) were included.

Once the action started, it was clear the USA were heading for victory with Hagen avenging his huge singles defeat against opposing captain Duncan two years earlier in teaming up with Shute to defeat Duncan and Arthur Havers, 10 and 9. The USA won the Foursomes 3-1 before demolishing their rivals 6-2 in Saturday's singles matches, with some of the victories by huge margins. Burke demolished Archie Compston, 7 and 6, in the opening singles game, for instance. Gene Sarazen (who had already won 8 and 7 in the Foursomes a day earlier) added another point in beating Fred Robson, also by 7 and 6.

Once again failing to cope with the searing heat, Britain were able to muster just two victories – for Arthur Havers against Craig Wood once the trophy had already been lost and for William Davies, 4 and 3 against Johnny Farrell. In contrast the US team were majestic in victory, ending the matches 9-3 ahead to send their rivals home disconsolate. The Ryder Cup had now tasted victory, defeat, controversy and disappointment on both sides of the Atlantic and although on PGA insistence it would never again be played in the heat of an American summer, the matches were becoming ingrained in golfing folklore.

Ryder Cup legends
Walter HAGEN

One of the greatest showmen golf has ever seen, Walter Hagen did as much as anyone to popularize the Ryder Cup in its early days, as both skilful player and enigmatic captain, but his influence on the game of golf goes far beyond that. In many ways, he was the world's first professional golfer and single-handedly propelled the sport into the modern era.

When Walter Hagen arrived at the British Open in 1920 there was still stuffiness about British golf, which viewed golf professionals with immense scepticism and even banned them from entering the clubhouse. But one story about the US legend sheds light on the true character of the man who transformed those opinions – and those ancient rules – during the course of his career. By then, Hagen was already making good money from playing exhibition golf back home and so rather than suffer the ignominy of being refused entry to the clubhouse at Deal, Kent, he hired himself a showy Daimler limousine, asked his chauffeur to park it on the drive of the club, where he used it as a changing room instead. One can only imagine the reaction he received from his British hosts but on his return two years later to win the British Open, he sparked an interest in US golf that would prove crucial to plans for a Britain v America challenge match.

Over the ensuing years Hagen became a true sporting legend. Known simply as "Sir Walter" or "The Haig", although exact figures are unavailable, it is quite possible he became golf's first millionaire such was his success on and off the course. He won 11 professional major championships, second only to Jack Nicklaus' total of 18, and between 1914 and 1929, won the PGA Championship five times, the British Open four times and twice-won the US Open. In the Ryder Cup, his record was won seven, lost one and halved one; he captained the USA in the first Ryder Cup in 1927, eventually playing in five contests, winning four. In fact, Hagen – one of the game's great scramblers – was instrumental in supporting the idea of a Britain v USA tournament from the start and it was his colourful personality and attitude to life that really caught the public's imagination.

Hagen made further strides in his stand against the establishment at the 1920 US Open in Toldo, Ohio, by encouraging players to donate a large grandfather clock to the host club in return for the professionals being allowed to use the clubhouse during the tournament; this showed he understood the need for diplomacy, too.

Born in Rochester, New York, on December 21, 1892, the son of a blacksmith, Walter Hagen hailed from a modest background and entered golf as a caddy, but always intended to live large. "I never wanted to be a millionaire," he famously said. "I just wanted to live like one." He looked like a millionaire on the golf course, too, sporting expensive tailored clothes in bright colours and plush fabrics, so perhaps it came as no surprise that his exhibition matches, which did so much to raise the profile of the game and the standing of golf professionals in the US, became

hugely popular. Perhaps the only irony is that he also became so associated with the Ryder Cup – a tournament with no prize money, where players turned up for the glory of representing their country and the chance to hold the gold trophy aloft. Although one quote from the great man perhaps explains this decision for he said: "My game was my business and as a business, it demanded constant playing in the championship bracket for a current title was my selling commodity."

Hagen served as the first club professional at the now-legendary Oakland Hills Country Club, in Bloomfield Hills, Michigan from 1918 and also made money endorsing golf equipment and designing clubs for Wilson Sports, which bore his name (marketed either as "Walter Hagen" or "Haig Ultra"). But it would be unfair to remember him only as a player who made a big impact off the course. Despite his glitzy persona, he was focused and technical on the course, with such immense self-confidence that it seemed nothing could faze him. "I expect to make at least seven mistakes a round," he once declared. "Therefore, when I make a bad shot, it's just one of the seven."

In essence, Walter Hagen was an incredible player and an even more amazing character, whose celebrated philosophy was: "Don't hurry, don't worry – you're only here for a short visit, so be sure to smell the flowers along the way." The Ryder Cup, and professional golf, owes him a lot.

> *" All the professionals should say a silent thanks to Walter Hagen each time they stretch a cheque between their fingers. It was Walter who made professional golf what it is. "*
>
> *Gene Sarazen, Hagen's team-mate, pays tribute*

RYDER CUP RECORD

Ryder Cups: 1927 (winner, playing captain), 1929, 1931 (winner, playing captain), 1933, 1935 (winner, playing captain), 1937 (winner, non-playing captain)

Total wins: 4

Matches: 9 (won 7, halved 1, lost 1)

Total points: 7.5

1933

Great Britain 6.5
USA 5.5

Southport & Ainsdale Golf Club

June 26-27

THE COURSE

Southport & Ainsdale Golf Club
Location: Southport, Merseyside, England
Par: 72
Yards: 6,836

A true championship links course set among ranges of tall sandhills and smaller sand dunes, the club was founded in 1906. Its signature hole, the 16th, features a giant bunker nicknamed "Gumbley's" after a former member, who took 14 strokes to escape it and hole out.

The Ryder Cup's first-ever non-playing captain, John Henry Taylor, guided Great Britain to victory at Southport in 1933 as Syd Easterbrook converted a nerve-wracking putt in the very last match. In doing so, he secured a narrow win for the host nation. This meant that the number of wins for each side was tied at two trophies each after the opening four Ryder Cup tournaments.

BY 1933, THE FIERCE RIVALRY that is so familiar to modern Ryder Cup fans was already beginning to emerge and a remarkably close match at the Southport & Ainsdale Golf Club only served to intensify the increasing passion for the competition on both sides of the Atlantic Ocean.

The tension increased when Great Britain appointed traditionalist John Henry Taylor as captain - a man who had never found much in common with America's flamboyant and progressive leader Walter Hagen. It worsened again when Hagen only just missed hitting his rival with a practice swing on the 1st tee but once the golf began, it was incredibly tight.

Unlike their miserable performance of two years ago, and in windy conditions that felt more familiar at the coastal course, Great Britain looked intent on revenge. Even without Henry Cotton, still omitted because he was based abroad in Belgium, and even when the sun came out on the opening day, home advantage remained crucial.

Playing in front of 7,000 spectators, Great Britain led in three and were all square in the fourth after 18 holes of Foursomes with Percy Alliss and Charles Whitcombe going round in 72, and Abe Mitchell and Arthur Havers following suit. But an afternoon fight-back by America changed everything.

Hagen and Gene Sarazen started the ball rolling by coming back from one down with one to play to at least earn a half against Alliss and Whitcombe. They also edged victory in the final match as Ed Dudley and Billy Burke beat the two Alfs - Padgham and Perry - having been four-down at one stage. Those results sandwiched British victories for Mitchell and Havers; also William Davies and Syd Easterbrook, leaving the home side just one point ahead by the end of the first day.

The singles proved just as close, too, and it all came down to the final match with Easterbrook and Denny Shute all square on the final green and both facing long par putts to gain an advantage.

LEFT: *The Ryder Cup scoreboard is chalked up by an official at Southport in 1933, telling the story.*

OPPOSITE: *Crowds surround the green as Abe Mitchell tees off during the 1933 Ryder Cup.*

> **"***I am the proudest man in the British Commonwealth of people at this moment.***"**
>
> *British captain John Henry Taylor after regaining the Ryder Cup*

Indeed, the tension was palpable as Easterbrook left his effort close to the hole and Shute went four feet past before missing his second effort to hand Britain the trophy. Easterbrook had no problem finishing off the job and it proved a landmark in Ryder Cup history.

It's a mark of the competition's newfound status that the trophy was presented not by Samuel Ryder this time but by HRH The Prince of Wales in his capacity as president of the PGA, saying: "In giving this Cup, I am naturally impartial. But, of course, we over here are very pleased to have won." Players were also presented with medals before Taylor led a traditional "three cheers" salute to the weekend's special guest.

Despite the on-course rivalry, the speeches reflected the spirit of the matches as the Prince paid tribute to the US team, and Taylor in turn praised the Americans for their sporting attitude and the spectators for their good behaviour. US captain Hagen, too, congratulated Great Britain on their "excellent golf" and looked forward to winning the trophy back – a prediction that was soon to come true. But what he could not have predicted was that this was the last time Britain would win the trophy for 24 years, and also the last time that Samuel Ryder would attend – sadly, he died in 1936. But, judging by the events at the S&A, he had certainly left a remarkable legacy behind him.

DAYS ONE AND TWO

CAPTAINS

Great Britain: John Henry Taylor   **USA:** Walter Hagen

MONDAY FOURSOMES

Alliss/C. Whitcombe *halved with* **Sarazen/Hagen**

Mitchell/Havers *beat* **Dutra/Shute**, *3 and 2*

Davies/Easterbrook *beat* **Wood/Runyan** *by one hole*

Padgham/Perry *lost to* **Dudley/Burke** *by one hole*

Session Score: 2.5-1.5

TUESDAY SINGLES

Alf Padgham *lost to* **Gene Sarazen**, *6 and 4*

Abe Mitchell *beat* **Olin Dutra**, *9 and 8*

Arthur Lacey *lost to* **Walter Hagen**, *2 and 1*

William Davies *lost to* **Craig Wood**, *4 and 3*

Percy Alliss *beat* **Paul Runyan**, *2 and 1*

Arthur Havers *beat* **Leo Diegel**, *4 and 3*

Syd Easterbrook *beat* **Denny Shute** *by one hole*

Charles Whitcombe *lost to* **Horton Smith**, *2 and 1*

Session Score: 4-4

Overall Score: Great Britain 6.5, USA 5.5

1935

**USA 9
Great Britain 3**

Ridgewood Country Club, New Jersey

September 28-29

The legendary Walter Hagen led the USA to another impressive home victory in 1935 as he played in his last Ryder Cup. He combined effectively with Gene Sarazen to comprehensively end Great Britain's challenge. It was a match that saw all three Whitcombe brothers – Charles, Ernest and Reg – compete for the losing side at New Jersey's Ridgewood Country Club.

GREAT BRITAIN MAY HAVE ENJOYED their victory in front of royalty in 1933 but they soon found playing in America – where a larger ball was used – a completely different prospect. They were royally beaten by Hagen's team, with Paul Runyan and Horton Smith playing superbly to clinch a six-point victory for the second time in a row on US soil.

Hagen combined with his old rival Gene Sarazen (the two were never the greatest of friends but were able to put differences aside to compete effectively together) to beat Jack Busson and Alf Perry by a mammoth 7 and 6 in the opening day's Foursomes. However, the captain was honest enough about his own form, at the age of 42, to leave himself out of the singles, allowing others to finish off the job. Hagen went on to become non-playing captain in 1937, but this was his last on-course action in the Ryder Cup – the tournament he had helped to instigate. He bowed out with a record of seven victories, one half and one defeat, having lifted the trophy three times out of five. It's a record that makes him one of the competition's all-time greats.

Great Britain, still without Henry Cotton because of selection issues over players who were based abroad, went for family connections this time in a bid to stop the Americans. Captain Charles Whitcombe chose both his brothers, Ernest and Reg, for the team. But even family know-how – and drizzling rain to make the Brits feel at home – was not enough to prevent the USA from running away with victory.

Following the lead of their captain, Paul Runyan and Horton Smith added a Foursomes victory for the States, as did Henry Picard and Johnny Revolta. At the end of the opening day, the home team led 3-1, just as they had four years earlier. Charles and Ernest Whitcombe combined for Britain's only point – a one-up

> ❝*The British team could not hole out in a hole the size of the Atlantic.*❞

The London Mail explains Great Britain's defeat

OPPOSITE: *Britain's trio of Ryder Cup brothers (left to right), Reg, Ernest and Charles Whitcombe in New Jersey in 1935.*

RIGHT: *Sam Parks and Alf Perry (driving) in action at Ridgewood during the Ryder Cup singles matches.*

victory over Olin Dutra and Ky Laffoon. Afterwards, Charles sat out the singles and could only watch despairingly as his team were demolished 6-2 to relinquish the trophy that they had won so dramatically in Southport.

Percy Alliss was one of the few British success stories with a victory over Craig Wood. The Americans, cheered on by a crowd of up to 8,000 on the Sunday afternoon, were too good for their rivals, though. Windy conditions made matters more difficult, highlighted by the fact that Horton Smith was the only player to go under 70 as he carded 69 for his first 18 against Bill Cox – and even he had to settle for a half as the wind picked up later in the day, amazingly carding 83 for the second round. Sarazen was widely credited with the "Shot of the Day" as he played a miraculous shot from beneath overhanging branches, using only a restricted backswing to drop the ball inches from the hole on his way to a hard-fought victory over Busson. In all, America won five of the eight matches, with Runyan, Revolta, Dutra and Picard all adding to Sarazen's opening point, while Sam Parks added a half in a high-quality match against Alf Perry.

It was a hugely convincing victory in which the British players struggled to deal with patches of wet clover on the course, which often made ball striking more difficult. There were also signs of American superiority on the putting greens: there was no doubting the USA were worthy winners and it was a feeling they soon became highly accustomed to.

DAYS ONE AND TWO

CAPTAINS

USA: Walter Hagen   **Great Britain:** Charles Whitcombe

SATURDAY FOURSOMES

Sarazen/Hagen *beat* **Perry/Busson**, *7 and 6*

Picard/Revolta *beat* **Padgham/Alliss**, *6 and 5*

Runyan/Smith *beat* **Cox/Jarman**, *9 and 8*

Dutra/Laffoon *lost to* **C. Whitcombe/E. Whitcombe** *by one hole*

Session Score: 3-1

SUNDAY SINGLES

Gene Sarazen *beat* **Jack Busson**, *3 and 2*

Paul Runyan *beat* **Dick Burton**, *5 and 3*

Johnny Revolta *beat* **Reg Whitcombe**, *2 and 1*

Olin Dutra *beat* **Alf Padgham**, *4 and 2*

Craig Wood *lost to* **Percy Alliss** *by one hole*

Horton Smith *halved with* **Bill Cox**

Henry Picard *beat* **Ernest Whitcombe**, *3 and 2*

Sam Parks *halved with* **Alf Perry**

Session Score: 6-2

Overall Score: USA 9, Great Britain 3

Ryder Cup legends
Gene **SARAZEN**

BELOW: *The most remarkable of Gene Sarazen's four singles victories came in 1937, in what proved to be his final Ryder Cup appearance for the USA.*

The influence of Gene Sarazen, a true golfing hero, extends way beyond the Ryder Cup but during those transatlantic battles the man affectionately known as "The Squire" helped make the USA the world's dominant golfing power.

Born Eugenio Saraceni, Gene Sarazen formed part of a supremely talented US triumvirate with Bobby Jones and Walter Hagen, who tussled for titles throughout the 1920s and 30s - rivalries that extended the interest in the sport of golf across the globe. Sarazen, one of just five players to win all four Majors - the "Grand Slam" of golf - as an individual, was similarly imperious as part of the USA team competing in the Ryder Cup.

In his first two Ryder Cup appearances of 1927 and 1929, Sarazen picked up just half a point from the singles, but won four in a row, 1931-37. The most notable of his singles triumphs came at Southport & Ainsdale Golf Club. In the build-up to the tournament, the 1937 US side was described by *Golf Monthly* as "the greatest golfing force which has ever come to this country". But Britain had other ideas and were indeed level with their opponents, with only the final four singles matches left to play. In the first of these, Sarazen faced Percy Alliss and found himself three shots down just after lunch. The Squire fought back to draw level before a major stroke of luck on the 15th swung the match and the tournament in the USA's favour. Alliss could only watch in horror as Sarazen's shot bounced off an unwitting spectator and onto the green. His disappointment was compounded when his US opponent nonchalantly sunk the putt to edge himself ahead for the first time in the contest. Sarazen held on tight to claim a one-up victory, which put his team into a 5-4 lead - and on the way to an 8-4 triumph.

Sarazen's Ryder Cup legacy was also mirrored in his overall contribution to golf. Only two years before this memorable round at Southport, he hit the "shot heard round the world" (an albatross - double eagle inAmerica - on the 15th hole) to ultimately claim the 1935 Masters. He is also credited with the invention of the modern sand wedge (which he debuted in the 1932 British Open) and held a 75-year endorsement contract with Wilson, the longest in professional sport.

RYDER CUP RECORD

Ryder Cups: 1927 (winner), 1929, 1931 (winner), 1933, 1935 (winner), 1937 (winner)

Total wins: 4
Matches: 12 (won 7, halved 3, lost 2)
Total points: 8.5

Archie COMPSTON

Sacked for idleness at 16 by Kidderminster Golf Club, Archie Compston went on to become one of Britain's leading lights in the Ryder Cup's early years and even became a personal coach and close friend of Edward VIII.

Despite being described as a fiery, volatile character, Compston – a towering figure – was much loved by golf fans and became arguably the sport's first British celebrity but his association with the game started in somewhat inauspicious circumstances in the small town of Kidderminster in Worcestershire.

His obvious talent, both as a player and a coach, prompted the club committee to make the "lad-from-down-the-road in Wolverhampton" their first-ever pro in 1909. He was paid 18 shillings (about $4.50) a week for his role as "pro and groundsman", but was sacked for his lamentable attitude towards keeping the greens. It proved no more than a minor blip on his journey to the top of both the sport and England's social ladder as a result of his close association with Edward VIII, later the Duke of Windsor, who also played at Coombe Hill Golf Club. However, Compston's reputation was not built on social profile alone, with performances in his three campaigns in Great Britain's Ryder Cup team marking him out as one of the world's finest players, during which time he forged a particular rivalry with the US's Gene Sarazen.

In 1927's inaugural edition, Compston lost in the Foursomes and the singles as the USA triumphed at the Worcester Country Club in Massachusetts. It was not until two years later, in the heavy rain drenching the Moortown Golf Club in Yorkshire, that the two men's paths first crossed. Having halved his Foursome alongside Charlie Whitcombe on the first day, Compston scored his first and only point against Sarazen with a 6 and 4 victory in the singles. Two years later, in 1931, the American would have his revenge in the heat of Ohio, when he and Johnny Farrell thrashed Compston – alongside W.H. Davies – 8 and 7 in the Foursomes. American Billy Burke also beat the Englishman 7 and 6 in what proved to be his last Ryder Cup.

RIGHT: Britain's Archie Compston poses at Moortown, Leeds, during the final day's practice before heading to America for the 1927 Ryder Cup.

RYDER CUP RECORD

Ryder Cups: 1927, 1929 (winner), 1931
Total wins: 1
Matches: 6 (won 1, halved 1, lost 4)
Total points: 1.5

1937

**Great Britain 4
USA 8**

Southport &
Ainsdale Golf Club

June 29-30

THE COURSE

Southport & Ainsdale Golf Club
Location: Southport,
Merseyside, England
Par: 72
Yards: 6,836

Staging the Ryder Cup for the second time in a row, Great Britain hoped that the S&A would once more prove a lucky course for them. But despite terrible storms, the Americans, more accustomed to sunnier climes, still came out on top.

For the first time in Ryder Cup history, the host team suffered defeat as the legendary Walter Hagen, now a non-playing captain, took his US side to Southport. The Americans returned home with an emphatic 8-4 victory that, due to World War II, proved to be the last time the two teams would meet for another decade.

HAVING WON SUCH A MEMORABLE VICTORY at Southport in 1933, Great Britain must have gone into the matches four years later dreaming of a similar result. Having tied at 4-4, with only four games remaining on course, there seemed no reason at all why it could not be repeated. But what happened on the second afternoon will be forever remembered on both sides of the Atlantic, albeit for opposite reasons. The USA won all four of those matches through Gene Sarazen, Sam Snead, Ed Dudley and Henry Picard to turn a tight encounter into a hugely impressive victory that proved once and for all that the Americans were no longer golf's apprentices, they were rapidly becoming masters.

Even the return of British talisman Henry Cotton, overlooked for the previous three Ryder Cups because of a residency rule, was not enough to inspire the hosts although he certainly made an impact

by beating Tony Manero, 5 and 3. Quite clearly, Cotton was Britain's best golfer of the 1930s, having won The Open in 1934 – and he went on to win the trophy again, just weeks after the 1937 Ryder Cup was completed. But having accepted a role as a professional in Belgium, he was ruled ineligible for the Ryder Cup until he returned to Britain to take up a post at Ashridge Golf Club, near London.

Cotton formed part of a strong British side that included up-and-coming stars Dai Rees and Sam King and was captained by Charles Whitcombe. Having guided his team to defeats in America (1931 and 1935), Whitcombe was looking to make it third time lucky.

The Americans, featuring rookies Sam Snead (runner-up in that year's US Open), Byron Nelson and Ed Dudley, began well, despite stormy seaside conditions that made the opening day's play difficult for both teams. Cotton's disappointing and surprising defeat with Alf

ABOVE: *Crowds flock to watch Great Britain's Dai Rees putting on a wet 18th green at Southport during the 1937 Ryder Cup.*

DAYS ONE AND TWO

CAPTAINS

Great Britain: Charles Whitcombe   **USA:** Walter Hagen

TUESDAY FOURSOMES

Padgham/Cotton *lost to* **Dudley/Nelson,** *4 and 2*

Lacey/Cox *lost to* **Guldahl/Manero,** *2 and 1*

C. Whitcombe/Rees *halved with* **Sarazen/Shute**

Alliss/Burton *beat* **Picard/Revolta,** *2 and 1*

Session Score: 1.5-2.5

WEDNESDAY SINGLES

Alf Padgham *lost to* **Ralph Guldahl,** *8 and 7*

Sam King *halved with* **Denny Shute**

Dai Rees *beat* **Byron Nelson,** *3 and 1*

Henry Cotton *beat* **Tony Manero,** *5 and 3*

Percy Alliss *lost to* **Gene Sarazen** *by one hole*

Dick Burton *lost to* **Sam Snead,** *5 and 4*

Alf Perry *lost to* **Ed Dudley,** *2 and 1*

Arthur Lacey *lost to* **Henry Picard,** *2 and 1*

Session Score: 2.5-5.5

Overall Score: Great Britain 4, USA 8

ABOVE: *Captain Charles Whitcombe (left) welcomes Ryder Cup debutant Henry Cotton to the Great Britain team.*

Padgham against new boys Dudley and Nelson, going down 4 and 2, set the tone. The USA ended Day One leading 2.5-1.5.

But with the rain still pouring down on the second day, the British reached lunch in what seemed an encouraging position. Already Cotton had secured victory over Manero and Rees beat Nelson, 3 and 1. By mid-afternoon the scores were tied at 4-4, with everything to play for, but then the Americans simply stepped up a gear with Snead the hero (as he was so often to become in the future).

There was an element of fate about the result, too – especially when Sarazen's narrow victory over Percy Alliss was achieved thanks to a birdie at the 15th when his tee shot landed in the lap of a female spectator and bounced back onto the green as she stood up to shake it off! But in fairness, Sarazen had already worked hard to come back from three-down and there was no luck involved in Snead's convincing 5 and 4 victory over Dick Burton, Dudley's 2 and 1 triumph over Alf Perry, or Picard's 2 and 1 win against Arthur Lacey.

This match proved to be the final Ryder Cup before the intervention of the World War II, with the 1939 event (planned for Ponte Vedra Country Club, Florida) cancelled. But the Americans ended the first period in Ryder Cup history on a major high and they certainly enjoyed it.

With the British Open staged in Carnoustie that year, most of the US team were due to stay in England for two more weeks. Together, they headed for Scotland by bus – it must have been quite a journey.

> ❝ *We left no pub un-stoned on that ride.* ❞

The US team celebrate their Ryder Cup win on their way to play in the British Open at Carnoustie

US captain Sam Snead blasts out of the sand at the 2nd hole during the first-day Foursomes at Eldorado in 1959. He and Cary Middlecoff halved with Harry Weetman and Dave Thomas, but the USA won 8.5-3.5.

CHAPTER THREE
THE HOGAN ERA

The 1937 Ryder Cup proved to be the last before World War II made the postponement of the event inevitable. Play did not resume until 1947, when the Great Britain team discovered that the game had taken great steps forwards in the USA. And so started a period of American dominance, inspired by Ben Hogan, that would last another decade.

RYDER CUP RECORD

Ryder Cups: 1947 (winner, playing captain), 1949 (winner, non-playing captain), 1951 (winner), 1967 (winner, non-playing captain)

Total wins: 4

Matches: 3 (won 3, halved 0, lost 0)

Total points: 3

Ryder Cup legends
Ben HOGAN

Against a backdrop of childhood tragedy, World War II and a near-fatal car accident, the quiet Ben Hogan became one of history's most celebrated golfers, with a swing that is still hailed as perhaps the finest ever.

OPPOSITE: *America's iconic golfer Ben Hogan receives the Ryder Cup trophy as winning team captain in 1949.*

Ben Hogan was just 9 years old when his father – a blacksmith – committed suicide with a gunshot to the chest on Valentine's Day of 1922, plunging the family into turmoil. The young Ben and his siblings were forced to go out to work to ease the financial burden on his mother, Clara, and it was then that he discovered that he could make a handsome profit as a caddy at the nearby Glen Garden Country Club, Fort Worth, Texas – and so began his love affair with golf at the age of 11.

As a youngster, Hogan would often practise with his brother Royal and their friend, Byron Nelson – himself a future golfing star – but he was not averse to honing his skills alone, with an approach to training that frequently bordered on the obsessive. Indeed, this would become a trademark of his time, both as player and captain, and the fruit of his labours was the putative perfect swing. Life was not always easy for Hogan, who struggled financially as a young pro, because of a hook that undermined all his good work on the course, although he worked incredibly hard to correct the problem.

Like many, Hogan's job was put on hold when the USA entered World War II, where he fought between 1942 and 1945. Up until then, he had busied himself in racking up tour victories and it seemed to take him no time at all to get back into the swing of things when he returned from the conflict. That said, he was still without the holy grail of a Major title, winning a record 30 tournaments before finally landing a big one. Success came at the Portland Golf Club, where he lifted the 1946 PGA Championship and then the following year, Hogan began a Ryder Cup career that would span 20 years, both as player and captain. As the USA's leading moneymaker and arguably his country's finest player, Hogan was appointed playing captain and set the perfect example in turning around a four-shot deficit to take his Foursomes match two-up on the final green. He chose to drop himself for the singles but the decision mattered little, with America claiming a crushing 11-1 overall victory.

In his mid-thirties, Hogan's singles career went from strength to strength, winning the second and third Majors of his career at the PGA Championship and the US Open. But on the morning of February 2, 1949, Hogan and his beloved Valerie were driving just outside Texas when a Greyhound bus, attempting to overtake a truck, collided head-on with their car. Just before impact, the three-time Major-winning golfer dived across to shield his wife from the impact, saving her life as well as his own for the steering column punctured the seat where he had been sitting just a split-second beforehand.

As a result of the many injuries he sustained in the crash, doctors said he might never walk again, but Hogan proved them wrong. After 59 days in hospital, he returned home on April 1 and when the eighth Ryder Cup kicked off in September of that year, the man known as "The Hawk" was ready to captain his fellow countrymen in a non-playing role. This was the first Ryder Cup played on British soil (at Ganton Golf Club in Yorkshire) for 12 years and Hogan's crop contained just three players with previous experience of playing across the pond. Despite being on crutches and only able to reach the holes nearest to the clubhouse, the captain inspired his team to a 7-5 overall win.

His final outing as a Ryder Cup player came two years later at Pinehurst, North Carolina, under captain Sam Snead. Having won the Masters earlier in 1951, Hogan was the star of a USA team considered superior to their opponents in almost every way. And so it was on the course, with the USA romping to a 9.5- 2.5 victory with Hogan, alongside Jimmy Demaret, cruising to a 5 and 4 Foursomes win before beating Charlie Ward, 3 and 2, in the singles.

After a 16-year hiatus he made a return to the Ryder Cup in 1967 to captain the US team that he famously introduced as "the finest golfers in the world". In the event, his words could not have been any more accurate for his team, containing such stars as Arnold Palmer and Gene Littler, humiliated Europe with a record 23.5-8.5 victory. It was a fitting way for Ben Hogan to bow out.

" I hate a hook – it nauseates me, I could vomit when I see one. It's like a rattlesnake in your pocket."

Ben Hogan battles against the hook shot

Spectators gather in front of the main Wentworth scoreboard as the results for the final day of the 1953 Ryder Cup are mounted.

1955

USA 8
Great Britain 4

Thunderbird CC, California

November 5-6

In 1955, American domination of the Ryder Cup continued in California as captain Chick Harbert guided his side to an 8-4 victory. This meant the trophy had now resided in the USA for an astonishing 21 years, but at least Great Britain put up a fight in probably their best performance so far on American soil.

IT IS A SIGN OF JUST HOW STRONG America were in the 1950s that gaining four points, even in defeat, was seen as something of a triumph by the British, who were led by captain Dai Rees and picked up four victories in the USA for the first time. Contrast that to their last two visits to the States, where they collected a total of just three points!

Great Britain were determined to at least be competitive and had decided to select seven players for their team based on points awarded for performances in five key tournaments. The other three were selected by committee and this time there was no place for Peter Alliss or Bernard Hunt, the two men who had crumbled under pressure at Wentworth two years earlier, or for

> **"***We've learned a lot, although we have lost, and we are going back to practise in the streets and on the beaches.***"**

Lord Brabazon, president of the British PGA, makes his post-match speech

LEFT: *Harry Weetman is filmed by his wife as the British team practise before sailing to America for the 1955 Ryder Cup.*

ABOVE: *US captain Chick Harbert holds the Ryder Cup with pride, watched on by sponsor Robert Hudson and Great Britain's Dai Rees (right).*

DAYS ONE AND TWO

CAPTAINS

USA: Chick Harbert   **Great Britain:** Dai Rees

SATURDAY FOURSOMES

Harper/Barber *lost to* **Fallon/Jacobs** *by one hole*

Ford/Kroll *beat* **Brown/Scott**, *5 and 4*

Burke/Bolt *beat* **Lees/Weetman** *by one hole*

Snead/Middlecoff *beat* **Bradshaw/Rees**, *3 and 2*

Session Score: 3-1

SUNDAY SINGLES

Tommy Bolt *beat* **Christy O'Connor**, *4 and 2*

Chick Harbert *beat* **Syd Scott**, *3 and 2*

Cary Middlecoff *lost to* **John Jacobs** *by one hole*

Sam Snead *beat* **Dai Rees**, *3 and 1*

Marty Furgol *lost to* **Arthur Lees**, *3 and 2*

Jerry Barber *lost to* **Eric Brown**, *3 and 2*

Jack Burke *beat* **Harry Bradshaw**, *3 and 2*

Doug Ford *beat* **Harry Weetman**, *3 and 2*

Session Score: 5-3

Overall Score: USA 8, Great Britain 4

48-year-old Henry Cotton, now considered too old. Instead four new players – John Jacobs, Syd Scott, Christy O'Connor Snr. and Johnny Fallon – joined the ranks.

Having dominated the tournament for so long, the Americans were also keen to make changes: not to their team, but to the format itself. Sam Snead suggested Fourballs should replace the more traditional Foursomes, for instance. However, the proposal received short shrift from the British PGA. That year's American team was not considered one of its strongest. Even taking into consideration rookies Jerry Barber, Marty Furgol, Doug Ford, Chandler Harper and Tommy Bolt, the average age was 37 and without the likes of Ben Hogan and Byron Nelson, it lacked star quality. The impressive Thunderbird Country Club had enough glamour to make up for that, however. In the celebrity heartland of Palm Springs, it had a touch of Hollywood glitz about it. A fleet of electric buggies followed players around the course, which was surrounded by homes owned by film stars and celebrities. Water hazards featured around the greens, narrow fairways and punishing areas of rough. It was very different to what the British team were used to back home.

Maybe they took time to grow accustomed to their new surroundings because the USA raced into a 3-1 lead on the opening day despite an exciting and hard-fought victory for Britain's Fallon and Jacobs in the first Foursomes match against Harper and

Barber. The match was a real battle all the way, with some stunning displays of short-game genius from Barber, who time and again was able to chip in from off the green. But in the end the British held firm for a narrow one-up victory. Their team-mates could not follow suit, however, because America's Doug Ford and Ted Kroll, Jack Burke Jnr. and Tommy Bolt, and Sam Snead and Cary Middlecoff all won their matches to take a healthy lead into the singles.

Perhaps the turning point was a combative display from Tommy "Lightning" Bolt, whose gritty play helped his team come from behind to snatch victory against Harry Weetman and Arthur Lees. And the same player kicked off the singles by beating O'Connor, 4 and 2. It took a spirited fight-back from Great Britain to make their hosts sweat in front of a large and increasingly vocal crowd. Jacobs began with an important victory against Middlecoff, thanks to birdies at the 12th and 13th before Lees added a 3 and 2 win against Furgol, and Eric Brown beat Jerry Barber. But the Americans were too strong to throw it all away and their attitude was typified by Sam Snead, who when faced with what seemed an impossible shot up against a palm tree at the 7th against Dai Rees still managed to produce a miraculous recovery shot to make an eagle and take the hole. By the time Burke beat Bradshaw and Ford beat Weetman, overall victory was already assured and the status quo was safe – but there were at least signs that Britain could fight back.

1957
Great Britain 7.5
USA 4.5

Lindrick Golf Club, Rotherham

October 4-5

THE COURSE

Lindrick Golf Club
Location: Rotherham, South Yorkshire, England
Par: 71
Yards: 6,541

The South Yorkshire course, founded in 1891, was a controversial choice because many critics in Britain feared it would suit the USA more than their own team. But they were proved wrong as Great Britain produced a rare and memorable Ryder Cup win.

Roared on by a vociferous crowd that upset American sensibilities, Great Britain produced possibly their greatest singles session ever in the Ryder Cup of 1957. Led by playing captain Dai Rees, they won six of the eight matches to lift the trophy for the first time in 24 years.

THE PERFORMANCE AT LINDRICK GOLF CLUB will always be remembered by the British as one of their finest, even against some of the incredible displays in the modern era; Rees' team came from 3-1 down to win 7.5-4.5 on an incredible Saturday that saw the US side routed. All this on a course selected after Sir Stuart Goodwin, a Yorkshire businessman, had donated £10,000 ($28,000 at mid-1950s exchange rates) to help finance the British team on condition the competition was staged at his local club. But it proved no barrier to a British victory for with a strong team (selected based on performances in professional stroke-play tournaments), captain Rees was able to call on players of the quality of Max Faulkner, Ken Bousfield, Christy O'Connor Snr., Harry Weetman and Eric Brown.

The American team, led by Jack Burke Jnr., perhaps lacked star names after Sam Snead and Ben Hogan both opted against taking part, while Cary Middlecoff and Julius Boros were ignored after controversially choosing to play in a lucrative exhibition match instead of the USPGA Championship. Even so, after seven victories in a row they were strong favourites.

Things started badly for Britain when Peter Alliss and Bernard Hunt – recalled despite their infamous collapses, four years earlier – went down to Doug Ford and Dow Finsterwald, 2 and 1, in the opening match. There were further defeats for Faulkner and Weetman (against Ted Kroll and Burke) and for O'Connor and Brown (a crushing 7 and 5 reverse against Dick Mayer and Tommy Bolt). The one ray of hope as the USA went 3-1 up was a battling performance from Rees, who, partnered by Bousfield, came from two-down to beat Art Wall and Fred Hawkins; but when a row over selection broke out on the Friday night, the outlook appeared bleak.

Following a team meeting, Rees had left Faulkner and Weetman out of his singles line-up after both men apparently volunteered

" *The worst I have ever seen in my life.* "

America's Tommy Bolt describes the crowd at Lindrick after they cheered his missed putts

ABOVE: *Britain's Eric Brown chooses a club during his singles match against Tommy Bolt.*

LEFT: *Great Britain's jubilant captain Dai Rees is surrounded by happy team-mates after winning the trophy.*

DAYS ONE AND TWO

CAPTAINS

Great Britain: Dai Rees   **USA:** Jack Burke Jnr.

FRIDAY FOURSOMES

Alliss/Hunt *lost to* **Ford/Finsterwald,** *2 and 1*

Bousfield/Rees *beat* **Wall/Hawkins,** *3 and 2*

Faulkner/Weetman *lost to* **Kroll/Burke,** *4 and 3*

O'Connor/Brown *lost to* **Mayer/Bolt,** *7 and 5*

Session Score: 1-3

SATURDAY SINGLES

Eric Brown *beat* **Tommy Bolt,** *4 and 3*

Peter Mills *beat* **Jack Burke,** *5 and 3*

Peter Alliss *lost to* **Fred Hawkins,** *2 and 1*

Ken Bousfield *beat* **Lionel Hebert,** *4 and 3*

Dai Rees *beat* **Ed Furgol,** *7 and 6*

Bernard Hunt *beat* **Doug Ford,** *6 and 4*

Christy O'Connor *beat* **Dow Finsterwald,** *7 and 6*

Harry Bradshaw *halved with* **Dick Mayer**

Session Score: 6.5-1.5

Overall Score: Great Britain 7.5, USA 4.5

to drop out. Later, he was stunned when a furious Weetman told journalists he would never play under his captaincy again. The two men had been long-time friends and the controversy was lapped up by the English media, with Weetman later being called to a disciplinary hearing by the PGA and subsequently banned from playing for a year. Without him, however, Britain produced their best-ever singles display to justify Rees' decision. They began with an early win for Brown in an ill-humoured match against the volatile, but talented Bolt. Roared on by an increasingly raucous home crowd, Brown won 4 and 3 with Bolt clearly rattled by the way the home supporters cheered missed putts. He even broke a golf club shaft over his knee in frustration.

That particular tie set the tone but perhaps the biggest shock came as rookie Peter Mills beat US captain Burke, 5 and 3, to level the scores at 3-3, with Bousfield, Hunt and O'Connor all leading as he did so. Fred Hawkins showed great resolve to beat Alliss and stem the tide but that result proved to be the US's last win of the day as Great Britain roared to victory. O'Connor crushed Finsterwald 7 and 6 in another ill-humoured match that saw both men refuse to shake hands, while Rees continued his own excellent Ryder Cup in beating Ed Furgol by the same margin.

Bernard Hunt scored a morale-boosting victory over Ford to make up for his disappointment of four years earlier and with the score now 6-4, Britain needed only a half from either Bousfield – who appeared to be on a slide after losing three holes in a row, having once been seven-up against Lionel Hebert – or Harry Bradshaw against Dick Mayer. But after Faulkner and Rees raced across the course to let Bousfield know the importance of his result, he regained his nerve to seal a victory that meant the Ryder Cup was, at last, returning to Britain. It had been a long, long wait.

Billy Capser of the USA studies a putt during the Friday afternoon Fourballs, which he and Gay Brewer lost 3 and 2 to Great Britain's Tony Jacklin and Peter Oosterhuis, in the 1973 Ryder Cup at Muirfield.

CHAPTER FOUR
THE USA RETAINS CONTROL

As the Ryder Cup moved into the 1960s and 1970s, American dominance showed no sign of diminishing. Even the inclusion of Irish players in the British team couldn't close the huge gap that had opened up. Eventually, questions were raised about the competition's future.

1963

USA 23
Great Britain 9

Atlanta Athletic Club, Georgia

October 11-13

Although drastic changes had been made to make the Ryder Cup more competitive, more alterations came in 1963 when two sets of Fourballs were introduced. However, nothing could stop the USA - led by inspired player-captain Arnold Palmer - from storming to what remains the second-biggest victory in Ryder Cup history, as they demolished their bewildered opponents in Atlanta.

IF EVER THERE WAS ANY DOUBT about the chasm in class between the US and British teams in the 1960s, this was certainly confirmed by a Ryder Cup that was to prove historically important for so many reasons in 1963. For a start it saw the introduction of Fourballs to attract greater television interest in the US, where Foursomes - played mostly in Scotland - were a largely unknown format and had long been regarded with some scepticism by the US PGA. Repeated requests to replace them were previously ignored by the British, who feared doing so would make their team even less competitive and so a compromise was reached as the matches were extended to two series of

DAYS ONE AND TWO

CAPTAINS

USA: Arnold Palmer   **Great Britain:** John Fallon

FRIDAY MORNING FOURSOMES
Palmer/Pott *lost to* **Huggett/Will**, *3 and 2*
Casper/Ragan *beat* **Alliss/O'Connor** *by one hole*
Boros/Lema *halved with* **Coles/Hunt**
Littler/Finsterwald *halved with* **Thomas/Weetman**
Session Score: 2-2

SATURDAY MORNING FOURBALLS
Palmer/Finsterwald *beat* **Huggett/Thomas**, *5 and 4*
Littler/Boros *halved with* **Alliss/B. Hunt**
Casper/Maxwell *beat* **Weetman/Will**, *3 and 2*
Goalby/Ragan *beat* **Coles/O'Connor** *by one hole*
Session Score: 3.5-0.5

FRIDAY AFTERNOON FOURSOMES
Maxwell/Goalby *beat* **Thomas/Weetman**, *4 and 3*
Palmer/Casper *beat* **Huggett/Will**, *5 and 4*
Littler/Finsterwald *lost to* **Coles/B. Hunt**, *2 and 1*
Boros/Lema *beat* **Haliburton/G. Hunt** *by one hole*
Session Score: 3-1

SATURDAY AFTERNOON FOURBALLS
Palmer/Finsterwald *beat* **Coles/O'Connor**, *3 and 2*
Lema/Pott *beat* **Alliss/B. Hunt** *by one hole*
Casper/Maxwell *beat* **Haliburton/G. Hunt**, *2 and 1*
Goalby/Ragan *halved with* **Huggett/Thomas**
Session Score: 3.5-0.5

DAY THREE

SUNDAY MORNING SINGLES

Tony Lema *beat* **Geoff Hunt,** *5 and 3*

Johnny Pott *lost to* **Brian Huggett,** *3 and 1*

Arnold Palmer *lost to* **Peter Alliss** *by one hole*

Billy Casper *halved with* **Neil Coles**

Bob Goalby *beat* **Dave Thomas,** *3 and 2*

Gene Littler *beat* **Christy O'Connor** *by one hole*

Julius Boros *lost to* **Harry Weetman** *by one hole*

Dow Finsterwald *lost to* **Bernard Hunt** *by two holes*

Session Score: 3.5-4.5

SUNDAY AFTERNOON SINGLES

Arnold Palmer *beat* **George Will,** *3 and 2*

Dave Ragan *beat* **Neil Coles,** *2 and 1*

Tony Lema *halved with* **Peter Alliss**

Gene Littler *beat* **Tom Haliburton,** *6 and 4*

Julius Boros *beat* **Harry Weetman,** *2 and 1*

Billy Maxwell *beat* **Christy O'Connor,** *2 and 1*

Dow Finsterwald *beat* **Dave Thomas,** *4 and 3*

Bob Goalby *beat* **Bernard Hunt,** *2 and 1*

Session Score: 7.5-0.5

Overall Score: USA 23, Great Britain 9

Fourballs, two series of Foursomes and a series of singles. It meant there were now 32 points at stake instead of 24 and the Ryder Cup, for the first time, would be played over three days rather than two.

This particular Ryder Cup also proved to be the last time a playing captain took charge of either team. The British had already dispensed with that tradition, choosing John Fallon as a non-playing captain in Atlanta, but the legendary Arnold Palmer (who had already won the Masters three times, the US Open once and the British Open twice) gave it one last go. He won four points, including a singles victory over George Will, as he guided his team to victory.

Great Britain at least made a decent start, squaring the opening session of Foursomes 2-2, with a surprise win for Will and Brian Huggett against Palmer and Johnny Pott. The Americans won the afternoon session 3-1 (Fallon having surprisingly and controversially broken up his successful partnerships from the morning), before the home team completely dominated the Fourballs, winning seven out of eight points available to lead 12-4 at the end of the second day.

The Ryder Cup was all but over for the British side but the USA were ruthless in keeping their foot on the accelerator and thundered to a 14-point victory, winning 10 of the singles matches, including seven out of eight in the final session. For Great Britain, the only highlights were a memorable win for Peter Alliss against Palmer and a sweet triumph for Harry Weetman against US Open champion Julius Boros, but the gap between the two sides was cavernous. Palmer had introduced his men by saying: "This team would beat the rest of the world combined." And he wasn't overstating his case.

OPPOSITE: *The US Ryder Cup team of 1963 pose for the cameras complete with their golf bags ahead of the matches in Georgia.*

ABOVE: *Arnold Palmer throws down his putter in frustration during his Day One Foursomes match. He and partner Johnny Pott lost to Great Britain's Brian Huggett and George Will.*

Ryder Cup legends
Arnold **PALMER** and
Gardner **DICKINSON**

US tennis star Peter Fleming once stated the best doubles partnership in the world was "John McEnroe and anybody" – generously self-deprecating from a man who partnered his fellow American to numerous major tennis titles. Golf's closest equivalent to McEnroe might be Arnold Palmer, but it was really only with the relatively unheralded Gardner Dickinson that "The King" was truly invincible.

Gardner Dickinson and Arnold Palmer are America's most successful Ryder Cup partnership. They played together five times, won five times and were on the winning team by comfortable margins when competing as members of the 1967 and 1971 US sides. Palmer is possibly America's greatest-ever Ryder Cup player in terms of games played and points won. Dickinson had a 9-1 overall record in Ryder Cup play – the best winning percentage for anyone participating in at least seven matches in the biennial team event.

US captain Ben Hogan paired the rookie Dickinson with the near million-dollar prizewinner Palmer for the 1967 Ryder Cup. His faith, however, was returned as Dickinson and "The

RIGHT: *Arnold Palmer (right) helps team-mate Gardner Dickinson line up a putt at the Ryder Cup in St. Louis in 1971.*

King' returned with their country's first point of the competition in beating Peter Alliss and Christy O'Connor Snr., 2 and 1. Indeed, it was the start of a beautiful relationship. Afterwards, they went out in the afternoon and thrashed Malcolm Gregson and Hugh Boyle, 5 and 4. The following morning, Hogan rested Palmer, but Dickinson maintained his winning debut by pairing Doug Sanders to a 3 and 2 win over Brian Huggett and George Will. The same pair beat Alliss/Gregson in the afternoon. The results must surely have helped to inspire Palmer and Dickinson to win both their singles matches against prize scalp Tony Jacklin on the final day. Palmer even found time to beat Brian Huggett, too, at a time when two rounds of eight separate singles matches were played on the same day.

> 66 *I loved the Ryder Cup because it simply wasn't about playing for money – it was about playing for something far grander and more personal.* 99
>
> *Arnold Palmer*

The unbeaten - and unbeatable - duo contributed more than any other US players in leading their country to a 23.5-8.5 win - the biggest win in the history of the competition. Two years later, the Ryder Cup was in danger of losing its allure, such was the one-sided nature of the event, and so it was possibly fortunate the two countries played out a draw at Royal Birkdale, albeit without Dickinson in the US side. He played his way back into 1971 side for the September meet at Old Warson Country Club, St. Louis, Missouri and captain Jay Herbert was sensible enough to reunite him with Palmer in the opening morning's Fourballs games. The pair continued to maintain their unbeaten streak with a two-up win over Peter Townsend and rookie Peter Oosterhuis. They went on to beat the same pair by the same score in the afternoon Foursomes.

The following morning featured America's most dynamic-ever duo in a controversial 5 and 4 win over Oosterhuis and Bernard Gallacher. Palmer tried to calm the argument after Gallacher's young caddie asked him what club he used for a stunning tee-shot and the referee subsequently awarded the USA the hole for the youngster's infringement. The rest is history and it proved to be Dickinson and Palmer's fifth - and final - match together. Palmer, who successfully partnered Dow Finsterwald in earlier Ryder Cups, was later paired with fellow legend and World No. 1 Jack Nicklaus, although he never achieved the same success or synergy as he had with Dickinson. He did, however, end up with a Ryder Cup record of 22 matches won against eight losses, with two ties and a total of 23 points. It was a mark that would stand from 1973 until Nick Faldo won two more points at Valderrama in 1997.

RYDER CUP RECORD

Arnold PALMER
Ryder Cups: 1961, 1963 (winner, playing captain), 1965, 1967 (winner) 1971 (winner), 1973 (winner), 1975 (winner, non-playing captain)
Total wins: 5
Matches: 32 (won 22, halved 2, lost 8)
Total points: 23

Gardner DICKINSON
Ryder Cups: 1967 (winner), 1971 (winner)
Total wins: 2
Matches: 10 (won 9, halved 0, lost 1)
Total points: 9

AS A PAIR:
Matches: 5 (won 5, halved 0, lost 0)
Total points: 5

1967

USA 23.5
Great Britain 8.5

Champions Golf Club, Texas

October 20-22

US captain Ben Hogan introduced his players as the finest golfers in the world and they more than lived up to that tag in 1967. Indeed, with a breath-taking performance, they inflicted what remains the heaviest defeat ever suffered by a British or European Ryder Cup team.

THE USA'S 15-POINT VICTORY at the Champions Golf Club in Houston was all the more remarkable because it was achieved without their best player, Jack Nicklaus, who despite having won seven Major championships had yet to complete his five-year period as a PGA member and was therefore ineligible for selection. But Gardner Dickinson and Arnold Palmer neatly stepped into his shoes as both went unbeaten in five matches to steer the US team to a memorable victory.

Captain Hogan set the tone for a dominant performance at a team dinner on the eve of the tournament. Having listened patiently to a long introduction from British captain Dai Rees, outlining the achievements of his players one by one, he calmly rose to introduce his squad in just a single sentence. And as he sat down to raucous applause, the demolition of Great Britain began.

Rees had been a controversial choice as a former captain – indeed, the hot-headed Harry Weetman refused to play under him. By contrast, Hogan was an impressive leader, single-handedly choosing his team (not by committee, unlike the British), insisting on long practice hours and introducing a 10.30 p.m. curfew for the players. Even world superstar Palmer was put firmly in his place when he questioned an order to practise with the smaller British-sized ball, only to be told: "Who said you are playing?"

Of course Palmer did play, but every player in the US side got the message from their captain. With rookies Gardner Dickinson,

ABOVE: *Tony Jacklin of Great Britain chips out of a bunker on the second hole in Houston during the 1967 Ryder Cup.*

DAY ONE

CAPTAINS

USA: Ben Hogan   **Great Britain:** Dai Rees

FRIDAY MORNING FOURSOMES
Casper/Boros *halved with* **Huggett/Will**
Palmer/Dickinson *beat* **Alliss/O'Connor**, *2 and 1*
Sanders/Brewer *lost to* **Jacklin/Thomas**, *4 and 3*
Nichols/Pott *beat* **Hunt/Coles**, *6 and 5*
Session Score: 2.5-1.5

FRIDAY AFTERNOON FOURSOMES
Casper/Boros *beat* **Huggett/Will** *by one hole*
Dickinson/Palmer *beat* **Gregson/Boyle**, *5 and 4*
Littler/Geiberger *lost to* **Jacklin/Thomas**, *3 and 2*
Nichols/Pott *beat* **Alliss/O'Connor**, *2 and 1*
Session Score: 3-1

Bobby Nichols, Al Geiberger, Doug Sanders and Gay Brewer joining established stars such as Palmer and Billy Casper, the American team boasted a formidable line-up. Although Britain introduced a young Tony Jacklin, fresh from scoring the first televised hole-in-one at the Dunlop Masters weeks earlier, they were soon to be outplayed.

Huggett/Will did give the visitors an early half against Casper/Boros, while Jacklin/Thomas sealed a 4 and 3 victory over Sanders/Brewer. Any joy was short-lived, however, for the Americans won the afternoon Foursomes 3-1 before taking seven out of eight Fourballs matches on the Saturday to set up a 13-3 lead. By the end of the final day, the USA – with Dickinson, Palmer and Geiberger all winning twice in the singles – had added another 10.5 points to their total to complete a record-breaking victory. For Great Britain, it was an all-time low.

With the exception of Palmer's 5 and 3 demolition of Huggett, most of the matches had been close. All the same, the result had never been in doubt and the scoreline told a sorry story for

Great Britain (and maybe for the competition itself). It had been a ruthless, top-quality performance from the victors, but could the Ryder Cup carry on like this?

DAYS TWO AND THREE

SATURDAY MORNING FOURBALLS
Casper/Brewer beat Alliss/O'Connor, 3 and 2
Nichols/Pott beat Hunt/Coles by one hole
Littler/Geiberger beat Jacklin/Thomas by one hole
Dickinson/Sanders beat Huggett/Will, 3 and 2
Session Score: 4-0

SATURDAY AFTERNOON FOURBALLS
Casper/Brewer beat Hunt/Coles, 5 and 3
Dickinson/Sanders beat Alliss/Gregson, 3 and 2
Palmer/Boros beat Will/Boyle by one hole
Littler/Geiberger halved with Jacklin/Thomas
Session Score: 3.5-0.5

SUNDAY MORNING SINGLES
Gay Brewer beat Hugh Boyle, 4 and 3
Billy Casper beat Peter Alliss, 2 and 1
Arnold Palmer beat Tony Jacklin, 3 and 2
Julius Boros lost to Brian Huggett by one hole
Doug Sanders lost to Neil Coles, 2 and 1
Al Geiberger beat Malcolm Gregson, 4 and 2
Gene Littler halved with Dave Thomas
Bobby Nichols halved with Bernard Hunt
Session Score: 5-3

SUNDAY AFTERNOON SINGLES
Arnold Palmer beat Brian Huggett, 5 and 3
Gay Brewer lost to Peter Alliss, 2 and 1
Gardner Dickinson beat Tony Jacklin, 3 and 2
Bobby Nichols beat Christy O'Connor, 3 and 2
Johnny Pott beat George Will, 3 and 1
Al Geiberger beat Malcolm Gregson, 2 and 1
Julius Boros halved with Bernard Hunt
Doug Sanders lost to Neil Coles, 2 and 1
Session Score: 5.5-2.5
Overall Score: USA 23.5, Great Britain 8.5

ABOVE: Dense fog at the Champions Course didn't prevent Arnold Palmer getting in some practice ahead of the Sunday games.

" Ladies and gentlemen, the United States Ryder Cup team – the finest golfers in the world!"

Ben Hogan introduces his star-studded team

1971

USA 18.5
Great Britain 13.5

Old Warson CC, Missouri

September 16-18

After all the high drama of "The Concession" in 1969, it was business as usual two years later. Inspired by Lee Trevino, the USA completed a straightforward victory in St. Louis. But the British team could at least hold their heads high after a competitive performance that maintained the interest of the American public and with it, that of the television networks.

THE COURSE

Old Warson
Country Club
Location: St. Louis, Missouri, USA
Par: 71
Yards: 6,718

Designed by Robert Trent Jones Snr, the par-four 14th from an elevated tee requires a 200-yard shot across a lake to a narrow landing area. Naturally, it is one of the great holes on any golf course in the world.

THE EXCITEMENT OF ROYAL BIRKDALE was still in the air in 1971 and, with Tony Jacklin having won the US Open in 1970, American broadcasters televised the Ryder Cup for the first time. The tournament will be remembered for the bizarre weather conditions. Starting with a 37.7°C (100°F) heat wave during practice sessions, it continued with a deluge of rain, which resulted in the opening ceremony being cancelled.

Great Britain captain Eric Brown had called up rookies Harry Bannerman, John Garner and Peter Oosterhuis, and got off to a glorious start with Neil Coles and Christy O'Connor Snr. producing a shock 2 and 1 victory over Billy Casper and Miller Barber. There was even better to come when Tony Jacklin and Brian Huggett beat Nicklaus/Stockton, 3 and 2 (a match in which the Americans failed to register a single birdie) before Maurice Bembridge and Peter Butler put their side 3-1 up with victory over Charles Coody and Frank Beard.

DAY ONE

CAPTAINS
Great Britain: Eric Brown   **USA:** Jay Hebert

THURSDAY MORNING FOURSOMES
Casper/Barber *lost to* **Coles/O'Connor,** *2 and 1*
Palmer/Dickinson *beat* **Townsend/Oosterhuis** *by one hole*
Nicklaus/Stockton *lost to* **Huggett/Jacklin,** *3 and 2*
Coody/Beard *lost to* **Bembridge/Butler** *by one hole*
Session Score: 1-3

THURSDAY AFTERNOON FOURSOMES
Casper/Barber *lost to* **Bannerman/Gallacher,** *2 and 1*
Palmer/Dickinson *beat* **Townsend/Oosterhuis** *by one hole*
Trevino/Rudolph *halved with* **Huggett/Jacklin**
Nicklaus/Snead *beat* **Bembridge/Butler,** *5 and 3*
Session Score: 2.5-1.5

ABOVE: *British captain Eric Brown poses for the cameras ahead of the 1971 Ryder Cup in Missouri.*

The Americans were stunned. Captain Jay Hebert had included rookies Coody, Dave Stockton, Mason Rudolph and J.C. Snead (nephew of the legendary Sam Snead) but could still call on the world's top four golfers in Jack Nicklaus, Lee Trevino, Billy Casper and Arnold Palmer – even if Trevino was still recovering from an appendix operation and Casper was nursing a broken toe. In the end, quality counted. The British had one last hurrah when Harry Bannerman and Bernard Gallacher opened the afternoon Foursomes by beating Casper/Barber, 2 and 1. The momentum shifted, however, when the USA won the session 2.5-1.5 to leave their rivals just a single point ahead.

As so often in the past, the Fourballs proved to be America's trump card, winning Friday's morning session 4-0 and the afternoon session 2.5-1.5 to lead by 10-6. There was controversy, too, when Gallacher's caddie – impressed by a shot from Palmer – asked him what club he had used on the par-three 7th – an infringement of Rule 9a, the giving of advice. After much discussion, the match referee awarded the hole to the Americans despite Palmer's attempts at diplomacy.

With British confidence drained, the singles proved a formality. Trevino crushed Brian Huggett, 7 and 6 (his fourth point of the week), before Snead's one-hole win against Jacklin retained the trophy. Though Britain managed to end on a high with wins for Barnes, Gallacher, Oosterhuis and Bannerman, the coveted trophy was long gone and at 18.5-13.5, the Americans underlined their superiority.

ABOVE: *Great Britain's Tony Jacklin plays out of a bunker on a practice day prior to the 1971 tournament at the Old Warson Country Club.*

DAYS TWO AND THREE

FRIDAY MORNING FOURBALLS
Trevino/Rudolph *beat* **O'Connor/Barnes,** *2 and 1*
Beard/Snead *beat* **Coles/Garner,** *2 and 1*
Palmer/Dickinson *beat* **Oosterhuis/Gallacher,** *5 and 4*
Nicklaus/Littler *beat* **Townsend/Bannerman,** *2 and 1*
Session Score: 4-0

SATURDAY MORNING SINGLES
Lee Trevino *beat* **Tony Jacklin** *by one hole*
Dave Stockton *halved with* **Bernard Gallacher**
Mason Rudolph *lost to* **Brian Barnes** *by one hole*
Gene Littler *lost to* **Peter Oosterhuis,** *4 and 3*
Jack Nicklaus *beat* **Peter Townsend,** *3 and 2*
Gardner Dickinson *beat* **Christy O'Connor,** *5 and 4*
Arnold Palmer *halved with* **Harry Bannerman**
Frank Beard *halved with* **Neil Coles**
Session Score: 4.5-3.5

FRIDAY AFTERNOON FOURBALLS
Trevino/Casper *lost to* **Gallacher/Oosterhuis** *by one hole*
Littler/Snead *beat* **Jacklin/Huggett,** *2 and 1*
Palmer/Nicklaus *beat* **Townsend/Bannerman** *by one hole*
Coody/Beard *halved with* **Coles/O'Connor**
Session Score: 2.5-1.5

SATURDAY AFTERNOON SINGLES
Lee Trevino *beat* **Brian Huggett,** *7 and 6*
J.C. Snead *beat* **Tony Jacklin** *by one hole*
Miller Barber *lost to* **Brian Barnes,** *2 and 1*
Dave Stockton *beat* **Peter Townsend** *by one hole*
Charles Coody *lost to* **Bernard Gallacher,** *2 and 1*
Jack Nicklaus *beat* **Neil Coles,** *5 and 3*
Arnold Palmer *lost to* **Peter Oosterhuis,** *3 and 2*
Gardner Dickinson *lost to* **Harry Bannerman,** *2 and 1*
Session Score: 4-4
Overall Score: USA 18.5, Great Britain 13.5

1973

GB & Ireland 13
USA 19

Muirfield, East Lothian

September 20-22

THE COURSE

Muirfield
Location: East Lothian, Scotland
Par: 71
Yards: 7,245

The legendary – and original – links course overlooking the Firth of Forth was opened in 1891. Its unusual design sees it arranged as two loops of nine holes: one played clockwise, the other anti-clockwise.

Finally, in 1973, the Ryder Cup went "home" to the birthplace of golf - Scotland. It was also the first time the hosts competed officially as Great Britain & Ireland, even though Irish players had been eligible to play for many years. The result was a familiar one, however, as a strong US side won by six points to retain the trophy.

THE AMERICAN TEAM AT MUIRFIELD, captained by Jack Burke Jnr., was regarded as the strongest ever to cross the Atlantic for the Ryder Cup. It included such superstars as Jack Nicklaus, Billy Casper, Lee Trevino and the new British Open champion, Tom Weiskopf. Between them, they boasted 28 Majors (compared to Tony Jacklin's two for Britain), and the US team was heavily backed to defend the trophy. In fact, the media was so convinced of an American victory that it was debating the one-sided nature of the Ryder Cup even before the matches got underway.

A few changes had been made to the format, including mixing up Foursomes and Fourballs on the opening two days and altering the name of the British team to Great Britain & Ireland. It was little more than a gesture because Irish players had been selected since 1953 and Northern Irish players since 1947, though it was nevertheless an important landmark.

The British team, which included rookies Eddie Polland, Clive Clark and Tommy Horton, made an encouraging start under new captain Bernard Hunt. Indeed, the good news started at the very first hole, where Trevino and Casper three-putted to go one down against Bernard Gallacher and Brian Barnes, who eventually sealed a narrow victory. Christy O'Connor and Neil Coles then produced an encouraging 3 and 2 victory over Weiskopf and J.C. Snead before a

DAY ONE

CAPTAINS

GB & Ireland: Bernard Hunt   **USA:** Jack Burke Jnr.

THURSDAY MORNING FOURSOMES

Barnes/Gallacher *beat* **Trevino/Casper** *by one hole*
O'Connor/Coles *beat* **Weiskopf/Snead**, *3 and 2*
Jacklin/Oosterhuis *halved with* **Rodríguez/Graham**
Bembridge/Polland *lost to* **Nicklaus/Palmer**, *6 and 5*
Session Score: 2.5-1.5

THURSDAY AFTERNOON FOURBALLS

Barnes/Gallacher *beat* **Aaron/Brewer**, *5 and 4*
Bembridge/Huggett *beat* **Palmer/Nicklaus**, *3 and 1*
Jacklin/Oosterhuis *beat* **Weiskopf/Casper**, *3 and 1*
O'Connor/Coles *lost to* **Trevino/Blancas**, *2 and 1*
Session Score: 3-1

DAYS TWO AND THREE

FRIDAY MORNING FOURSOMES

Barnes/Butler *lost to* **Nicklaus/Weiskopf** *by one hole*
Oosterhuis/Jacklin *beat* **Palmer/Hill** *by two holes*
Bembridge/Huggett *beat* **Rodríguez/Graham,** *5 and 4*
Coles/O'Connor *lost to* **Trevino/Casper,** *2 and 1*
Session Score: 2-2

SATURDAY MORNING SINGLES

Brian Barnes *lost to* **Billy Casper,** *2 and 1*
Bernard Gallacher *lost to* **Tom Weiskopf,** *3 and 1*
Peter Butler *lost to* **Homero Blancas,** *5 and 4*
Tony Jacklin *beat* **Tommy Aaron,** *3 and 1*
Neil Coles *halved with* **Gay Brewer**
Christy O'Connor *lost to* **J.C. Snead** *by one hole*
Maurice Bembridge *halved with* **Jack Nicklaus**
Peter Oosterhuis *halved with* **Lee Trevino**
Session Score: 2.5-5.5

FRIDAY AFTERNOON FOURBALLS

Barnes/Butler *lost to* **Snead/Palmer** *by two holes*
Jacklin/Oosterhuis *lost to* **Brewer/Casper,** *3 and 2*
Clark/Polland *lost to* **Nicklaus/Weiskopf,** *3 and 2*
Bembridge/Huggett *halved with* **Trevino/Blancas**
Session Score: 0.5-3.5

SATURDAY AFTERNOON SINGLES

Brian Huggett *beat* **Homero Blancas,** *4 and 2*
Brian Barnes *lost to* **J.C. Snead,** *3 and 1*
Bernard Gallacher *lost to* **Gay Brewer,** *6 and 5*
Tony Jacklin *lost to* **Billy Casper,** *2 and 1*
Neil Coles *lost to* **Lee Trevino,** *6 and 5*
Christy O'Connor *halved with* **Tom Weiskopf**
Maurice Bembridge *lost to* **Jack Nicklaus** *by two holes*
Peter Oosterhuis *beat* **Arnold Palmer,** *4 and 2*
Session Score: 2.5-5.5
Overall Score: Great Britain 13, USA 19

crushing win for the powerful pairing of Nicklaus/Palmer (6 and 5 against Polland and Maurice Bembridge) restored American pride.

The Great Britain & Ireland team ended the day three points ahead, including another win for Barnes/Gallacher in the afternoon Fourballs, but disaster struck when Gallacher contracted food poisoning overnight. He was replaced at short notice by Peter Butler who, playing alongside Barnes the next day, was to make an instant impact. Butler made Ryder Cup history when he became the first player ever to score a hole-in-one in the competition. He aced the par-three 16th in a Friday Foursomes match against Nicklaus and Weiskopf. However, defeat at the last against Nicklaus/Weiskopf

was to set the tone for an American revival, as the second day ended with the scores tied at 8-8.

The opening two singles matches proved crucial to the final result, with Casper easing past a tired-looking Barnes and Gallacher (back from illness but still looking pale) before succumbing to a 3 and 1 defeat against Weiskopf. So, by the time Homero Blancas crushed Butler, 5 and 4, the writing was on the wall. America won the session 5.5-2.5 before taking the afternoon singles by exactly the same margin, thanks to a crucial run of victories for Snead, Gay Brewer, Casper and Trevino. The Ryder Cup might have come home but the trophy would not linger there.

OPPOSITE: *Peter Butler of Great Britain celebrates his momentous hole-in-one – the first in Ryder Cup history.*

RIGHT: *US team captain Jack Burke Jnr. holds the Ryder Cup, flanked by his victorious players at Muirfield.*

Ryder Cup legends
Peter **ALLISS** and Christy **O'CONNOR**

After switching his putter for a microphone in the early 1960s, Englishman Peter Alliss soon established himself as the voice of golf. Meanwhile, Christy O'Connor Snr. (affectionately known as "Himself") is one of Ireland's favourite sons and counts among his country's finest sportsmen. But it was as a Ryder Cup pairing that both men truly excelled as the tournament's second most successful team.

The incomparable Spanish partnership of Severiano Ballesteros and José María Olazábal will probably never be challenged as the greatest-ever in the Ryder Cup but more recent successes have featured Nick Faldo and Ian Woosnam, as well as Darren Clarke and Lee Westwood. Before them, however, came the genial double act of Peter Alliss and Christy O'Connor. They played together 12 times, winning five and halving one match. In comparison, the best-ever US team of Arnold Palmer and Gardner Dickinson won only five points. Between 1953 and 1969, Alliss played in a total of eight Ryder Cups while O'Connor appeared in 10 consecutive competitions from 1955-73 – a record that would be surpassed only by Nick Faldo in 1997.

RYDER CUP RECORD

Peter ALLISS
Ryder Cups: 1953, 1957 (winner), 1959, 1961, 1963, 1965, 1967, 1969 (tied but USA retain trophy)
Total wins: 1
Matches: 30 (won 10, halved 5, lost 15)
Total points: 12.5

Christy O'CONNOR Snr.
Ryder Cups: 1955, 1957 (winner), 1959, 1961, 1963, 1965, 1967, 1969 (tied but USA retain trophy), 1971, 1973
Total wins: 1
Matches: 36 (won 11, halved 4, lost 21)
Total points: 13

AS A PAIR:
Matches: 12 (won 5, halved 1, lost 6)
Total points: 5.5

ABOVE: *Christy O'Connor drives the 10th watched by partner Peter Alliss (left) at the 1965 Ryder Cup matches at Royal Birkdale.*

Although not paired, both players were on the same team in 1957 and O'Connor, in particular, played a key part in helping to secure the Cup at Lindrick Golf Club in Yorkshire. With an impressive second-day comeback, the British team won the event for the first time since 1933 when O'Connor thrashed Dow Finsterwald, 7 and 6. Two years later, the British failed to retain the trophy when attending the Eldorado Country Club in Indian Wells, California, but the significance of their one Foursome victory should not be underestimated for it came from the new team of Christy O'Connor and Peter Alliss, who beat Art Wall and Doug Ford, 3 and 2. America retained the title in 1961, although O'Connor and Alliss were again winners together. For the promising Great Britain side, the one-sided US victory of 1963 was one to forget, however.

Fourballs were introduced in 1965 and it was in that year, at Royal Lytham & St Annes, Lancashire, when Alliss and O'Connor combined to win three matches out of four and lose just one. At a time when the American golfers were so dominant, this was an outstanding feat – one that would not be achieved again for more than 20 years.

For Alliss and O'Connor, life (and golf) was fairly simple for both were naturals who took to the game from an early age and played with seemingly effortless ease. Former US captain and Ryder Cup player Lee Trevino said of O'Connor: "Christy flows through the ball like fine wine." Despite winning over 20 professional tournaments and finishing in the top five of the British Open five times, Peter Alliss still places the event above all others, admitting that his greatest (and worst) moments came in the Ryder Cup. As he explained: "Worst was in the 1953 Ryder Cup, the 18th at Wentworth, when I took four to get down. Best was in the final hole of the 1965 Ryder Cup. It was Alliss and O'Connor against Palmer and Marr – I hit a four-wood to within 10 feet." His father, Percy, also played for Great Britain and the two men are one of only two father-and-son duos to compete in the Ryder Cup (Antonio and Ignacio Garrido of Spain being the other).

Christy O'Connor was one of Europe's most respected Ryder Cup players (although against such tough opposition, he holds the record for most matches lost at 21). It was in his final appearance at the Ryder Cup of 1973 at Muirfield in Scotland that he excelled. On the morning of the final day, O'Connor lost to J.C. Snead by one hole and reportedly asked to sit out the afternoon singles but captain Bernard Hunt wanted him to play against Tom Weiskopf, winner of The Open Championship and six other tournaments that year. O'Connor, approaching his 49th birthday, held the strongest US player to a tie, earning half a point for his team in the process with a spectacular half on the final hole. Peter Alliss has said of his former partner, "'Himself' was a genius – a legend of Irish golf, and golf in general."

At the age of 38, Alliss retired from full-time tour golf and swiftly moved on to the commentary duties, for which he is possibly more widely known than his on-course talents. However, his Ryder Cup record, especially in partnership with Christy O'Connor, will never be forgotten.

"It would be very easy to drool with sentimentality over the Ryder Cup but at the end of the day, it is simply two teams trying to knock seven bells out of each other in the nicest possible way."

Peter Alliss on the Ryder Cup

Ryder Cup legends
Billy CASPER

Billy Casper is probably the most underrated golfer in the history of the game. Though he did not win as many Majors as Tiger Woods, Jack Nicklaus, Arnold Palmer or Gary Player, he beats them in almost every other statistical analysis and is unequivocally America's greatest-ever Ryder Cup performer.

Casper, who also captained the US team in 1979, played in eight consecutive winning sides from 1961-75. He competed in 37 matches, winning 20 and gaining seven halves for a record 23.5 points. Since he never featured on a losing Ryder Cup team as player or captain, it is perhaps only because of his desire to keep a relatively low profile compared to his 1960s rivals that he is not such a household name as his peers.

Quite possibly, it was Casper's unusual childhood in New Mexico and San Diego that persuaded him to become such a family man when he later had the chance. Born during the Depression to teenage parents who soon separated, he was largely raised by close relatives, although his father did start a sporting legend when he stuck a golf club in his hand, aged four. Golf would prove to be his escape from childhood troubles, not that he ever seemed disturbed on, or off, a golf course. He also found salvation in his childhood sweetheart, Shirley, who he married over 60 years ago before going on to have 11 children, six of them adopted. Add 34 grandchildren and 11 great-grandchildren to the equation and it is easier to understand why he claims he was always happiest at home as opposed to chasing media and commercial opportunities.

Few golfers were calmer under pressure than Casper, the unchallenged king of the putter. His two US Open and one Masters' triumphs were impressive but kept him in the Majors shadow of the "Big Three": Nicklaus, Palmer and Player. That said, between 1964 and 1970, Casper won 27 tournaments on the PGA Tour – two more than Nicklaus and six more than Palmer and Player combined. It is particularly revealing to hear what some of his fellow golfing greats say of him, although this testament to his putting, from Chi Chi Rodríguez, is perhaps the best: "Casper was the greatest putter I ever saw. When golf balls used to leave the factory, they prayed they would get to be putted by Billy!"

In all, Casper, who was sometimes known as "Buffalo Bill" for his love of buffalo meat, won 51 times in his career. Only Sam Snead, Jack Nicklaus, Tiger Woods, Ben Hogan, Arnold Palmer and Byron Nelson won more PGA Tour titles. And one of his three Majors goes down in history as being among the greatest feats in modern golf and came against the legendary Palmer, his first Ryder Cup playing partner. It was at the 1966 US Open when Casper trailed Palmer by seven shots with nine holes to play. His nerve and putting enabled him to draw level and force an 18-hole play-off, which he won relatively comfortably.

Casper's final PGA Tour win came in 1975, and he went on to win eight more times on the Senior Tour. His post-playing career has included designing many golf courses through his company,

Billy Casper Golf. He was the second player to reach $1 million in career tour earnings (Arnold Palmer being the first), attaining that mark on January 11, 1970, with his win at the Los Angeles Open. But his Ryder Cup debut came back in 1961, when he teamed up with Arnold Palmer to defeat Dai Rees and Ken Bousfield, 2 and 1. It was the start of a beautiful friendship between Casper and the tournament for he went on to win three of America's points in their 14.5-9.5 victory at Lytham St Annes.

Casper was also responsible for four-and-a-half points as America retained the trophy, two years later in Atlanta. He suffered his first Ryder Cup defeat in his second Foursomes match of the 1965 event at Royal Birkdale when British stalwarts Peter Alliss and Christy O'Connor Snr. were the victors over Casper partnered by Gene Littler. In 1967, he responded at the Champions Golf Club in Houston in going undefeated with four-and-a-half points in the thumping 23.5 to 8.5 victory. Casper also notched up three points in the infamous drawn Ryder Cup of 1969, fading only in 1971 when he failed to score. Further good scoring in 1973 and 1975 proved his star was far from burnt out, though.

He proved equally adept at captaining the 1979 side when the USA faced a European team for the very first time and saw them off by a 17-11 scoreline. Billy Casper's Ryder Cup legacy was certainly now assured, if not already.

> **❝** *Casper was always there. He was a great player and a really great player under pressure.* **❞**
>
> US player and captain Jack Nicklaus

RYDER CUP RECORD

Ryder Cups: 1961, 1963, 1965, 1967, 1969, 1971, 1973, 1975,
1979 (non-playing captain). All won except
1969 (tied but USA retained trophy)
Wins: 8 (plus 1 tie to retain the trophy, 1969)
Matches: 37 (won 20, halved 7, lost 10)
Points: 23.5

1977

GB & Ireland 7.5
USA 12.5

Royal Lytham & St Annes Golf Club

September 15-17

THE COURSE

Royal Lytham & St Annes Golf Club
Location: Lytham St Annes, Lancashire, England
Par: 70
Yards: 7,118

A true links course founded in 1886, the club was first used for the Ryder Cup in 1961. Featuring 203 bunkers, the course has hosted the British Open.

In 1977, the USA completed its 20th Ryder Cup victory at a canter at Royal Lytham & St Annes and it proved to be their last against the Great Britain & Ireland team. The result was a landmark moment in Ryder Cup history as it sparked a series of vociferous calls for players from continental Europe to be allowed to join the competition in the future.

IN ONE LAST DESPERATE BID to make the matches closer (and no doubt in an attempt to see off suggestions from America that players from the "rest of the world" be invited to join the British team), some major changes were made to the format as Dow Finsterwald's US side arrived in Lancashire ready to defend the trophy once again.

At the request of the British PGA, the number of matches was drastically reduced, with only five Foursomes and five Fourballs to be played over the opening two days, followed by just one session of 10 singles, with 20 points on offer in all. But if the tinkering was designed to give Great Britain & Ireland a chance of victory, it failed to reap dividends for the home side, captained this time by Brian Huggett, were once again truly beaten.

The American team started quickly, winning the Foursomes by two points and stretching their lead to five in the Fourballs. Even an improved display by their opponents in the singles, tying the session 5-5, was nowhere near enough to turn it around. However, the performances of a young Nick Faldo, who at the age of 20 won three points, at least gave a hint of a brighter future. Not bad for a player who just days earlier had been diagnosed with glandular fever.

In fact, Faldo went on to play in 11 Ryder Cups, winning a record 25 points. He made his debut on the same day that American great Tom Watson also took his Ryder Cup bow. Both lined up in the opening day of Foursomes, with Faldo partnering the more experienced Peter Oosterhuis to a 2 and 1 victory over Ray Floyd

LEFT: *Sand goes flying as Ray Floyd plays a shot out of a bunker at Royal Lytham & St Annes in 1977.*

OPPOSITE: *Britain's successful duo Nick Faldo and Peter Oosterhuis discuss tactics on the way to another victory.*

and Lou Graham before Watson joined Jack Nicklaus to whip Tommy Horton and Mark James, 5 and 4. For both sides, a new era had begun. It couldn't come quick enough for Britain, though, as they went into the singles already five points behind and with little hope of winning the trophy. To add to their problems, Huggett had controversially dropped Tony Jacklin from his line-up and further upset the Englishman by openly criticizing him for failing to support his team-mates on course until the afternoon. Reports suggest the two men fell out badly over those comments and refused to speak to each other for many months.

Back on the course, victories for Graham, Lanny Wadkins, Dave Hill, Hubert Green and Ray Floyd completed victory for the US, with Peter Dawson, Brian Barnes, Faldo and Oosterhuis adding a touch of respectability to the scoreline for the hosts. And, just like two years earlier in Pennsylvania, there was a sweetener for Britain as the great Nicklaus was beaten, this time by a young Bernard Gallacher by one hole. The win was all the more remarkable because Gallacher was playing with a hastily purchased new putter after his own was stolen – such are the stories that make the Ryder Cup so special. But after another one-sided match, it was obvious to everyone on both sides of the Atlantic that major changes were needed to keep the format alive in the long term.

DAYS ONE TO THREE

CAPTAINS

GB & Ireland: Brian Huggett   **USA:** Dow Finsterwald

THURSDAY'S FOURSOMES

Gallacher/Barnes lost to **Wadkins/Irwin**, *3 and 1*

Coles/Dawson lost to **Stockton/McGee** *by one hole*

Faldo/Oosterhuis beat **Floyd/Graham**, *2 and 1*

Darcy/Jacklin halved with **Sneed/January**

Horton/James lost to **Nicklaus/Watson**, *5 and 4*

Session Score: 1.5-3.5

FRIDAY'S FOURBALLS

Barnes/Horton lost to **Watson/Green**, *5 and 4*

Coles/Dawson lost to **Sneed/Wadkins**, *5 and 3*

Faldo/Oosterhuis beat **Nicklaus/Floyd**, *3 and 1*

Jacklin/Darcy lost to **Hill/Stockton**, *5 and 3*

James/Brown lost to **Irwin/Graham** *by one hole*

Session Score: 1-4

SATURDAY'S SINGLES

Howard Clark lost to **Lanny Wadkins**, *4 and 3*

Neil Coles lost to **Lou Graham**, *5 and 3*

Peter Dawson beat **Don January**, *5 and 4*

Brian Barnes beat **Hale Irwin** *by one hole*

Tommy Horton lost to **Dave Hill**, *5 and 4*

Bernard Gallacher beat **Jack Nicklaus** *by one hole*

Eamonn Darcy lost to **Hubert Green** *by one hole*

Mark James lost to **Ray Floyd**, *2 and 1*

Nick Faldo beat **Tom Watson** *by one hole*

Peter Oosterhuis beat **Jerry McGee** *by two holes*

Session Score: 5-5

Overall Score: Great Britain 7.5, USA 12.5

" In America, the Ryder Cup now rates somewhere between Tennessee Frog Jumping and the Alabama Melon-Pip Spitting Championship."

English writer Peter Dobereiner on the uncompetitive Ryder Cup

Bernhard Langer celebrates as a putt from off the green finds the hole on the Saturday of the 1985 Ryder Cup at The Belfry. The German played five matches and picked up three points in Europe's 16.5-11.5 victory over the USA.

CHAPTER FIVE
ENTER THE EUROPEANS

With the USA dominant and matches often one-sided something had to be done to save the Ryder Cup. The answer came in 1979 as players from continental Europe were invited to join the Great Britain & Ireland team. It was a decision that eventually transformed the Ryder Cup into the spectacle it is today.

1979

USA 17
Europe 11

The Greenbrier, West Virginia

September 14-16

THE COURSE

The Greenbrier Course
Location: White Sulphur
Springs, West
Virginia, USA
Par: 72
Yards: 6,675

Set in 6,500 acres of rolling woodland, The Greenbrier was constructed in 1924 by Seth Raynor. In 1977, it was redesigned by Jack Nicklaus and was possibly the most luxurious resort to hold a Ryder Cup. In all, 26 US presidents stayed there.

By 1979, with the US team dominant and interest in an increasingly one-sided competition beginning to wane in America, the Ryder Cup had reached a crossroads. Something had to be done to save it. The solution, unveiled in West Virginia, came in the shape of a new-look Great Britain and Europe team that included star of the future, Severiano "Seve" Ballesteros.

AFTER 18 DEFEATS in the previous 22 Ryder Cups, it was clear that the British PGA needed to do something to make the event more competitive, or face the uncomfortable prospect that the tournament had no long-term future. In truth, discussions had been going on for the best part of a decade but maybe it was a statement from the great Jack Nicklaus that finally forced the issue. Having helped his team to yet another big away-win at Lytham St Annes, Nicklaus observed: "The Americans are quite happy to treat this match as a goodwill gesture, a get-together, a bit of fun, but here in Britain it's treated differently. The people here seem to want a serious knock-'em-down match. If that's

what's wanted, there has to be a stronger opposition."

He followed up these comments by writing to Lord Derby, President of the British PGA, and within a year two members of the British Ryder Cup committee - Brian Huggett and Peter Butler - were heading to Augusta National Golf Club in Georgia, USA to gain approval for plans to include Europeans in the side. Other options had been considered - a Commonwealth team, for instance, or even a "rest of the world" side, as suggested by Nicklaus - but both ideas involved matches in far-flung places such as South Africa or Australia. And with so many golfers to select from, how many British players would make the team?

LEFT: *Antonio Garrido (far left) and Severiano Ballesteros (far right), the first Spanish players in Europe's Ryder Cup team.*

OPPOSITE: *US captain Billy Casper poses with the Ryder Cup trophy after yet another victory for the Americans.*

DAY ONE

CAPTAINS

USA: Billy Casper   **Europe:** John Jacobs

FRIDAY MORNING FOURBALLS

Wadkins/Nelson *beat* **Garrido/Ballesteros**, *2 and 1*

Trevino/Zoeller *beat* **Brown/James**, *3 and 2*

Bean/Elder *beat* **Oosterhuis/Faldo**, *2 and 1*

Irwin/Mahaffey *lost to* **Gallacher/Barnes**, *2 and 1*

Session Score: 3-1

FRIDAY AFTERNOON FOURSOMES

Irwin/Kite *beat* **Brown/Smyth**, *7 and 6*

Zoeller/Green *lost to* **Ballesteros/Garrido**, *3 and 2*

Trevino/Morgan *halved with* **Lyle/Jacklin**

Wadkins/Nelson *beat* **Gallacher/Barnes**, *4 and 3*

Session Score: 2.5-1.5

Overall Score: USA 5.5, Europe 2.5

> **"*Brown played like he didn't care.*"**
>
> *Hale Irwin expresses his surprise at the behaviour of Ken Brown*

With the European Tour growing in stature and players such as a young Seve Ballesteros catching the eye, a European team was seen as a more attractive option, despite plenty of opposition from traditionalists on both sides of the Atlantic. Even the legendary Arnold Palmer objected, saying: "There are occasions even in professional sport when who wins by how much isn't everything." In the end, he was in the minority, though.

So, when the next Ryder Cup matches took place at The Greenbrier in West Virginia, the USA were up against new-look opposition that, for the first time, included two players from continental Europe: Spaniards Severiano Ballesteros and Antonio Garrido. Not that it made much difference to the result. With the format changed once again to include two sets of Foursomes and Fourballs followed by 12 singles matches, European captain John Jacobs had a brief boost when, after a rain-delayed start, he sent his Spaniards out together in the very first match and they duly won the opening two holes against Lanny Wadkins and Larry Nelson. Eventually they lost 2 and 1 in what proved to be yet another walkover for the Americans, led by captain Billy Casper.

There was, at least, an encouraging win for Brian Barnes and

Bernard Gallacher against Hale Irwin and John Mahaffey, but the USA were 3-1 up after the opening session. Europe were further embarrassed by the behaviour of two of their younger players, Ken Brown and Mark James, who, having turned up at the airport in casual clothes instead of team attire, then missed a team meeting to go shopping. Some critics demanded that the pair should be dropped after further disrespectful and disinterested antics during the opening ceremony, but instead they were sent out second in the morning and lost convincingly to Lee Trevino and "Fuzzy" Zoeller, with their body language once again criticized. In fact, Brown's petulant behaviour in an afternoon Foursomes match with Des Smyth (a new pairing because Mark James was suffering from a muscle injury) against Irwin and Tom Kite was so bad that the Europeans issued an apology after their team had lost, 7 and 6.

The European pair's behaviour dominated coverage in Britain, meaning a first-ever win for Ballesteros and Garrido over Zoeller and Hubert Green was overshadowed as the Americans went 5.5-2.5 ahead at the end of the first day of the first Ryder Cup to feature Europe instead of Great Britain.

PLAYER OF THE MATCH

Larry Nelson, who finished second to Tom Watson on the money list in 1979, was the USA's man of the weekend as he won a perfect five points from five matches in his very first Ryder Cup. He also secured four points in 1981 and went on to complete his Ryder Cup career with a record of nine victories, three defeats and one halved match - one of the ten best records of any American player in the history of the tournament.

> **"*The overall score wasn't that close, but many matches went down to the wire.*"**
>
> *US captain Billy Casper on the new-look Ryder Cup*

For the nervous organizers who were looking for signs that making changes to the Ryder Cup would eventually lead to it becoming more competitive, there was least some hope on the Saturday at Greenbrier. With a much-improved performance, Europe won the morning Foursomes session 3-1 to put themselves back in contention. Convincing wins for Tony Jacklin and Sandy Lyle (5 and 4 against Lee Elder and John Mahaffey) and for Nick Faldo and Peter Oosterhuis against Andy Bean and Tom Kite (this time by 6 and 5) gave the Europeans a morale-boosting start to the day. When Fuzzy Zoeller and Mark Hayes were beaten by Gallacher/Barnes 2 and 1, it seemed a clean sweep was on the cards - had Wadkins and the impressive Nelson not seen off Ballesteros and Garrido, 3 and 2.

The Americans continued their recovery in the afternoon as Wadkins and Nelson demolished Ballesteros and Garrido, 5 and 4,

to make it a difficult first Ryder Cup for the Spaniards. Irwin and Kite then teamed up to beat Jacklin/Lyle at the last but the session finished all square as Europe's most consistent performers - Faldo and Gallacher - fought back. Faldo again partnered Oosterhuis to a one-hole victory over Elder/Hayes, while Gallacher/Barnes made it three wins out of four as they beat Trevino/Zoeller.

With the US team only one point ahead going into the final day, there was still a chance that Europe could spring a surprise victory, but that hope was quickly demolished by a powerful display by the home side during Sunday's singles matches. Even without their leading money earner, Tom Watson - who had quit the team on the eve of the tournament as he rushed to attend the birth of his daughter - and despite fielding seven rookies, the USA were still, by some way, the better side.

Gallacher, with a 3 and 2 victory over Wadkins, gave Europe a good start, but the Americans hit back through the ever-consistent Larry Nelson (with his fifth win in three days), Kite, Hayes, Bean and Mahaffey all posting solid victories. Once the stoic Faldo had responded with a point for Europe, further victories for Irwin, Green and Trevino wrapped up the now-customary US victory parade. Only a late win for Brown against Zoeller gave Europe anything to smile about (although given his behaviour over the previous two days, there was an element of irony there). Clearly, there was a long way to go before the Ryder Cup matches would be as close as everyone dreamt of.

There had also been a gesture of sportsmanship from Europe captain Jacobs on the final day, which unlike previous years featured all 12 players in singles action. Both teams were asked to place the name of a player in a brown envelope in case an opponent was ill or injured, to even out the numbers. But Casper had clearly misunderstood the process and placed the name of his best player – Lee Trevino – in the envelope in error. James, to his credit, recognized it was a simple mistake and allowed his opposite number to rest Gil Morgan instead. The Ryder Cup was still not yet fully competitive, but it had certainly retained its spirit.

DAYS TWO AND THREE

SATURDAY MORNING FOURSOMES

Elder/Mahaffey *lost to* **Jacklin/Lyle**, *5 and 4*

Bean/Kite *lost to* **Faldo/Oosterhuis**, *6 and 5*

Zoeller/Hayes *lost to* **Gallacher/Barnes**, *2 and 1*

Wadkins/Nelson *beat* **Ballesteros/Garrido**, *3 and 2*

Session Score: 1-3

SATURDAY AFTERNOON FOURBALLS

Wadkins/Nelson *beat* **Ballesteros/Garrido**, *5 and 4*

Irwin/Kite *beat* **Jacklin/Lyle** *by one hole*

Trevino/Zoeller *lost to* **Gallacher/Barnes**, *3 and 2*

Elder/Hayes *lost to* **Faldo/Oosterhuis** *by one hole*

Session Score: 2-2

SUNDAY SINGLES

Lanny Wadkins *lost to* **Bernard Gallacher**, *3 and 2*

Larry Nelson *beat* **Seve Ballesteros**, *3 and 2*

Tom Kite *beat* **Tony Jacklin** *by one hole*

Mark Hayes *beat* **Antonio Garrido** *by one hole*

Andy Bean *beat* **Michael King**, *4 and 3*

John Mahaffey *beat* **Brian Barnes** *by one hole*

Lee Elder *lost to* **Nick Faldo**, *3 and 2*

Hale Irwin *beat* **Des Smyth**, *5 and 3*

Hubert Green *beat* **Peter Oosterhuis** *by two holes*

Fuzzy Zoeller *lost to* **Ken Brown** *by one hole*

Lee Trevino *beat* **Sandy Lyle**, *2 and 1*

Gil Morgan *halved with* **Mark James**

(Mark James injured, match not played)

Session Score: 8.5-3.5

Overall Score: USA 17, Europe 11

OPPOSITE: *Europe's controversial pair Ken Brown (far right) and Mark James (in red) shake after defeat to Fuzzy Zoeller (far left) and Lee Trevino.*

BELOW: *A young Sandy Lyle hits another sweet shot for Europe but he couldn't help his team to victory.*

1981

Europe 9.5
USA 18.5

Walton Heath Golf Club, Surrey

September 18-20

THE COURSE

The Old Course
Location: Walton Heath
Golf Club, Surrey,
England
Par: 72
Yards: 7,462

Chosen as a late replacement to The Belfry, Walton Heath – a classic fast-running heath-and-heather course designed by Herbert Fowler – was seen as a better choice. Its small and unreceptive greens were meant to favour the playing style of the Europeans.

Just when the arrival of the Europeans provided hope of a more competitive tournament, the USA sent possibly its strongest-ever side to Walton Heath and demolished their opponents by a record margin. The result underlined their superiority and left the hosts regretting a row with Seve Ballesteros, which prevented the great Spaniard from taking part.

TO SAY THAT 1981 was a setback for the new-look Team Europe is an understatement. The Americans were so strong and so superior that John Jacobs' side were completely torn apart by a ruthless display of team golf in a performance that must surely rank as one of the finest in Ryder Cup history.

In truth, nothing went right for the home side during the build-up to the event, let alone on the golf course. For a start it was due to be staged at The Belfry - the new West Midlands headquarters of the Professional Golfers Association - but the course was neither ready nor suitable and so the Ryder Cup was switched at the last minute to Walton Heath, Surrey. Then there were huge issues over selection. The biggest of these involved Seve Ballesteros, who was now playing his golf on the American tour

but looked unlikely to qualify through the team by earnings alone and would need to be a captain's pick. Despite a shaky start to his Ryder Cup career two years earlier, the Spaniard would certainly have been a good addition to the team considering he had completed a dramatic Open victory at Royal Lytham in 1979 and clinched his first US Open a year later. His style of play - full of clever recovery shots, dramatic escapes from impossible positions and glorious touch-shots - made him popular, both in Europe and America. But there was a problem: a political one.

Seve had become embroiled in a huge row over appearance money: as a player on the US tour he had been demanding fees to play in events in Europe (as other American players did) which went against the principles of many of those running golf

LEFT: *Jack Nicklaus and Tom Watson take refuge under the umbrellas during a rainy opening day in Surrey.*

OPPOSITE: *Dave Marr and his victorious US team get their hands on the trophy after a convincing win at Walton Heath.*

in Britain and Europe. Even when captain Jacobs asked him to compete in two pre-Ryder Cup events in Europe as a gesture of goodwill, Ballesteros refused.

When the European team was announced, there was no Seve Ballesteros. And, just as surprisingly, Tony Jacklin had been left out in favour of Mark James, a player so heavily criticized for his behaviour two years earlier at The Greenbrier. And this despite Jacklin's incredible record of only eight defeats in 35 Ryder Cup matches. In contrast, the US team – hailed the best to come to England – could not have been stronger, with 36 major championships between them. It included golfing superstars such as Jack Nicklaus, Tom Watson, Ray Floyd, Lee Trevino, Hale Irwin, Ben Crenshaw and Tom Kite.

The difference in class soon showed, although not immediately. Astonishingly, given the way the match was to end, Europe finished the opening day with a one-point lead. Trevino and Larry Nelson started well enough for the US, beating debutants Bernhard Langer and Manuel Piñero by one hole, but the morning Foursomes ended 2-2. Sandy Lyle and Mark James beat Bill Rogers and Bruce Lietzke, while Bernard Gallacher and Des Smyth overcame Hale Irwin and Ray Floyd. The match of the day was a battle between Faldo and Oosterhuis against the "dream team" of Watson/Nicklaus, which proved hugely competitive. Nicklaus had already lost out to the same pairing four years earlier (when partnered by Floyd) and clearly sought revenge as the Americans came from two-down after four to win 4 and 3 with a flurry of birdies.

Surprisingly, Faldo and Oosterhuis were then "rested" for the afternoon session, which saw Europe – against all expectations – take the lead, as they were replaced by the untried pairing of Irishman Des Smyth and Spaniard José María Cañizares. It proved to be a wise decision as the Europeans won 6 and 5 before Sandy Lyle and Mark James beat Crenshaw and Jerry Pate, 3 and 2. Sam Torrance and Howard Clark halved with Kite and Johnny Miller. America's only victory came from the ever-reliable Irwin/Floyd. Suddenly, the Europeans were going into the second day 4.5-3.5 ahead.

DAY ONE

CAPTAINS
Europe: John Jacobs   **USA:** Dave Marr

FRIDAY MORNING FOURSOMES
Langer/Piñero *lost to* **Trevino/Nelson** *by one hole*

Lyle/James *beat* **Rogers/Lietzke**, *2 and 1*

Gallacher/Smyth *beat* **Irwin/Floyd**, *3 and 2*

Oosterhuis/Faldo *lost to* **Watson/Nicklaus**, *4 and 3*

Session Score: 2-2

FRIDAY AFTERNOON FOURBALLS
Torrance/Clark *halved with* **Kite/Miller**

Lyle/James *beat* **Crenshaw/Pate**, *3 and 2*

Smyth/Cañizares *beat* **Rogers/Lietzke**, *6 and 4*

Gallacher/Darcy *lost to* **Irwin/Floyd**, *2 and 1*

Session Score: 2.5-1.5

Overall Score: Europe 4.5, USA 3.5

> **"***We've got a submarine on hand in case.***"**
>
> *US captain Dave Marr on his escape plans if his team lost*

Ryder Cup legends
Nick **FALDO** and Peter **OOSTERHUIS**

Nick Faldo is Mr Ryder Cup – most appearances, matches played, individual points, victories and fewest matches lost, there is barely a record he doesn't hold. Yet Ryder Cup folklore belongs both to Faldo and players such as Peter Oosterhuis, who competed in five successive European defeats, as they helped raise the competition to the exalted status it now holds.

When Scottish player Sam Torrance struck the winning putt in the 1985 Ryder Cup at The Belfry, it was not only a victory for the brilliant golfers present of the European side, but also a glorious triumph for all those who had battled so manfully towards inevitable defeat in the previous 28 years that the trophy had remained under US control. Few players embody the two sides to that particular coin better than Nick Faldo and Peter Oosterhuis.

For all of Faldo's triumphs, the man who put Welwyn Garden City on the map is well aware that he owes a debt of gratitude to characters such as "man mountain" Oosterhuis. The 6ft 5in Englishman played in every Ryder Cup from 1971–81 – and lost them all. Despite this, his personal record was 14 victories, 11 defeats and three halves. A man able to scramble a par from almost any position (and perhaps a European warning of what was to come when Seve Ballesteros arrived on the scene), Oosterhuis transformed from middling pro to a competitive lion when on Ryder Cup duty. His singles victims included the likes of Arnold Palmer, Johnny Miller and Gene Littler, but perhaps Oosterhuis' most famous match was against Lee Trevino in 1973. The night before they faced each other at Muirfield, East Lothian, Trevino told team-mates: "If I don't beat Oosterhuis, I'll kiss every ass in this room!" Needless to say, when he returned to the dressing room after halving the match, every one of them was there to greet him – with buttocks bared.

Yet perhaps Oosterhuis' greatest legacy was in teaching Faldo what the Ryder Cup really means, and quite why it gets under your skin and into the soul. Certainly, few would have blamed Faldo had he decided to pull out of the 1977 tournament for he was after all suffering with glandular fever. He himself was having none of it, however. It was his debut in the competition and he subsequently resolved to battle through – and did so in some style. Ultimately, this was a disappointing tournament for Great Britain and Ireland as they lost 12.5 to 7.5, but Faldo and Oosterhuis could come away with their heads up high as they won every match in which they competed. Raymond Floyd and Lou Graham were defeated in the Foursomes, Floyd and Jack Nicklaus in the Fourballs, then finally, Faldo and Oosterhuis claimed pyrrhic victories in the singles over Tom Watson and Jerry McGee respectively. It was an astonishing performance by the two men and it came as little surprise when they were paired together again in 1979. They had more of a mixed time in West Virginia, however, losing their Fourballs clash before claiming a stunning victory over Tom Kite and Andy Bean, 6 and 5.

> **"***Years from now I want people to be able to say, 'I saw Faldo play.'***"**

Nick Faldo's determination shines through

Unfortunately, Peter Oosterhuis' last appearance in the competition (1981) ultimately proved one to forget: he and Faldo were broken up as a partnership after losing 4 and 3 to Nicklaus and Watson before both lost while partnering Sam Torrance. Yet Faldo carried on the mantle of being the man that Europe rallied behind, the talismanic star who could take the fight to the Americans, as proven by his five Major titles between 1987 and 1992. And after being part of the team that made history in twice retaining the trophy Torrance sealed in 1985, Faldo's finest moment was still to come.

America had regained control of the Ryder Cup, winning in both 1991 and 1993, and went into the singles of 1995 ahead by two points. As the day went on, it became clear that victory hinged on Faldo beating Curtis Strange, yet on the 16th, he was one hole down and in the trees, while Strange was in the middle of the fairway. But the Faldo hit his approach to four feet and saved par. His opponent fell to pieces, and Faldo made another save for par at the last to seal a stunning victory. He became a figurehead for Europe, and his tally of points and appearances are unlikely to be matched. Not even defeat as captain in 2008 can change that.

RYDER CUP RECORD

Nick FALDO
Ryder Cups: 1977, 1979, 1981, 1983, 1985 (winner), 1987 (winner), 1989 (tied but Europe retains trophy), 1991, 1993, 1995 (winner), 1997 (winner), 2008 (non-playing captain)
Total wins: 4 (plus 1 tie to retain the trophy, 1989)
Matches: 46 (won 23, halved 4, lost 19)
Total points: 25

Peter OOSTERHUIS
Ryder Cups: 1971, 1973, 1975, 1977, 1979, 1981
Total wins: 0
Matches: 28 (won 14, halved 3, lost 11)
Points: 15.5

AS A PAIR:
Matches: 6 (won 4, halved 0, lost 2)
Total points: 4

ABOVE: *Ryder Cup all-time great Nick Faldo (right) with team-mate Peter Oosterhuis (left) at Royal Lytham & St Annes in 1997. Jack Nicklaus is centre.*

1983

USA 14.5
Europe 13.5

PGA National Golf Club, Florida

October 14-16

America's dream team was finally made to put up a fight in 1983. With Tony Jacklin brought in as captain and Seve Ballesteros welcomed back, Europe produced a gallant attempt to win back the Ryder Cup as they went into the final day level at 8-8 in Florida – only to lose by a single point in the end. The genius of Lanny Wadkins helped captain Jack Nicklaus oversee his side's seventh victory in a row.

WITH THE US TEAM STRONGER than ever and having gone so many years without a trophy, the Europeans – whose side was this time selected based on the Order of Merit plus three captain's picks – knew that the 1983 Ryder Cup was a crucial one. It was time to show the golfing world that European Tour players could match their rivals across the Atlantic in the US. That aim was certainly achieved in Florida, and although the target of ending Europe's Ryder Cup drought would have to wait a while, no one – on either side of the Atlantic – was left in any doubt that future tournaments would be closely fought occasions. In fact, Europe were level with their rivals all the way through to the tenth singles match on the Sunday, and it took something special from Lanny Wadkins, who produced a classic wedge shot under pressure at the death, and a missed putt from Bernard Gallacher to deny them something more than just honour in defeat.

The USA went into the matches as strong favourites, not surprising considering their record of having won 20, lost three and tied one in recent Ryder Cup history; also taking into account that talismanic Nicklaus was their captain. No US captain had ever lost on home soil since the competition began in 1927, as Nicklaus bluntly reminded his players following a somewhat nervy start. However, Tony Jacklin was determined to lead an improved European side and insisted on a string of changes, from the players travelling on Concorde (accompanied by their loved ones) to smart new suits, a "team room" at the hotel to encourage team spirit and caddies paid for by the European Tour. But perhaps his biggest coup was in persuading Seve Ballesteros to reconsider his Ryder Cup future and join the team.

The USA also had new blood on board, including Curtis Strange and Calvin Peete (only the second black American to play in the

RIGHT: *The US team line up for the 1983 Ryder Cup complete with garish suits at the opening ceremony.*

DAY ONE

CAPTAINS

USA: Jack Nicklaus   **Europe:** Tony Jacklin

FRIDAY MORNING FOURSOMES

Watson/Crenshaw *beat* **Gallacher/Lyle**, *5 and 4*

Wadkins/Stadler *lost to* **Faldo/Langer**, *4 and 2*

Floyd/Gilder *lost to* **Cañizares/Torrance**, *4 and 2*

Kite/Peete *beat* **Ballesteros/Way**, *2 and 1*

Session Score: 2-2

FRIDAY AFTERNOON FOURBALLS

Morgan/Zoeller *lost to* **Waites/Brown**, *2 and 1*

Watson/Haas *beat* **Faldo/Langer**, *2 and 1*

Floyd/Strange *lost to* **Ballesteros/Way** *by one hole*

Crenshaw/Peete *halved with* **Torrance/Woosnam**

Session Score: 1.5-2.5

Overall Score: USA 3.5, Europe 4.5

ABOVE: *Europe's Seve Ballesteros gives youngster Paul Way a hand during a day of mixed fortunes.*

Ryder Cup after Lee Elder), but with Nicklaus, Lee Trevino and Johnny Miller no longer playing perhaps they were not as strong as two years previously. Nicklaus, as non-playing captain, had thought seriously about his tactics and realizing how important team spirit would be in this particular Ryder Cup, had opted to base many of his pairings on friendships rather than rankings. Indeed, his first line-up of Tom Watson and Ben Crenshaw got the side off to the best possible start by beating Gallacher and Sandy Lyle, 5 and 4.

Played in searing temperatures that regularly topped 32°C (90°F), it quickly became clear that this would be no walkover, though. Faldo/Langer beat Wadkins and Craig Stadler, 4 and 2, to level things up and the morning session ended 2-2, with Sam Torrance and José María Cañizares providing a shock victory over Ray Floyd and Bob Gilder before Peete/Kite calmed some of the hype surrounding Ballesteros in winning 2 and 1 against the Spaniard and the young Englishman, Paul Way.

Despite this setback, Jacklin proved his talent at man-management over lunch, coaxing Ballesteros back into action after reports that the Spaniard was unhappy at having been paired with Way rather than his compatriot Cañizares. As captain, Jacklin needed Seve to guide his younger team-mate (Way was just 20 years old at the time) through the afternoon session and the Spaniard did exactly that as they beat Floyd and Strange at the last.

Europe ended the day with a one-point lead as Brian Waites and Ken Brown also won (2 and 1 against Gil Morgan and Fuzzy Zoeller), while Torrance and Ian Woosnam held Crenshaw/Peete to a half. The big winners for the USA were Watson and Jay Haas, who won 2 and 1 against possibly Europe's top pairing of Faldo/Langer. Even so, Nicklaus knew he had a fight on his hands.

> *"I will not be the first captain to blow this thing. Now you guys, show me some brass!"*

US captain Jack Nicklaus rallies his team

If the opening day had been close, it was no different on the Saturday because the USA came back to level at 8-8 by the end of the day. Probably for the first time since 1969, the result remained inconclusive going into the final session.

The morning Fourballs were won 2.5-1.5 by Nicklaus' men, with Craig Stadler showing the kind of determination and never-say-die spirit his captain had called for. He and Wadkins were three-down at one stage against Waites/Brown but came back to win at the last, thanks to a wonderful chip-in by Stadler at the 18th. Watson/Gilder also won against Torrance/Woosnam. But it wasn't only the Americans showing their mettle: Ballesteros produced two stunning woods to reach the par-five 18th in two against Morgan and Haas, knowing he needed to win the hole to earn a half. Playing alongside Way, the Spaniard was inspired as he chipped and putted to clinch a birdie and save his team from defeat. The pair won again in the afternoon, this time beating Watson/Gilder as another tight session was drawn 2-2. Sunday arrived with the teams all square and the Europeans dreaming of their first victory since 1957.

Jacklin opted to lead with his big guns up front in the singles, while Nicklaus placed his most experienced players further down the list to plug any holes in an emergency. Maybe the American made the right move because the match proved very close indeed. Early on, Ballesteros was on fire against Zoeller in the opening match, birdying four holes in a row to be three-up after 11 – only for the American to reply with four in a row and reach the 18th narrowly ahead. But Seve produced a quite remarkable shot from the bunker to set up a birdie and an all-important half at the death.

The rest of the singles then unfolded with the lead constantly changing hands. Faldo beat Haas, 2 and 1; Crenshaw replied by beating Lyle, 3 and 1. Then Langer beat Morgan to re-take the lead; Gilder responded by finishing off Gordon J. Brand before Peete sealed a one-up thriller against Waites. Finally, the USA led, but when Way beat fellow rookie Curtis Strange the seesaw was swinging again – and so it continued until the score reached 12.5-all and Nicklaus, buzzing around the course in his buggy, one ear glued to a walkie-talkie, started to fret.

In fact, when Torrance hit a stunning pitch at the 18th to halve his match with Kite, Europe appeared to be heading for a tie at the very least – unless Lanny Wadkins, who was one down against

SHOT OF THE DAY

Severiano Ballesteros' incredible bunker shot at the 18th against Fuzzy Zoeller is often listed as one of the best in Ryder Cup history. In fact, Bernhard Langer describes it as "the greatest shot I ever experienced". Seve, one down and fighting for a half, chose to take a three-wood from the sand – in a deep-linked bunker – and sent the ball 240 yards to the edge of the green.

LEFT: *Tom Watson takes aim at Palm Beach as the USA hold their nerve against an improving Europe.*

ABOVE: *Calvin Peete (partly hidden) congratulates his US team-mate Lanny Wadkins after a dramatic half against Spain's José María Cañizares.*

José María Cañizares, could produce something special. And that he did.

The American players and partners raced to the 18th fairway to watch as Wadkins left himself an 80-yard wedge to a pin guarded by a large bunker. He not only nailed the shot but almost holed it as Nicklaus rushed over and kissed the divot his player had left behind. Even then there was almost late drama as Watson allowed a two-hole lead to slip against Gallacher. Had the Scotsman not double-bogeyed the 17th, it could have been even closer. But the real moment when America's victory was sealed came with that incredible shot from Wadkins, who described it as "the most important of my life". It was a shot that kept Europe at bay for another two years – but at least they were getting closer.

> **"***It's the first tournament I've ever been to when I wasn't playing and couldn't do anything about what was happening. This was the damnedest thing I was ever involved in!***"**
>
> *US captain Jack Nicklaus*

DAYS TWO AND THREE

SATURDAY MORNING FOURBALLS

Wadkins/Stadler *beat* **Waites/Brown** *by one hole*

Crenshaw/Peete *lost to* **Faldo/Langer,** *4 and 2*

Morgan/Haas *halved with* **Ballesteros/Way**

Watson/Gilder *beat* **Torrance/Woosnam,** *5 and 4*

Session Score: 2.5-1.5

SATURDAY AFTERNOON FOURSOMES

Kite/Floyd *lost to* **Faldo/Langer,** *3 and 2*

Morgan/Wadkins *beat* **Torrance/Cañizares,** *7 and 5*

Watson/Gilder *lost to* **Ballesteros/Way,** *2 and 1*

Haas/Strange *beat* **Waites/Brown,** *3 and 2*

Session Score: 2-2

SUNDAY SINGLES

Fuzzy Zoeller *halved with* **Severiano Ballesteros**

Jay Haas *lost to* **Nick Faldo,** *2 and 1*

Gil Morgan *lost to* **Bernhard Langer** *by two holes*

Bob Gilder *beat* **Gordon J. Brand** *by two holes*

Ben Crenshaw *beat* **Sandy Lyle,** *3 and 1*

Calvin Peete *beat* **Brian Waites** *by one hole*

Curtis Strange *lost to* **Paul Way,** *2 and 1*

Tom Kite *halved with* **Sam Torrance**

Craig Stadler *beat* **Ian Woosnam,** *3 and 2*

Lanny Wadkins *halved with* **José María Cañizares**

Ray Floyd *lost to* **Ken Brown,** *4 and 3*

Tom Watson *beat* **Bernard Gallacher,** *2 and 1*

Session Score: 6.5-5.5

Overall Score: USA 14.5, Europe 13.5

Severiano Ballesteros of Europe plays a shot out of a bunker during his 1983 Ryder Cup singles match against Fuzzy Zoeller at the PGA National course in Palm Beach Gardens, Florida.

1985
Europe 16.5
USA 11.5

The Belfry, Sutton Coldfield

September 13-15

THE COURSE

Brabazon Course
Location: The Belfry,
Sutton Coldfield,
England
Par: 72
Yards: 7,118

Extensive re-seeding and tree planting after its last-minute replacement by Walton Heath in 1981, The Belfry played like a dream. Now complete with an on-course hotel, there was enough room for both teams to stay on site.

For Europe, 28 years of waiting and the accompanying frustration finally ended when Sam Torrance sank a putt on the 18th at The Belfry in 1985 and raised his arms aloft in celebration. For the first time since 1957, the Ryder Cup was no longer in the hands of the US team and a new era in the history of golf's greatest team competition had just begun. The architect of Europe's win, Tony Jacklin, became a hero.

IN 1985, GOLF FANS IN ENGLAND and all over Europe sensed a change in the tide as their team prepared for the 26th Ryder Cup matches with a growing sense of optimism and excitement. Having come so close two years earlier at Palm Beach Gardens in Florida, European belief had been strengthened by Bernhard Langer's victory at the Masters in Augusta and Sandy Lyle's triumph at the British Open. Could this be the year when everything changed?

Record crowds of more than 25,000 flocked to The Belfry each day to cheer on their heroes, creating an atmosphere rarely experienced in the Ryder Cup before. It came as quite a shock to some of the American players, more accustomed to sedate British crowds who understood the etiquette of the game, when missed shots were cheered by the galleries and the volume grew louder, the nearer Europe came to victory. Suddenly, less than a decade after many critics suggested the event was too one-sided to survive for much longer, it was now so passionate and so competitive that a completely new generation of fans were giving it an edge hitherto unimagined.

Opinions were mixed on whether this new phenomenon was a good thing, with some players, including American Peter Jacobsen, complained it was off-putting and disappointing. US captain Lee Trevino was made of sterner stuff, however, and accused his own team members of being "cry babies". Whatever the behaviour of the crowd, the USA knew they had under-achieved at The Belfry because the side they sent to England was still a strong one, if perhaps lacking a real star name. It was missing talisman Tom Watson, who had narrowly failed to qualify, but captained by the experienced Trevino. US Open champion Andy North, PGA winner Hubert Green and new boys Mark O'Meara, Peter Jacobsen and Hal Sutton now added to the mix.

Once again captained by Tony Jacklin after his impressive leadership of two years earlier, the home side was largely similar

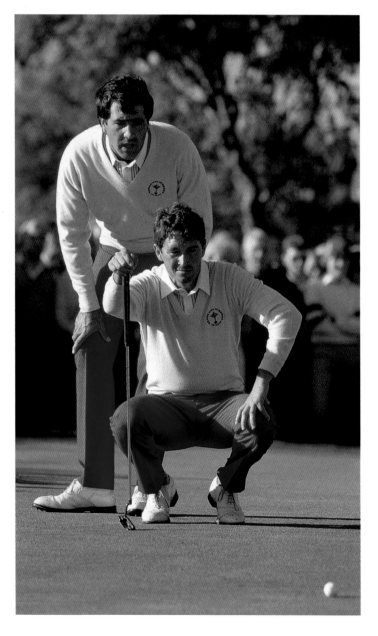

RIGHT: *Europe's Severiano Ballesteros (rear) and Manuel Piñero line up a putt during the second day of the 1985 Ryder Cup at The Belfry.*

LEFT: *Sunshine, flowers, water and greenery provide a picture-postcard moment at The Belfry as Curtis Strange putts for the USA.*

to the one that came so close to victory at Palm Beach, with Spaniard José Rivero the only real newcomer; the British public were expectant of something special. However, the galleries were made to wait for their moment of glory as the opening day saw Team USA in complete control as they began the defence of their trophy with resolve, claiming three of the four morning Foursomes. Calvin Peete and Tom Kite started the ball rolling with a 3 and 2 victory over the top European pairing of Bernhard Langer and Nick Faldo before the always-steady Wadkins and Floyd beat Lyle/Brown; Stadler/Sutton overcame Clark and Torrance, 3 and 2. For the Europeans, the only highlight was another impressive display from Seve Ballesteros, who drove the par-four 10th as he partnered Piñero to a 2 and 1 victory over Strange/O'Meara.

The afternoon Fourballs were more even, but the USA still ended the day with an important one-point lead, thanks primarily to a narrow victory by Floyd/Wadkins against Torrance/Clark at the last hole. However, Europe were encouraged by the performance of youngster Paul Way, who partnered the more experienced Ian Woosnam to beat Fuzzy Zoeller and Hubert Green by one hole. Meanwhile, another victory for Ballesteros and Piñero, this time against North/Jacobsen by 2 and 1, ensured the home side won the session (there was also a half for Langer and José María Cañizares against Stadler and Hal Sutton) and ended the day within touching distance of the holders – just 4.5-3.5 behind. The new Ryder Cup was starting to catch fire.

DAY ONE

CAPTAINS

Europe: Tony Jacklin   **USA:** Lee Trevino

FRIDAY MORNING FOURSOMES

Ballesteros/Piñero *beat* **Strange/O'Meara,** *2 and 1*

Langer/Faldo *lost to* **Peete/Kite,** *3 and 2*

Lyle/Brown *lost to* **Wadkins/Floyd,** *4 and 3*

Clark/Torrance *lost to* **Stadler/Sutton,** *3 and 2*

Session Score: 1-3

FRIDAY AFTERNOON FOURBALLS

Way/Woosnam *beat* **Zoeller/Green** *by one hole*

Ballesteros/Piñero *beat* **North/Jacobsen,** *2 and 1*

Langer/Cañizares *halved with* **Stadler/Sutton**

Torrance/Clark *lost to* **Floyd/Wadkins** *by one hole*

Session Score: 2.5-1.5

Overall Score: Europe 3.5, USA 4.5

Jack **NICKLAUS** and Tom **WATSON**

Virtually unbeatable as individuals, as a partnership Jack Nicklaus and Tom Watson were truly unstoppable. Together, they played four times in the Ryder Cup, winning all four times. Great friends off the course, the sight of them teaming up proved a dagger to the heart of any European hopes of victory – and their 100 per cent winning record testifies to the champions' potency.

Jack Nicklaus and Tom Watson arrived at the 1981 Ryder Cup determined not just to win but to eviscerate their opponents. The US team included players who had won a combined 37 Majors and the best of them – Nicklaus and Watson, who had won 26 of them – were, quite simply, unbeatable together. They had first partnered four years earlier at Royal Lytham & St Annes and served notice of just how potent a team they could be in beating Tommy Horton and Mark James, winning 5 and 4 in their Foursomes match.

They began in 1981 with a convincing 4 and 3 Foursomes win over Peter Oosterhuis and Nick Faldo before being rested until the second day. That was when America took complete control of the tie, winning the morning Fourballs and afternoon Foursomes 7-1, just half a point short of the all-time Ryder Cup record. Nicklaus and Watson were to the fore. Des Smyth and Jose Maria Cañizares were beaten 3 and 2 in the Fourballs before Bernhard Langer and Manuel Piñero lost by the same scoreline in the Foursomes.

Watson has since said Nicklaus was the reason they won, but that's putting himself down. True, his partner found the green on the four out of five occasions that Watson's drive ended up in the heather, but this was a real team. Nicklaus went on to beat Eamonn Darcy in the singles to complete his perfect Ryder Cup and the final score was 18.5 to 9.5 in America's favour. Nicklaus and Watson's last time playing together was also the last time the USA won the Ryder Cup so convincingly.

The pair also enjoyed enormous success as individuals in the Ryder Cup. Nicklaus' first tournament was in 1969 at Royal Birkdale and is still remembered as one of the greatest acts of sportsmanship in its history. The whole tournament was on a knife-edge and as Nicklaus sunk a four-foot putt on the last, his opponent – Tony Jacklin – was left with a two-footer to tie. Nicklaus conceded the putt, ensuring the Ryder Cup was tied for the first time in history, although America still retained the trophy.

It proved the start of a wonderful story for Nicklaus, playing 15 matches and taking 10 points between 1971 and 1975. Having taken to heart the Ryder Cup concept, he captained the American team

in 1983 and 1987. In both cases it was Nicklaus v Jacklin. In 1983 the score was 1-1 as the USA won by one point. Four years later the USA was beaten on American soil for the first time, losing 15-13.

Tom Watson followed his friend in being both a victorious player and captain. He played under Nicklaus in 1983 and made his final appearance some six years later when his victory over Sam Torrance helped secure a tie at The Belfry. Then, as captain in 1993, his team were a point down after two days at The Belfry, but staged a memorable comeback, winning six singles matches and halving two others to claim victory.

Ultimately, though, Jack Nicklaus and Tom Watson will be remembered for their stunning performances as players. As a pair they were so dominant that they never once had to play the 17th hole, let alone an 18th, to win a match. Individually, the two men were astonishing; together, they were completely unstoppable.

RYDER CUP RECORD

Jack NICKLAUS
Ryder Cups: 1969 (tied but USA retains trophy), 1971, 1973, 1975, 1977, 1981, 1983 (non-playing captain), 1987 (non-playing captain). All won, except 1969 tie and 1987.
Total wins: 6 (plus 1 tie to retain the trophy, 1969)
Matches: 28 (won 17, halved 3, lost 8)
Total points: 18.5

Tom WATSON
Ryder Cups: 1977, 1979, 1981, 1983, 1989 (tied but Europe retain trophy), 1993 (non-playing captain), 2014 (non-playing captain). All won, except 1989 tie and 2014 loss.
Total wins: 5
Matches: 15 (won 10, halved 1, lost 4)
Total points: 10.5

AS A PAIR:
Matches: 4 (won 4, halved 0, lost 0)
Total points: 4

> **"***Resolve never to quit, never to give up, no matter what the situation.***"**
>
> *Jack Nicklaus on being a winner*

ABOVE: *Unbeatable US pairing Jack Nicklaus (right) and Tom Watson deep in discussion at the 1981 Ryder Cup at Walton Heath Golf Club.*

ABOVE: *Severiano Ballesteros celebrates a winning putt in his singles match against Curtis Strange, his fourth point of the 1987 Ryder Cup.*

On the Saturday, the USA needed to start well – and did, with Strange/Kite comfortable winners against Rivero and Brand Jnr. in the morning Foursomes and Sutton and Larry Mize denying Faldo/Woosnam their third victory in a row by winning the final hole for a half. But the next two matches set the tone for what was to come: Lyle/Langer won 2 and 1 against Wadkins and Larry Nelson, including an eagle at the 11th, before Ballesteros/Olazábal crept home against Ben Crenshaw and Payne Stewart. The result helped to quieten the home crowd, who had been issued with free Stars and Stripes flags and were asked by Nicklaus to provide more voluble support.

But in the afternoon session (tied 2-2), the Europeans played some outstanding golf. Nick Faldo and Ian Woosnam's performance against Curtis Strange and Tom Kite had to be seen

DAYS TWO AND THREE

SATURDAY MORNING FOURSOMES

Strange/Kite *beat* **Rivero/Brand,** *3 and 1*

Sutton/Mize *halved with* **Faldo/Woosnam**

Wadkins/Nelson *lost to* **Lyle/Langer,** *2 and 1*

Crenshaw/Stewart *lost to* **Ballesteros/Olazábal** *by one hole*

Session Score: 1.5-2.5

SATURDAY AFTERNOON FOURBALLS

Strange/Kite *lost to* **Faldo/Woosnam,** *5 and 4*

Bean/Stewart *beat* **Darcy/Brand,** *3 and 2*

Sutton/Mize *beat* **Ballesteros/Olazábal,** *2 and 1*

Wadkins/Nelson *lost to* **Lyle/Langer** *by one hole*

Session Score: 2-2

SUNDAY SINGLES

Andy Bean *beat* **Ian Woosnam** *by one hole*

Dan Pohl *lost to* **Howard Clark** *by one hole*

Larry Mize *halved with* **Sam Torrance**

Mark Calcavecchia *beat* **Nick Faldo** *by one hole*

Payne Stewart *beat* **José María Olazábal** *by two holes*

Scott Simpson *beat* **José Rivero,** *2 and 1*

Tom Kite *beat* **Sandy Lyle,** *3 and 2*

Ben Crenshaw *lost to* **Eamonn Darcy** *by one hole*

Larry Nelson *halved with* **Bernhard Langer**

Curtis Strange *lost to* **Severiano Ballesteros,** *2 and 1*

Lanny Wadkins *beat* **Ken Brown,** *3 and 2*

Hal Sutton *halved with* **Gordon Brand**

Session Score: 7.5-4.5

Overall Score: USA 13, Europe 15

RIGHT: *An emotional and ecstatic European captain Tony Jacklin clasps the Ryder Cup after Europe retained the trophy at the Nicklaus-built Muirfield Village, course in Ohio, USA.*

to be believed: Kite and Strange - who was to go on and win the next two US Opens - were a high-quality pairing, but were torn apart, 5 and 4. "I don't think the Americans knew what hit them," Faldo said, when asked to recall the game. "Woosie and I birdied the first five holes - we played some unbelievable golf." Then Sandy Lyle and Bernhard Langer held off a late fight from Lanny Wadkins and Larry Nelson to win
by one hole, with Lyle hitting the shot of the day: a glorious approach to the 18th.

With the Europeans, who were collectively 25-under-par for the afternoon, now five ahead - and needing just four points to retain the trophy - Jack Nicklaus opted for shock tactics on the Sunday. He put his weaker players out first when Europe expected to see the big guns up front. It was a tactic that almost worked because the USA claimed five of the first seven games. Andy Bean stunned Ian Woosnam by winning at the 18th in the opening match - and the scoreboard showed the USA up in five and level in three of the remaining 11 matches. When European talisman Nick Faldo also lost - by one hole to Calcavecchia - Sandy Lyle lost to Tom Kite and José María Olazábal went down to Stewart, what had seemed impossible became more realistic.

But Europe had Howard Clark's early victory over Pohl to hang onto and a surprise hero in the shape of Eamonn Darcy. He was up against golfing legend Crenshaw but it was the American who cracked under the pressure - in spectacular style. Angry at a missed putt on the 6th green, he snapped the blade of his putter while hitting it on the ground in frustration and from then on, was forced to use his irons to putt. Amazingly, he still reached the 18th level, but threw it away with a tee-shot that found water, and when Darcy had a putt to win the match, he calmly holed it for his name to be passed down in Ryder Cup folklore.

With Europe now 13-11 ahead, they needed just one-and-a-half points from five games and a third of these came in surprising fashion when Langer called for a half at the 18th after rolling his putt just inside that of opponent Nelson's with the match squared. To everyone's surprise, Nelson agreed. Fittingly, the match-winning putt came from Ballesteros as he beat World No. 1 Curtis Strange on the 17th green to win 2 and 1 before lifting an arm aloft in triumph. The celebrations, it has to be said, were far less restrained - and as players danced and champagne flowed, Jacklin was almost speechless at what he and his team had achieved. It was a Ryder Cup that would never be forgotten.

"*It is the greatest week of my life!*"

Tony Jacklin hails Europe's victory

Ryder Cup legends
Tony JACKLIN and Bernard GALLACHER

Tony Jacklin and Bernard Gallacher were great Ryder Cup players but even greater captains. In 1985, Jacklin turned a one-sided tournament into the finest competition in golf by beating the USA for the first time in 28 years, then led Europe to its first-ever victory in America, two years later.

Tony Jacklin first shot to fame when he won The Open and The US Open in successive years in the late 1960s. With two Majors under his belt by the age of 26, his reputation was further enhanced when he became Ryder Cup captain in 1983, having played in the competition eight times, seven of which were American victories and one a memorable tie.

Jacklin was appointed non-playing captain for the 1983 contest. His first move was to bring Seve Ballesteros in from the cold and although the USA won by a point, Jacklin was about to change things. By 1985 he had a squad of fine players to support Ballesteros, including Ian Woosnam, Sandy Lyle, Bernhard Langer and Nick Faldo. His team at The Belfry in 1985 was better prepared than ever before and triumphed by a massive five-point margin.

Even better was to come when Jacklin took his team to the USA two years later, where they beat captain Jack Nicklaus' side on a course he had designed: Muirfield Village. A Ballesteros win over Curtis Strange completed a 15-13 victory and ensured a first defeat for the USA on home turf – "It was the sweetest moment," he observed. In his final contest as captain, back at The Belfry, Europe retained the trophy with a 14-14 draw. Jacklin had won the Ryder Cup in three of his four captaincies.

Bernard Gallacher followed in Jacklin's wake, having been a successful Ryder Cup player and assistant to his predecessor. He became the youngest Briton in the Ryder Cup when he made his debut in 1969 aged 20, and went on to play eight times. After he beat the legendary Lee Trevino five times, the American admitted: "In the Ryder Cup, Bernard was the only player to get the better of me." But it was not so easy as captain. His first tournament – the 1991 "War on the Shore" at Kiawah Island – ended in defeat. Two years later at The Belfry all of Gallacher's big names – Ballesteros, Faldo, Woosnam and Langer – failed to win on the final day. Gallacher wanted to step down as captain after the defeat, but was persuaded to stay – it turned out to be third time lucky.

His finest moment came in 1995, when Europe regained the Ryder Cup. He said the key to success was an open mind: "Before play at Oak Hill, I never at any time had Sam Torrance playing with Costantino Rocca but they came together because other guys were off-form or tired and they turned out to be a perfect combination." When Gallacher handed over to Seve Ballesteros for the 1997 Cup, it was the last time a European captain would have more than one term – the job was now just too big.

RYDER CUP RECORD

Tony JACKLIN
Ryder Cups: 1967, 1969, 1971, 1973, 1975, 1977, 1979, 1983 (non-playing captain), 1985 (winner, non-playing captain), 1987 (winner, non-playing captain), 1989 (tied but Europe retain trophy, non-playing captain)
Total wins: 2 (plus 1 tie to retain trophy, 1989)
Matches: 35 (won 13, halved 8, lost 14)
Total points: 17

Bernard GALLACHER
Ryder Cups: 1969, 1971, 1973, 1975, 1977, 1979, 1981, 1983, 1991 (non-playing captain), 1993 (non-playing captain), 1995 (winner, non-playing captain)
Total wins: 1
Matches: 31 (won 13, halved 5, lost 13)
Total points: 15.5

> *"The Ryder Cup is more than just golf – it is your country, your team, your tour, your captain that you're playing for. It is the ultimate in golf."*
>
> *Tony Jacklin*

1989

Europe 14
USA 14

The Belfry, Sutton Coldfield

September 22-24

In 1989, US captain Raymond Floyd controversially introduced his team as the "12 greatest players in the world". However, Europe (who by now felt they had plenty of players worthy of inclusion on such a list) matched them all the way in a dramatic contest at The Belfry, which ended in a tie – only the second in Ryder Cup history.

THE COURSE

Brabazon Course
Location: The Belfry, Sutton Coldfield, England
Par: 72
Yards: 7,118

Staging the Ryder Cup for the second time, The Belfry, set in 550 acres of Warwickshire countryside, could describe itself as the spiritual home of the Ryder Cup in England. And it certainly provided some incredible memories.

A QUICK LOOK AROUND The Belfry in the build-up to the 28th Ryder Cup matches showed just how far the competition had come: packed galleries, almost 1,000 accredited journalists, the largest tented village at any sports event in Britain and a crowd whipped up by pre-match hype generated by a headline-hungry media. It would take an incredible contest to live up to all this, but the 1989 Ryder Cup certainly delivered.

With Europe going into the matches as favourites for the first time in living memory, the interest in England was huge but the build-up was given extra fuel by US captain Floyd at the pre-

tournament Gala Ball. Perhaps attempting to put his team on the front foot, he introduced his players as the "12 greatest players in the world", partly in deference to the great Ben Hogan, who unveiled his side of 1967 with exactly the same words. But this time it backfired, serving only to infuriate the European team and provide captain Tony Jacklin with a very simple motivational speech on the eve of the opening day.

Tony Jacklin was captaining for the fourth – and final – time in a row. He had endured a difficult time in his personal life following the death of his wife Vivian in a car accident in Spain,

DAY ONE

CAPTAINS

Europe: Tony Jacklin   **USA:** Raymond Floyd

FRIDAY MORNING FOURSOMES

Faldo/Woosnam *halved with* **Kite/Strange**

Clark/James *lost to* **Wadkins/Stewart** *by one hole*

Ballesteros/Olazábal *halved with* **Watson/Beck**

Langer/Rafferty *lost to* **Calcavecchia/Green,** *2 and 1*

Session Score: 1-3

FRIDAY AFTERNOON FOURBALLS

Torrance/Brand *beat* **Strange/Azinger** *by one hole*

Clark/James *beat* **Couples/Wadkins,** *3 and 2*

Faldo/Woosnam *beat* **Calcavecchia/McCumber** *by two holes*

Ballesteros/Olazábal *beat* **Watson/M. O'Meara,** *6 and 5*

Session Score: 4-0

Overall Score: Europe 5, USA 3

RIGHT: *Crowds flock around the greens at The Belfry as the action gets serious in one of the closest Ryder Cups ever.*

OPPOSITE: *US team captain Ray Floyd gets around the course in his buggy during the Ryder Cup matches of 1989.*

but his team was still a powerful one. The Scot Sandy Lyle was missing, following an alarming dip in form, but Bernhard Langer had recovered from the yips to make the squad; Christy O'Connor Jnr. and Howard Clark were the other captain's picks, with Ronan Rafferty the only rookie.

The US, meanwhile, were in a transitional period and included five debutants in Paul Azinger, Chip Beck, Fred Couples, Mark McCumber and Ken Green – perhaps counter-balanced by Floyd's selection of the experienced Lanny Wadkins and Tom Watson as his personal choices. Even so, the Americans began the opening day in impressive fashion as they took a 3-1 lead by the end of the morning Foursomes. Nick Faldo and Ian Woosnam were held to a half in the opening match by Tom Kite and Curtis Strange before Wadkins, who had missed six cuts in his last eight tournaments, proved that the Ryder Cup is different as he partnered Stewart to a vital victory against Howard Clark and Mark James. Even when the incomparable partnership of Severiano Ballesteros and José María Olazábal took a three-hole lead against Beck and Watson the USA refused to crumble, with two birdie putts from Watson eventually helping them halve the match.

Europe's also lost the last Foursomes, where Langer and Rafferty battled back from three-down against Calcavecchia/

Green before going down 2 and 1. Thus, the favourites reached the opening afternoon without having won a single match. The Americans had laid down a serious challenge but it was a situation that would change very quickly indeed, with Europe recovering sufficiently to whitewash their opponents after lunch.

In a high-octane and patriotic atmosphere the home crowd at The Belfry could barely believe their eyes as Tony Jacklin's men won every single Fourballs match to end the day 5-3 ahead, even though the captain made only cursory changes. He kept three of his pairs the same but replaced the out-of-touch Langer and Rafferty with Torrance and Gordon Brand Jnr. Just as at Muirfield Village in Ohio two years earlier, his gamble paid handsome dividends as the new pairing were sent out first and edged to a one-hole victory over Curtis Strange and Azinger.

Further victories for Clark and James against Couples/Wadkins, 3 and 2, and for Faldo and Woosnam against Calcavecchia/McCumber by two holes put the European team on a high. Ballesteros/Olazábal added the icing to the cake with a hugely convincing 6 and 5 victory over Watson and O'Meara. In the space of a few hours Europe had gone from frustration to elation and, in the process, whipped up an already enthusiastic crowd into a high-pitch whirl of excitement.

CHAPTER SIX
LET BATTLE COMMENCE

With Europe growing in stature in the 1980s, holding the trophy for three contests in a row, it was up to the USA to hit back in the 1990s. The Americans did exactly that, resulting in some fiercely contested - and sometimes controversial - Ryder Cups.

The US team celebrates after their amazing fightback earned them victory by a single point at the 1999 Ryder Cup.

1991

USA 14.5
Europe 13.5

Kiawah Island, South Carolina

September 27-29

THE COURSE

The Ocean Course
Location: Kiawah Island
Golf Resort,
Kiawah Island,
South Carolina, USA

Par: 72
Yards: 7,356

Designed by Pete Dye, the course had only just been completed when the Ryder Cup arrived in town. Naturally, there were still some unfinished parts but with a sea view from every hole The Ocean Course was both scenic and testing.

Before a ball was even struck, the 1991 Ryder Cup at Kiawah Island had been billed "War on the Shore" by an American magazine and it certainly lived up to this tag, proving to be one of the most controversial, yet compelling Ryder Cups of all time. Eventually, it was decided on the last green, in the last match of the last day by a missed putt from Bernhard Langer.

US CAPTAIN DAVE STOCKTON, aware his team needed every advantage, hardly sought to calm the atmosphere. In fact, he infuriated the European team by inviting them to watch a 40-minute film on the History of the Ryder Cup - one edited to feature virtually all American victories and celebrations. Nick Faldo almost walked out in protest and by the time the players teed off, there was no love lost between them.

Matters were hardly helped by a local radio DJ broadcasting a shameful "Wake Up the Enemy" campaign, giving out the phone number of the European hotel and urging US supporters to ring the players in the middle of the night. Indeed, many overly pumped-up fans did exactly that. It seemed the "War on the Shore" tag was being taken too seriously and therefore when Corey Pavin and Steve Pate turned up to play a Fourballs wearing "Operation Desert Storm" forage caps it seemed at the very least tactless and at worst, tasteless. However, no one could say the intense atmosphere wasn't working in America's favour because when Team USA finally got to play golf, they made an impressive start.

ABOVE: Seve Ballesteros tees off at the 4th on Day One, watched by José María Olazábal and the USA's Paul Azinger and Chip Beck.

DAY ONE

CAPTAINS

USA: Dave Stockton   **Europe:** Bernard Gallacher

FRIDAY MORNING FOURSOMES

Azinger/Beck *lost to* **Ballesteros/Olazábal**, *2 and 1*

Floyd/Couples *beat* **Langer/James**, *2 and 1*

Wadkins/Irwin *beat* **Gilford/Montgomerie**, *4 and 2*

Stewart/Calcavecchia *beat* **Faldo/Woosnam** *by one hole*

Session Score: 3-1

FRIDAY AFTERNOON FOURBALLS

Wadkins/O'Meara *halved with* **Torrance/Feherty**

Azinger/Beck *lost to* **Ballesteros/Olazábal**, *2 and 1*

Pavin/Calcavecchia *lost to* **Richardson/James**, *5 and 4*

Floyd/Couples *beat* **Faldo/Woosnam**, *5 and 3*

Session Score: 1.5-2.5

Overall Score: USA 4.5 Europe 3.5

ABOVE: Fred Couples hits a tee-shot at Kiawah Island, watched by partner Ray Floyd and Europe's Ian Woosnam and Nick Faldo.

Gallacher's decision to play rookies Colin Montgomerie and David Gilford together in the Foursomes backfired as they were comprehensively beaten, 4 and 2, by Lanny Wadkins and Hale Irwin, while Ray Floyd and Fred Couples eased to a 2-1 victory over Langer and Mark James before Payne Stewart and Mark Calcavecchia beat Nick Faldo and Ian Woosnam. It might have been a clean sweep for the home side, had Seve Ballesteros and José María Olazábal not collected Europe's only point of the morning in a controversial and ill-humoured match against Paul Azinger and Chip Beck that set the tone for the weekend.

Ballesteros was furious when he spotted at the 10th that Azinger had been using a different ball and accused his opponent of cheating (players are required to declare the make and number of the ball they are using at the first tee and inform opponents when changes are made). The match referee ruled in Azinger's favour but Ballesteros continued to complain and both men could barely bring themselves to shake hands when the Europeans clinched victory with a Seve putt at the 17th. "The American team has 11 nice guys and Paul Azinger," a bitter Ballesteros said later.

With the atmosphere intensifying, Europe performed better in the afternoon as the Spaniards, once again faced by Azinger/Beck, won 2 and 1 to close the gap, and when Richardson/James followed up with a convincing 5-4 victory over Pavin/Calcavecchia, the battle was on. Wadkins/O'Meara halved with Torrance/Feherty and it took a surprisingly easy victory by Floyd/Couples against an out-of-touch Faldo/Woosnam to keep the USA ahead by a point.

With his team one point down and his best partnership of Nick Faldo and Ian Woosnam on the back of two consecutive and disappointing defeats, Europe captain Bernard Gallacher knew he must make changes on Day Two to change the situation but his decision could well have lost him the Cup.

Gallacher opted to put Faldo (never the easiest partner for even an experienced player) with rookie David Gilford, a shy and quiet character who appeared nervous in his team-mate's shadow. It's easy to say with hindsight, but at best the choice was a gamble and at worst complete lunacy; quite simply, the chemistry didn't work. Even the most casual observer could see the two weren't talking and barely a word was spoken throughout the entire round (they were comprehensively beaten by Azinger/O'Meara, 7 and 6). Later the British press lambasted Faldo for failing to give Gilford support, although he responded by saying that he should never have been paired with the rookie in the first place. Gallacher has since admitted he made the wrong call.

With Faldo forced to retreat inside his shell to hold his own game together and to keep all thoughts of any outside problems away, he was never going to have the time or patience to babysit a team-mate through such a difficult match. Of course, it was tough on Gilford, who had been playing well in practice. Through a quirk of fate, he never got to pick up his clubs again for his singles opponent Pate was ruled out through injury on the Sunday, forcing him to watch the rest of the Ryder Cup from the sidelines.

Fair or not, the USA were in the mood to take full advantage, especially as Wadkins/Irwin had already beaten Torrance/Feherty 4 and 2 in the opening match of the day. They made it three wins in a row as a slick performance from Stewart/Calcavecchia proved too much for Richardson/James. Europe must have been relieved to see Ballesteros/Olazábal pick up their customary point - 3 and 2 against Couples/Floyd - to keep them in the competition.

Already the home crowd were in good voice, pumped up by a patriotic press as well as the skills of their heroes. The *Charleston News*, for instance, reminded everyone just what was at stake during the Ryder Cup in reporting: "The teams are playing for their countries, their families, their team-mates, Uncle Sam, The Queen, Mom and Dad, the Fatherland and the legends of the leprechaun, all rolled into three days of golf."

With the locals starting to taste blood, Europe realized something must be done to turn the tide and in a bid to quieten them, Gallacher made another gamble in the afternoon Fourballs. After trying out new partnerships in the shape of Langer/Montgomerie and Woosnam/Broadhurst, he was rewarded with improbable victory. Despite playing in his first Ryder Cup (and chosen on the basis of an impressive week during practice sessions), Broadhurst in particular proved sensational, chipping and putting superbly alongside his more experienced team-mate as they beat the more established pairing of Azinger/Irwin, 2 and 1.

Langer/Montgomerie, too, earned a point against Pavin/Pate (the first of many for a young Monty), and when James/Richardson followed suit, winning 3 and 1 against Wadkins/Levi, the scores were level, with Ballesteros/Olazábal still on course. Surely Europe would be unable to go into the singles ahead?

The answer to that question became a simple "no", thanks to some outstanding golf from Payne Stewart and Fred Couples. The Americans were ahead for much of the match and it needed

RIGHT: *Europe's José María Olazábal lines up a putt with Seve Ballesteros during Saturday's play - with the eyes of the world watching.*

BELOW: *Corey Pavin and Steve Pate of the USA in action during Saturday's afternoon Fourballs against Bernhard Langer and Colin Montgomerie.*

DAY TWO

SATURDAY MORNING FOURSOMES

Irwin/Wadkins *beat* **Feherty/Torrance,** *4 and 2*

Calcavecchia/Stewart *beat* **James/Richardson** *by one hole*

Azinger/O'Meara *beat* **Faldo/Gilford,** *7 and 6*

Couples/Floyd *lost to* **Ballesteros/Olazábal,** *3 and 2*

Session Score: 3-1

SATURDAY AFTERNOON FOURBALLS

Azinger/Irwin *lost to* **Woosnam/Broadhurst,** *2 and 1*

Pavin/Pate *lost to* **Langer/Montgomerie,** *2 and 1*

Wadkins/Levi *lost to* **James/Richardson,** *3 and 1*

Stewart/Couples *halved with* **Ballesteros/Olazábal**

Session Score: 0.5-3.5

Overall Score: USA 8, Europe 8

> **❝** *We'd just finished the Gulf War. Patriotism was running high, and I wanted to take advantage of that…I wanted my team to bond.* **❞**

US captain Dave Stockton tells Golf Digest *the secrets of 1991*

a nervy six-foot putt from Olazábal on the 18th to deny them a full point. Even so, with four battles already waged, no one knew who would win the war because the final day was to start with both teams locked at eight points all and everything still to play for. The fact that the USA had home advantage and they had only lost the singles four times in the competition's history made them clear favourites, but now the staunchest of their supporters had accepted there was a lot of hard work ahead to make it happen.

As a footnote, the Ryder Cup came at just the right time for South Carolina and was said to completely revitalize the region's economy. Only two years earlier, Hurricane Hugo had devastated the area. Having the celebrated competition in town brought in much-needed revenue and, at the same time, established Kiawah Island as a real golfing retreat. Locally, such was the popularity of the Ryder Cup that 19-and-a-half hours was dedicated daily on the NBA and USA networks.

When the final push of the "War on the Shore" arrived it came as no surprise to anyone, given the events of the previous two days, and controversy arrived with it. US captain Dave Stockton announced one of his key players - Steve Pate - would be unable to take part in the singles but had conveniently forgotten to warn his opposite number. There was always a possibility of Pate being ruled out after he was involved in a car crash shortly before the Ryder Cup matches began, hurting his ribs, but he had played the previous day in the afternoon Foursomes and looked in decent shape. Europe smelled a rat.

The Ryder Cup system is for captains to file a sealed brown envelope containing the name of a player prepared to stand down, should a member of the opposing side become ill or injured. Chosen man David Gilford was already heading for the course when Gallacher saw the draw and quickly realized he would have to reduce his team to 11 players.

Already the psychological war had begun, but what no one expected was for the final day to be so close, for so long. It was eventually sealed by just one missed putt on the 18th green. Gallacher's tactics proved correct as he gave the previously grumpy and distracted Faldo an opportunity to lead his team out and the Englishman responded by beating Raymond Floyd by two holes, but the lead was destined to change hands many times.

Feherty, who had started out so nervously, found his form to beat Stewart before Montgomerie came from four holes down against Calcavecchia, with only four to play, to earn himself an unfeasible half. It wasn't until the Americans won the next two matches - Azinger beating Olazábal by two holes and Pavin eclipsing Richardson, 2 and 1 - that the crowd began to play their part. Whipped up by Azinger and Pavin, the atmosphere was more akin to a football match than a game of golf, with chants of "USA, USA!" ringing round the course.

The score soon moved to 12-12 with four matches to go after Beck beat Woosnam and Ballesteros overcame Levi. A tense finish was assured. Europe's impressive rookie Paul Broadhurst delighted his captain with a 3 and 1 triumph over O'Meara, but two 3 and 2 victories for Couples and Wadkins (over Torrance and James respectively) left the USA 14-13 ahead, with only one last match on course.

All eyes were now on Hale Irwin and Bernhard Langer. Their match had progressed in the shadow of seemingly bigger battles but suddenly everything depended on the result. It was tight, too. Irwin had been two-up at 14, but Langer pulled one back at 15 and

> **“** *Telling David he wasn't playing was one of the toughest things I have ever had to do in my career.* **”**
>
> European captain Bernard Gallacher
> on leaving David Gilford out

then saw his rival three-putt at 17 – the Ryder Cup would go to the very last match on the final day.

Langer's drive at the 18th was good, but Irwin's veered into the crowd and was expected to be found in the rough; somehow it bounced back to the fringes of the fairway – almost certainly it had been thrown there. Even so, Langer's approach shot made the green and Irwin's didn't. Advantage Europe, or so it seemed – especially when Irwin's next shot (a chip to the green) left him 25 feet short. Gallacher must have thought so as he crouched green-side, dreaming of lifting the famous trophy just as his predecessor Tony Jacklin had done. Still, there was drama to come. Langer's putt from the back of the green was good but sailed just a little further past the hole than anticipated, leaving him an awkward six-footer to finish. Irwin, meanwhile, sent a long putt to within two feet – a shot generously conceded by his opponent. It meant everything, the entire Ryder Cup, depended on Langer's next shot.

The tension as he bent over the ball with his familiar uncomfortable-looking gait was unbearable and when he finally struck, it slithered just wide. Langer collapsed, his face twisted in agony. Meanwhile, the Americans celebrated wildly and the chants of "USA, USA!" were back. One of the greatest Ryder Cups of all time – and one of the most controversial – had been decided on the very last shot of the day.

DAY THREE

FINAL DAY SINGLES

Raymond Floyd *lost to* **Nick Faldo** *by two holes*

Payne Stewart *lost to* **David Feherty,** *2 and 1*

Mark Calcavecchia *halved with* **Colin Montgomerie**

Paul Azinger *beat* **José María Olazábal** *by two holes*

Corey Pavin *beat* **Steven Richardson,** *2 and 1*

Wayne Levi *lost to* **Seve Ballesteros,** *3 and 2*

Chip Beck *beat* **Ian Woosnam,** *3 and 1*

Mark O'Meara *lost to* **Paul Broadhurst,** *3 and 1*

Fred Couples *beat* **Sam Torrance,** *3 and 2*

Lanny Wadkins *beat* **Mark James,** *3 and 2*

Hale Irwin *halved with* **Bernhard Langer**

Steve Pate *halved with* **David Gilford** *(Pate injured, match unplayed)*

Session Score: 6.5-5.5

Overall Score: USA 14.5, Europe 13.5

Ian Woosnam plays spectacularly out of the bunker at the 17th hole during a singles match at the 1991 Ryder Cup at Kiawah Island, South Carolina.

1993

Europe 13
USA 15

The Belfry, Sutton Coldfield

September 24-26

THE COURSE

Brabazon Course
Location: The Belfry,
Sutton Coldfield,
England
Par: 72
Yards: 7,118

The Brabazon Course had already hosted Ryder Cups in 1985 and as recently as 1989, when its famous 18th hole caused the Americans so many problems as the match was tied. It was opened in 1977 and features water on 13 holes.

Following the controversy of the "War on the Shore", not to mention the conflicts caused by the behaviour of the crowd at Kiawah Island, there was a genuine desire in the golfing world to rein in the Ryder Cup and get back to the principles its founding fathers held so dear. The legendary Tom Watson was the man to bring about a return to sanity - and the Cup with it.

FAIRNESS, GOOD SPORTSMANSHIP AND FRIENDSHIP were meant to be the by-words of a competition played for glory, not cash, and designed to bring people together, not split them apart. And if all this had been forgotten along the way, the organizers of the 30th Ryder Cup matches were determined to get it back. Passionate spectators were all well and good - and the modern trend for chanting and singing was shared by both sets of fans and a regular occurrence - but galleries abusing players, even affecting results by throwing golf balls back towards the fairway? These were issues to be addressed, both practically and philosophically.

The British and American PGAs spent many an hour discussing the situation and eventually agreed a series of proposals aimed at solving some of those issues. When Tom Watson was appointed US captain for 1993, he seemed the perfect man to bring about peace in our time. One of golf's greatest legends, Watson was almost as popular in Europe as he was back home and had a reputation for respecting the great traditions and history of the game. Indeed, he vowed to stand back from all the mind games, hyperbole and overblown rhetoric that seemed to have set the tone for a controversial Ryder Cup.

Characteristically, Watson immersed himself in the history and tactics of the event, determined to leave no stone unturned in his preparation. He wanted a team of players who could cope with the pressure of winning away from home and selected Ray Floyd and Lanny Wadkins as his captain's picks.

Over in Europe, Bernard Gallacher - who had offered to quit his role after losing in Kiawah Island in 1991 - had been persuaded to stay on as captain and in a tactical blow chose the first Swede in

LEFT: *US captain Tom Watson looks concerned as he keeps up with the action at the 1993 Ryder Cup at The Belfry.*

OPPOSITE: *Joakim Haeggman celebrates an historic moment - he was the first Swede ever to play in the Ryder Cup, and marked it with a singles victory.*

Ryder Cup history for his team: Joakim Haeggman. Other rookies included Peter Baker, Barry Lane and Italian Costantino Rocca.

The teams were in, the date set and everything looked ready for a smooth ride – until the President called. At short notice, the US team were invited to the White House to meet President Bill Clinton, who wanted to wish them well before they flew to England, but many of the players were not impressed. Some perhaps held different political beliefs, while others were angered by Clinton's plans to raise taxes on high earners, which naturally included the golfing fraternity. Their hesitant response was seen as unpatriotic by a shocked US nation and led to a flurry of highly embarrassing headlines. Fortunately, common sense prevailed and Watson did eventually lead his team to the White House, finally allowing the sport of golf to take over the headlines.

It proved to be a tight and tense match, too, and despite the US captain's preparations at the end of the opening day – which was delayed by two hours due to fog – it was Europe holding a slight advantage. Gallacher began battle with his most experienced men but the morning session ended all square in a tense start that featured a shock defeat for the previously unbeatable Ballesteros and Olazábal as they faced Tom Kite and Davis Love, losing by two holes. The turning point came at the 10th when Seve opted to play safe with an iron at the relatively short par-four and the more adventurous Kite made him pay for this by sending a powerful three-wood right to the centre of the green. Torrance/James also lost, 4 and 3, to Wadkins/Pavin, but the excellent new partnership of Faldo/Montgomerie eased to a virtually faultless 4 and 3 victory over Ray Floyd and Fred Couples, while Woosnam/Langer beat Azinger and Payne Stewart by a whopping 7 and 5.

DAY ONE

CAPTAINS
Europe: Bernard Gallacher   **USA:** Tom Watson

FRIDAY MORNING FOURSOMES
Torrance/James lost to **Wadkins/Pavin**, *4 and 3*

Woosnam/Langer beat **Azinger/Stewart**, *7 and 5*

Ballesteros/Olazábal lost to **Kite/Love**, *2 and 1*

Faldo/Montgomerie beat **Floyd/Couples**, *4 and 3*

Session Score: 2-2

FRIDAY AFTERNOON FOURBALLS
Woosnam/Baker beat **Gallagher/Janzen** by one hole

Langer/Lane lost to **Wadkins/Pavin**, *4 and 2*

Faldo/Montgomerie halved with **Azinger/Couples**

Ballesteros/Olazábal beat **Love/Kite**, *4 and 3*

Session Score: 2.5-1.5

Overall Score: Europe 4.5, USA 3.5

> *This isn't war, this is golf… when it's over, we should be able to go off together, lift a glass and toast one another.*

Tom Watson before the 1993 Ryder Cup

With the opening day underway, the Ryder Cup organizers could relax in the knowledge that the atmosphere on course was vibrant but friendly, so perhaps their efforts to tone down the excesses of the tournament had been successful. But there had been something of a blip on the eve of the competition when Watson, who handed his players almost minute-by-minute practice schedules and a strict list of rules, inadvertently caused a rumpus.

One of Watson's rules was a week's ban on signing autographs – he wanted his players fully focused – and this included the Wednesday night gala staged at the Metropole Hotel. The formal dinner and speeches night had become something of a Ryder Cup tradition, with players mixing with guests and spending the last part of the evening offering autographs. There was also an unwritten tradition that both teams signed each other's menus as a keepsake. Unfortunately, Watson decided that having turned down autographs all night, he would not be able to assist when the European menu arrived from Sam Torrance for his team to sign.

Torrance was furious and the British tabloids had a field day. With typical relish and jingoistic delight, the *Sun* splashed the story on its front page under the headline "Fork Off". Suddenly,

the bad feeling that Watson had tried so hard to deter had returned and he was subsequently forced to issue a hasty apology. Thankfully the stand-off ended with humour when Gallacher was asked if the European team's evening had been ruined. "Well," he replied mischievously, "Seve did struggle a bit with his fromage."

The problems of the previous night appeared to have been forgotten by lunchtime on the opening day, with the scores level at 2-2. When the afternoon session began Seve Ballesteros and José María Olazábal made amends for their morning slip by firing a string of birdies in a comfortable victory over Tom Kite and Davis Love, which ended on the 15th. Perhaps the highlight for Europe was the performance of local boy Peter Baker on his debut, who partnered Woosnam to a one-hole victory over US rookies Gallagher Jnr./Janzen, holing a spectacular 25-foot putt on the 18th green to seal the point. With light deteriorating towards the end of the evening, Europe were 4-3 ahead, with only Faldo/Montgomerie on course against Azinger/Couples. Faldo's birdie putt at the 17th brought the game level and although the crowd were desperate to see the match finished, it was obvious the light would prevent this from happening.

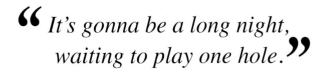

> *It's gonna be a long night, waiting to play one hole.*

Paul Azinger after play was called off for the day

DAY TWO

SATURDAY MORNING FOURSOMES

Faldo/Montgomerie *beat* **Wadkins/Pavin**, *3 and 2*

Langer/Woosnam *beat* **Couples/Azinger**, *2 and 1*

Baker/Lane *lost to* **Floyd/Stewart**, *3 and 2*

Ballesteros/Olazábal *beat* **Love/Kite**, *2 and 1*

Session Score: 3-1

SATURDAY AFTERNOON FOURBALLS

Faldo/Montgomerie *lost to* **Cook/Beck** *by two holes*

James/Rocca *lost to* **Pavin/Gallagher**, *5 and 4*

Woosnam/Baker *beat* **Couples/Azinger**, *6 and 5*

Olazábal/Haeggman *lost to* **Floyd/Stewart**, *2 and 1*

Session Score: 1-3

Overall Score: Europe 8.5, USA 7.5

LEFT: *Lanny Wadkins of the USA reacts to his putt during the 30th Ryder Cup Match at The Belfry.*

ABOVE: *Deadly rivals Paul Azinger of the USA (left) and Nick Faldo of Europe do battle in the singles at the 1993 Ryder Cup.*

When play resumed the next day, with crowds already in place at 8 a.m., it came to a shoot-out on the green between Azinger and Faldo – and it was the Englishman who held his nerve to save a half. With his team-mates gathered round the green after completing their practice sessions, Azinger missed from 20 yards and Faldo calmly converted from eight.

"What's for breakfast?" shouted Faldo toward the cheering galleries as he headed for the clubroom, before pretending to faint. But who needs a fry-up breakfast when golf provides all the right sustenance?

With the score 4.5-3.5 and spurred on by Faldo's bravado, Europe won three of the next four matches to move into a healthy lead. Faldo himself set the ball rolling with a 3 and 2 Foursomes victory alongside Montgomerie against Wadkins/Pavin, while

the highlight for the USA was a strong performance from Floyd/Stewart as they beat Baker/Lane, 3 and 2. It needed a brave decision from Watson to turn things around and this came completely out of the blue on the Saturday afternoon. Realizing he must shake things up, he brought in Chip Beck and John Cook, two players who had looked out of touch in previous weeks, and lined them up against Faldo/Montgomerie. His decision might have seemed madness, but it worked.

Cook and Beck matched their opponents every step of the way, with Beck's short game often the key as he chipped and putted from off the green to save par on three holes in a row. By the 18th (where Faldo had begun, more than 10 hours earlier, a hero), he now seemed mentally drained and held out a hand to concede after missing an eight-foot putt to halve the game. Earlier,

Woosnam and Baker had won, 6 and 5, against Couples/Azinger, but it was Team USA's afternoon. Going into the singles, Pavin/Gallagher Jnr. and Floyd/Stewart also posted victories to leave their side just one point behind.

The Americans may have reached the final day trailing by one point but considering their record in Ryder Cup singles, there was reason for optimism. And it proved justified as they stormed to six wins and two halves, inspired by veteran Chip Beck battling back from three holes down to beat Barry Lane.

For Europe, the bad news began on the Saturday night when Sam Torrance reported a toe injury would almost certainly keep him out of action the following day. Just as Gallacher had experienced two years earlier, it meant that Watson was forced to choose a player in his own team to sit out but Lanny Wadkins made it easy for him in generously volunteering to step down. The situation was almost repeated later that night when Europe's Peter Baker rushed to the hospital bed of his 11-month-old daughter following a meningitis scare, only returning the next morning after the doctors had given her the all-clear and confirmed it was nothing more than a bad ear infection.

Had Baker pulled out, the Americans would have been within their rights to claim the match – although in reality, Ray Floyd had offered to stand down, if need be. Thankfully, Baker was able to return and produced an astonishing round under the circumstances, beating Pavin by two holes. Indeed, the day was full of ups and downs, highlighted in the opening match when Woosnam allowed a two-hole lead to slip with six to play and halved against Couples. The indomitable Beck produced an even better result, coming from three behind to win at the last against Lane. Three European wins in a row – for Montgomerie, Baker and Haeggman – then tested the USA to the full, with the words of Watson still ringing in their ears: "If it gets too tough out there for you, remember what Lanny did for you!"

Stewart beat James, while Ballasteros was defeated, somewhat surprisingly, by Jim Gallagher Jnr. to move the score to 12.5-12.5, with three matches on course. With Ray Floyd ahead against Olazábal and Faldo up on Azinger, all eyes were instead on Italian Costantino Rocca – up by just one, with two to play against Davis Love.

A virtual unknown in America, Rocca had played well and looked set for a half at the 17th before buckling under a pressure putt just

SHOT OF THE DAY

Nick Faldo produced one of the most memorable shots of the 1993 Ryder Cup when he aced the 14th during a singles match against Paul Azinger. Already he and Colin Montgomerie had birdied the same hole four times and Faldo wanted to go one better. "I remember walking down the fairway with him on the 14th after he had hit the green again and him saying to me, 'You know, wouldn't it be great to find the hole next time?'" said Monty. "Sure enough, next day, he does it!"

ABOVE: *US hero Davis Love celebrates on the 18th green after defeating European Costantino Rocca at The Belfry.*

RIGHT: *A delighted US captain Tom Watson holds the Ryder Cup trophy aloft following a hard-fought victory that saw his team win by two points.*

DAY THREE

FINAL DAY SINGLES

Ian Woosnam *halved with* **Fred Couples**

Barry Lane *lost to* **Chip Beck** *by one hole*

Colin Montgomerie *beat* **Lee Janzen** *by one hole*

Paul Baker *beat* **Corey Pavin** *by two holes*

Joakim Haeggman *beat* **John Cook** *by one hole*

Mark James *lost to* **Payne Stewart**, *3 and 2*

Costantino Rocca *lost to* **Davis Love** *by one hole*

Seve Ballesteros *lost to* **Jim Gallagher**, *3 and 2*

José María Olazábal *lost to* **Ray Floyd** *by two holes*

Bernhard Langer *lost to* **Tom Kite**, *5 and 3*

Nick Faldo *halved with* **Paul Azinger**

Sam Torrance *halved with* **Lanny Wadkins** (*Torrance injured, match unplayed*)

Session Score: 4.5-7.5

Overall Score: Europe 13, USA 15

when it mattered. Love knew he had the psychological advantage and his next shot – a huge wood that ripped down the fairway of the 18th – rammed it home. You could almost sense Rocca's fear. Just as he was about to swing his own driver, a huge cheer disturbed his concentration and he was forced to stop mid-swing – Faldo had just aced the 14th and so the pressure doubled. By the time they reached the green, Rocca faced a dangerous downhill putt while Love – determined to leave his shot below the hole – got to within six feet. Inevitably, Rocca missed and the American finished off the job to silence the home crowd.

Team USA players engulfed their hero and when Floyd went three up with three to play against Olazábal, everyone at The Belfry knew the Cup was heading back across the Atlantic. Olazábal did pull two back, but at the 18th hooked his shot into the water and Floyd had no problem in putting-out to clinch victory.

With the trophy long gone, Azinger converted a putt on the same green to earn a battling half against Faldo and wrap up a thrilling 15-13 victory for his team. As he did so, out of sight, Davis Love chased after a disconsolate Rocca. Finding his opponent in tears, he gave him a consolatory embrace. The spirit of the Ryder Cup was back again.

> **❝** *This is the best feeling I've ever had in golf!* **❞**

Tom Watson on captaining his side to victory

Ryder Cup legends

Severiano **BALLESTEROS** and José María **OLAZÁBAL**

The outpouring of emotion across the globe when Severiano Ballesteros passed away on May 7, 2011 after a long battle against a cancerous brain tumour shows he was not only one of the world's greatest golfers, a colossus with a club, but also one of the sport's most popular and enduring characters. And who can forget so many of his greatest moments came in the Ryder Cup with his great friend, José María Olazábal?

The enigmatic Ballesteros and his close friend Olazábal are by far the most successful partnership in Ryder Cup history, with 11 wins and two halves from their 15 matches together – double the tally of any other. Individually, they were hugely successful, too. Ballesteros won 22.5 points – two more than compatriot Olazábal – and both would captain Europe once their playing days were over. Ballesteros was a fitting captain in 1997 when the Ryder Cup was first hosted in Spain, with Europe winning 14.5-13.5 at Valderrama. In September 2012, Olazábal will follow in his footsteps in leading Europe at the Medinah Country Club.

Ultimately, the statistics only take us so far – the panache, style and attitude that "The Spanish Armada" brought to the Ryder Cup of 1979 were much more than their guarantee of points.

Ballesteros was there in the first year that the British and Irish team included players from Europe, yet he didn't make his mark in 1979, winning only one of five matches as Europe were well and truly beaten. Two years later, he was left out of the team after playing much of his golf in America and declared he would never play in the Ryder Cup again. However, captain Tony Jacklin persuaded him to return in 1983 and following this appearance, he didn't miss a session in the next five tournaments. In 1985, Seve was an integral part of the first side to beat the Americans since 1957 – a victory he celebrated with gusto.

In 1985 he joined forces with José María Olazábal in what became the best-ever Ryder Cup partnership. At Muirfield Village in Columbus, Ohio, the Spanish pair won their first three matches as Europe built up a commanding lead. Ballesteros then beat Curtis Strange and for the first time in history, Europe won on American soil. But the best was still to come. In 1989 and 1991, Ballesteros and Olazábal were truly unbeatable, winning seven points out of eight in the Foursomes and Fourballs.

The pair partnered for the final time in 1993, beating Davis Love and Tom Kite, 2 and 1. In 1997 they were reunited, this time with Ballesteros as captain. With severe rheumatoid polyarthritis in both feet, Olazábal helped Europe to retain the trophy after his friend's captaincy inspired the side. Olazábal declared this team to have the best spirit of any he had been part of.

Sadly, Olazábal will always be remembered for missing the putt that lost the Ryder Cup in 1999 – and for the prior controversy when the US team stormed the green. However, he made a triumphant return in 2006 with Sergio Garcia to win all three of his matches in Europe's record-equalling win at The K Club. All those matches were completed without his dear friend Ballesteros by his side – indeed, Seve's death hit his junior partner hard. The best way to pay tribute, he insists, is to captain Europe to Ryder Cup glory.

> **"** *The Ryder Cup would not be the match it is today, if not for Seve Ballesteros.* **"**
>
> *USA Today*

RYDER CUP RECORD

Severiano BALLESTEROS
Ryder Cups: 1979, 1983, 1985 (winner), 1987 (winner), 1989 (tied but Europe retain trophy), 1991, 1993, 1995 (winner), 1997 (winner, non-playing captain)
Total wins: 4 (plus 1 tie to retain trophy, 1989)
Matches: 37 (won 20, halved 5, lost 12)
Total points: 22.5

José María OLAZÁBAL
Ryder Cups: 1987 (winner), 1989 (tied but Europe retain trophy), 1991, 1993, 1997 (winner), 1999, 2006 (winner), 2014 (non-playing captain (winner).
Total wins: 3 (plus 1 tie to retain trophy, 1989)
Matches: 29 (won 18, halved 3, lost 8)
Total points: 20.5

AS A PAIR:
Matches: 15 (won 11, halved 2, lost 2)
Total points: 12

1995

USA 13.5
Europe 14.5

Oak Hill Country Club, New York

September 22-24

Just when it seemed that Team USA were ready to rack up a hat-trick of Ryder Cup victories, they were hit from behind by an ageing European side in New York. In fact, the killer blow came from a player who was someone they had barely heard of, another highly talented Irishman called Philip Walton.

THE COURSE

East Course
Location: Oak Hill, Rochester, New York, USA
Par: 70
Yards: 7,198

The US PGA chose one of its hardest courses for the 1995 Ryder Cup and set it up for home advantage: the rough was long, the greens were dry and the course was prepared as if for a US Open. But Team USA were unable to take advantage.

NICK FALDO MIGHT HAVE DONE the groundwork and the USA - Curtis Strange, in particular - may have added to their own downfall in throwing victory away when it had seemed almost assured, but it was Walton (only qualifying when José María Olazábal dropped out through injury), who came out of nowhere to make the winning putt and steal back the trophy.

When the American media first saw Walton's name on the team sheet, their reaction had been cynical - who was the man with such a short CV, who had never before played in the USA? In the event, the US fans certainly remembered him as they trooped home

that Sunday evening. "Maybe the Americans know me now," cried Walton, draped in an Irish flag, as he celebrated long into the night. "Tell 'em I'm related to all those Waltons on that TV show!"

In fact, this proved to be a Ryder Cup that still hurts in the States right up to the present day: Oak Hill became Choke Hill and in turn, Heartbreak Hill. For those bedecked in the Stars & Stripes, it was an enormous disappointment after they had started out with such high hopes. Seven players in Bernard Gallacher's side were over the age of 37 and only one (Per-Ulrik Johansson) was under 30. The American media described them as being "over the hill" and

148

ABOVE: *Nick Faldo lines up a putt during a Foursomes match against Corey Pavin and Tom Lehman at the 1995 Ryder Cup.*

OPPOSITE: *US captain Lanny Wadkins (left) jokes with Curtis Strange on the 8th fairway during practice day at Oak Hill.*

DAY ONE

CAPTAINS

USA: Lanny Wadkins   **Europe:** Bernard Gallacher

FRIDAY MORNING FOURSOMES

Pavin/Lehman *beat* **Faldo/Montgomerie** *by one hole*

Haas/Couples *lost to* **Torrance/Rocca,** *3 and 2*

Love/Maggert *beat* **Clark/James,** *4 and 3*

Crenshaw/Strange *lost to* **Langer/Johansson** *by one hole*

Session Score: 2-2

FRIDAY AFTERNOON FOURBALLS

Faxon/Jacobsen *lost to* **Gilford/Ballesteros,** *4 and 3*

Maggert/Roberts *beat* **Torrance/Rocca,** *6 and 5*

Couples/Love *beat* **Faldo/Montgomerie,** *3 and 2*

Pavin/Mickelson *beat* **Langer/Johansson,** *6 and 4*

Session Score: 3-1

Overall Score: USA 5, Europe 3

> **" *It was a statement that Europe's best team could be beaten.* "**
>
> *Tom Lehman delights in victory over Faldo and Montgomerie*

predicted not only a comfortable victory for Team USA, but also potentially the end of the Ryder Cup as a seriously competitive tournament. Many of the Europeans were also not on form, with some complaining of injuries. Already Olazábal had pulled out with a toe problem and Nick Faldo was battling a wrist injury; Faldo's preparation was further affected by tabloid news stories that his marriage was under strain.

The story only broke as the European entourage, including Faldo's wife, Gill, boarded Concorde at London's Heathrow. Quite how Faldo, already based in America on the US tour, was able to perform so well is hard to contemplate. The pictures of him greeting his wife at the airport in New York with a formal handshake were painful to see, yet the English golfer was still able to display his usual nerves of steel in what would become one of his career highs. However, it was not until he completed a remarkable comeback from three-down against Curtis Strange in Sunday's singles to all but hand Europe the trophy that his emotions finally got the better of him.

That moment of elation could scarcely have been predicted two days earlier when Faldo first stepped onto the tee at Oak Hill alongside Colin Montgomerie. Two years earlier, the pair had been

impressive playing together at The Belfry but some of the magic appeared to have faded as they lost by one hole to Pavin and Tom Lehman. Faldo was tetchy, attacking Lehman after he tapped home a putt that the European had already conceded. "When I say it's good, it's good," he muttered. Lehman remained stoic, later claiming: "I wasn't going to put up with any crap, especially after he stretches out his arms as if to say 'put the ball in your pocket, you idiot' – I was hot!"

The morning Foursomes ended all square, however. Torrance/ Costantino Rocca combined to beat Haas/Couples, 3 and 2, to get Europe on track, and when Love/Maggert cruised past Clark and James, 4 and 3, the scores were levelled by Langer/Johansson following a narrow but crucial win against Crenshaw/Strange at the last. Already Team USA's promise to dominate appeared ambitious but the afternoon Fourballs must have lifted their spirits, with Maggert/Roberts, Couples/Love, Pavin and new boy Phil Mickelson all recording convincing victories.

Surprisingly, Faldo and Monty lost again – 3 and 2 to Couples/ Love – and in truth, Europe must have been thankful for a solitary win by Ballesteros/Gilford, 4 and 3 against Faxon/Jacobsen, to at least keep them in the hunt.

For Team USA, taking a two-point overnight lead into Saturday was regarded as nothing more than par for the course, but perhaps the media had overestimated the strength and depth of the American team. The average age of the European team might be high, but the US squad also included several players over the age of 40 (a fact that never seemed to get a mention in the media) and was vastly changed from the side that had done so well to win at The Belfry, two years earlier.

New captain Lanny Wadkins also had to manage five rookies – Brad Faxon, Phil Mickelson, Tom Lehman, Jeff Maggert and Loren Roberts – and received stinging criticism over his choice of captain's picks when he went for Strange/Couples, both personal friends but also players who had hardly been successful on tour that year. Indeed, none of the players in his 12-man squad had won a tournament since June, and the top US player on the PGA Tour money list – Lee Janzen – was not even selected owing to a qualification process that measured points, not dollars. Given the task ahead, were they under- or overachieving in New York?

Wadkins, whose selfless act of volunteering to step down from the singles in 1993 when Sam Torrance was injured had elevated him to Ryder Cup hero status in the eyes of his peers, knew he had a heavy task ahead, no matter what the score or what anyone else said. He was right to be cautious because Europe hit back at the start of the second day, winning three out of the four Foursomes, including a 6 and 5 demolition of Love/Maggert by Torrance/Rocca, with the Italian producing a hole-in-one at the 6th to add further adrenalin to European veins. There was also a welcome win for Faldo/Montgomerie against Strange/Haas and for Langer/Gilford – 4 and 3 against first-day heroes Pavin/Lehman. Team USA's only point came from Roberts/Jacobsen, who won at the last against Woosnam/Walton, and the score moved on to six-all.

Suddenly Europe was in the driving seat, although not for long because this would be a Ryder Cup with more twists and turns than any other in recent memory. In fact, the same afternoon the USA rebounded in winning three out of the four Fourballs to complete another turnaround. European captain Gallacher may have to take some responsibility for the result, completely surprising many experts in changing his line-up despite a successful morning and putting out four completely different pairings after lunch. Maybe he believed fresh legs and clear heads would keep concentration

SHOT OF THE DAY

Costantino Rocca became the toast of Europe when he aced the 6th hole on the Saturday morning, only the third hole-in-one in Ryder Cup history. The Italian took a five-iron to the tee, which proved to be the last club he needed to use. His spectacular shot helped clinch a 6 and 5 victory for himself and Sam Torrance against Davis Love III and Jeff Maggert, sparking a European revival. It must have been a real high for the player who had been criticized for his nervous finale at The Belfry, just two years earlier – "It's hard to lose the hole with a one," he beamed.

levels high but his gamble did not pay off and instead the USA took full advantage.

Faxon/Couples kicked off the home revival in beating Torrance/Montgomerie, 4 and 2. Although Love/Crenshaw lost to Woosnam/Rocca, an impressive victory for Haas/Mickelson against Ballesteros/Gilford, 3 and 2, soon followed. Mickelson in particular made a good impression on debut and would end his Ryder Cup unbeaten – a record he would not be able to repeat until 12 years on.

But the US team saved the best for last. Corey Pavin's astonishing chip-in from above the 18th green earned them an improbable point against Langer/Faldo, having gone into the last all square. The sound of the galleries chanting "Cor-ey! Cor-ey! Cor-ey!" followed the team all the way back to the clubroom and, with the USA 9-7 ahead, there was every reason for the home fans to be thrilled. After all, when had the USA last lost a Ryder Cup after being ahead going into the singles?

"We're still going to win," insisted a defiant Gallacher when he met journalists that evening, but few believed him – even if Wadkins politely refused to crow too loudly and instead urged caution. When asked if the Ryder Cup was already in the bag, he said: "I'm real confident – I have 12 guys playing well but this is golf and a two-point lead is not big enough."

DAY TWO

SATURDAY MORNING FOURSOMES

Strange/Haas *lost to* **Faldo/Montgomerie,** *4 and 2*

Love/Maggert *lost to* **Torrance/Rocca,** *6 and 5*

Roberts/Jacobsen *beat* **Woosnam/Walton** *by one hole*

Pavin/Lehman *lost to* **Langer/Gilford,** *4 and 3*

Session Score: 1-3

SATURDAY AFTERNOON FOURBALLS

Faxon/Couples *beat* **Torrance/Montgomerie,** *4 and 2*

Love/Crenshaw *lost to* **Woosnam/Rocca,** *3 and 2*

Haas/Mickelson *beat* **Ballesteros/Gilford,** *3 and 2*

Pavin/Roberts *beat* **Faldo/Langer** *by one hole*

Session Score: 3-1

Overall Score: USA 9, Europe 7

LEFT: *Oak Hill Country Club in all its glory as a spectacular opening ceremony takes place before the Ryder Cup of 1995 in front of packed galleries.*

RIGHT: *Corey Pavin reacts with delight after chipping in from the edge of the 18th green to win in the Saturday afternoon Fourballs.*

BELOW: *European talisman Nick Faldo plays out of the rough in a tense match with Curtis Strange, which he lost by one hole.*

OPPOSITE: *Philip Walton celebrates a famous win over Jay Haas by jumping into the arms of captain Bernard Gallacher.*

Every final day of a Ryder Cup produces heroes and villains and in 1995, it was almost pantomime time when Europe won the singles, 7.5-4.5 - and the trophy. Curtis Strange threw away victory from three-up against Nick Faldo and then froze when the USA needed only half a point to win. Brad Faxon and Jay Haas also had their chances to secure the win, but failed to do so.

Then there were the heroes - most of them European. Howard Clark had been overlooked all weekend but came out on singles day to provide a hole-in-one and an ensuing victory against Peter Jacobsen. Seve Ballesteros, the magical Spaniard, who despite being a long way past his best put up such a brave show against Tom Lehman that his team was totally inspired, even when he was forced to concede defeat. Then there was Faldo...

With so many distractions in his private life, the Englishman managed just two birdies all week. He hadn't been at his best. Against Strange, however, he played the hero. In truth, all he had to do was stay solid and play par golf while his nerve-shredded opponent staged an incredible collapse, having taken a one-shot lead at the 11th - but then, that's what Faldo does best.

Strange could - and should - have won the point his side needed but three bogeys in the last three holes had destroyed his chances. Instead the pair arrived at the 17th with the American still one-up and the overall match tied. Strange's unimpressive, prodded putt gifted Faldo a chance to draw level - a chance he took. With the tension mounting, it was a similar story at the 18th, although this time Strange had the advantage after a perfect tee-shot to the centre of the fairway, while Faldo found the rough and had already made a mess of a chip to the green. A terrible three-iron shot left Strange short of the green, also chipping out of the rough. Faldo played an exquisite wedge that looped up and landed within six feet of the hole. However, Strange followed suit, sending his ball to eight feet. Everything was down to the last putt.

Unable to watch, Faldo turned his back as Strange sent his effort narrowly past. Faldo strode forward, sent the ball to the middle of the hole and held his arms aloft in victory. "Everything was shaking," he later admitted. "Everything except the putter!" For Europe, there was still one more hero to come: Philip Walton. The man the Americans struggled to recognize was about to become an icon when, with the USA still needing one more half to earn a 14-14 draw and retain the trophy, he held out. Remarkably, Walton put himself three-up by the 16th and survived a nerve-racking finale as his opponent staged a late, fruitless rally. A putt from four feet at the 17th might have secured it, but even after missing to brays from the US crowd, he refused to buckle.

At the 18th Haas made a mess of his drive, sending it into the trees. By the time the pair reached the green both needed bogeys, but a Ryder Cup depended on it. Haas sent his chip six feet past the hole. Thankfully for Walton, his second putt - although eight feet out - was uphill. Finally, his moment of glory arrived.

> **" I can't tell you what this means to me… it's just… I can't! "**
>
> *Bernard Gallacher on Europe's comeback*

SHOT OF THE DAY

As if to prove all good things come in pairs, Europe's Howard Clark scored a Ryder Cup hole-in-one, just 24 hours after his team-mate Costantino Rocca did the same. Considering only three men had ever aced a Ryder Cup hole before, this was quite an achievement. Clark's moment of glory came with a six-iron at the par-three 11th during a match against Peter Jacobsen.

DAY THREE

FINAL DAY SINGLES

Tom Lehman beat **Seve Ballesteros,** 4 and 3

Paul Jacobsen lost to **Howard Clark** by one hole

Jeff Maggert lost to **Mark James,** 4 and 3

Fred Couples halved with **Ian Woosnam**

Davis Love beat **Costantino Rocca,** 3 and 2

Brad Faxon lost to **David Gilford** by one hole

Ben Crenshaw lost to **Colin Montgomerie,** 3 and 1

Curtis Strange lost to **Nick Faldo** by one hole

Loren Roberts lost to **Sam Torrance,** 2 and 1

Corey Pavin beat **Bernhard Langer,** 3 and 2

Jay Haas lost to **Philip Walton** by one hole

Phil Mickelson beat **Per-Ulrik Johansson,** 2 and 1

Session Score: 4.5-7.5

Overall Score: USA 13.5, Europe 14.5

1997

Europe 14.5
USA 13.5

Valderrama Golf Club, Sotogrande

September 26-28

THE COURSE

Valderrama
Location: Sotogrande,
Spain
Par: 72
Yards: 6,818

Owned by Jaime Ortiz-Patiño and designed by Robert Trent Jones, Valderrama beat off strong competition to become the first course outside Great Britain and America to stage a Ryder Cup. Its narrow fairways and small greens, as well as some 2,000 Cork Oak trees, make this a real test.

The 1997 Ryder Cup was an historic occasion, the first ever to be staged outside of the USA and the British Isles - and there was a sense that the script had been written long in advance. It was Spain's Ryder Cup, also Severiano Ballesteros' Ryder Cup, and he was about to make sure that it belonged to Europe. The moment golf's greatest tournament was pencilled in for Valderrama, there was only one possible candidate to captain Team Europe and Seve got the vote long in advance.

AT 40, HE WAS POSSIBLY TOO OLD and too out of form to qualify as a player, but he put so much enthusiasm and energy into winning the trophy as captain that it was almost as if the Spaniard was out there on the greens, putting Europe to victory. Indeed, many of his players felt if anything, he was perhaps a little too hands-on, while traditionalists believed he stretched etiquette to the limit. The prevailing memory of Valderrama was Seve buzzing around the course in his buggy - always there, closely observing every shot - and inevitably giving his opinion on how it should be played, too. "I knew the Americans were always aware of my presence and I think it made them uncomfortable," he insisted. "It always seemed to me, we won the hole when I was there."

Who knows if this is what that other golfing legend, Jack Nicklaus, had in mind when he suggested that inviting Europe rather than just Great Britain and Ireland to play in the Ryder Cup would make it more competitive, but it certainly underlined the huge strides that the USA's opponents had made since his suggestion was taken up in 1979. Besides, it was only right that Spain should be the first country in continental Europe to get the nod. After all, Seve Ballesteros had made such a huge contribution to Ryder Cup history, as had his compatriots.

Antonio Garrido joined him in 1979 and then there had been Manuel Piñero, José Maria Cañizares, José Rivero and, most significantly of all, Seve's great playing partner, José María Olazábal - who would be European captain in 2012. It was ironic, then, that it was two Spaniards who gave Ballesteros most cause for thought in the build-up to his home Ryder Cup. Miguel Martín narrowly qualified but Olazábal, having recovered from injury, was next on the list and Seve was keen to have him on board. The only problem was that he was permitted just two captain's picks - and Nick Faldo and Sweden's Jesper Parnevik had both not qualified. This could have led to a very tough decision but as fate would have it, Martín injured his wrist shortly before the tournament and it was Olazábal who took his place when the golf began, allowing both Faldo and Parnevik to compete. In fact, it was a major relief for Europe because Faldo proved enormously influential, though not so

ABOVE: *European captain Seve Ballesteros looks on anxiously during the opening day of the 1997 Ryder Cup.*

OPPOSITE: *Former US President George Bush with José María Olazábal following Europe's famous victory.*

> 66 *Here we were in Spain…
> losing just wasn't an option
> – it was Seve and the King of
> Spain, you felt you were part
> of an irresistible force.* 99

Colin Montgomerie on the 1997 Ryder Cup

DAY ONE

CAPTAINS

Europe: Seve Ballesteros   **USA:** Tom Kite

FRIDAY MORNING FOURBALLS

Olazábal/Rocca *beat* **Love/Mickelson** *by one hole*

Faldo/Westwood *lost to* **Couples/Faxon** *by one hole*

Parnevik/Johansson *beat* **Lehman/Furyk** *by one hole*

Montgomerie/Langer *lost to* **Woods/O'Meara**, *3 and 2*

Session Score: 2-2

Overall Score: Europe 2, USA 2

much as the captain himself. Seve even arranged for the Fourballs to be played first in the morning and the Foursomes second for the first time ever because he felt it best suited his team.

Many of the fans, and even some of the players, had not been aware that such a decision was in the home captain's gift. Seve had four rookies in his side, and also knew that the USA would be bringing a strong team, far stronger than the one that had lost at Oak Hill, two years earlier. Open champion Justin Leonard bolstered the side, as did Mark O'Meara, Lee Janzen (who many believed should have also played in 1995) and Jim Furyk. And then there was a certain Tiger Woods making his debut. Spain welcomed them all with open arms - as well as Spanish horses, flamenco dancers and the King of Spain - at a glitzy opening ceremony. The

scene was set for an historic Ryder Cup, or so it would have been, had it not rained for 12 straight hours overnight. In the event, play was delayed until 11.30 a.m., but it was only possible to start so early, thanks to the superb drainage system on the course. When play finally began, Seve sent out Spaniard José María Olazábal and Italian Costantino Rocca first and they responded with a morale-boosting one-hole victory over Davis Love and Phil Mickelson.

Jesper Parnevik and Per-Ulrik Johansson also beat Furyk and Tom Lehman, but Europe's more traditional performers were less successful. Nick Faldo and Lee Westwood lost to Fred Couples and Brad Faxon, while Colin Montgomerie and Bernhard Langer went down to Woods and O'Meara, 3 and 2. Spain's debut Ryder Cup was destined to be a close call.

With play unable to be completed on the opening Friday, the two teams were still playing Foursomes on the Saturday morning and this proved an encouraging session for Europe, their big guns now starting to fire. Langer and Montgomerie responded to early disappointment in crushing O'Meara and Woods, 5 and 3, while Faldo and Westwood also found form as they beat Leonard and Maggert, 3 and 2. Parnevik (whose selection ahead of Padraig Harrington had been controversial) remained unbeaten in partnering Ignacio Garrido to a half against the strong combination of Lehman and Mickelson. Indeed, the only reverse for Europe came in the opening match when Olazábal and Costantino Rocca went down by one hole to Hoch and Janzen.

Seve's men had edged out in front and over the next two sessions, they would build a strong lead when the captain's decisions, even the controversial ones, appeared to reap dividends. On the opening day he had raised eyebrows in leaving Ian Woosnam and Darren Clarke on the bench but once the points started to roll in, the critics were soon quietened. Ballesteros had put so much effort into the build-up to these games, even when it came to the course: he had been personally responsible for re-designing the 17th hole, deliberately narrowing the fairway just at the distance where the big-hitting Americans (particularly players like Woods) would be landing their ball.

BELOW: *US legend Tiger Woods plays from the rough on the 4th hole at Valderrama, but won only half a point over two days.*

RIGHT: *Huge crowds at the 17th green create a vibrant atmosphere at Valderrama as Europe take control of the 1997 Ryder Cup.*

DAY TWO

FRIDAY AFTERNOON FOURSOMES (FROM DAY ONE)

Rocca/Olazábal *lost to* Hoch/Janzen *by one hole*

Langer/Montgomerie *beat* O'Meara/Woods, *5 and 3*

Faldo/Westwood *beat* Leonard/Maggert, *3 and 2*

Parnevik/Garrido *halved with* Lehman/Mickelson

Session Score: 2.5-1.5

SATURDAY MORNING FOURBALLS

Montgomerie/Clarke *beat* Couples/Love *by one hole*

Woosnam/Bjørn *beat* Leonard/Faxon, *2 and 1*

Faldo/Westwood *beat* Woods/O'Meara, *2 and 1*

Olazábal/Garrido *halved with* Mickelson/Lehman

Session Score: 3.5-0.5

SATURDAY AFTERNOON FOURSOMES

Montgomerie/Langer *beat* Janzen/Furyk *by one hole*

Faldo/Westwood *lost to* Hoch/Maggert, *2 and 1*

Parnevik/Garrido *halved with* Leonard/Woods

Olazábal/Rocca *beat* Love/Couples, *5 and 4*

Session Score: 2.5-1.5

Overall Score: Europe 10.5, USA 5.5

The US team certainly didn't appreciate it – there were complaints about the hole from several players before the Cup got underway – and maybe it harmed their game because during the remainder of Saturday (also affected by rain, which meant two matches hung over to the Sunday), Team USA picked up just 3.5 points from a possible 12. With such a strong team on paper, back in the USA there had been predictions that it was almost impossible for Europe to win, but by the Sunday morning Seve's side were 10.5-5.5 ahead, with a massive five-point lead in the bag.

In the Fourballs, Clarke finally made his first appearance, partnering Montgomerie to a narrow victory over an in-form Couples and Love; he was swiftly followed by Woosnam and Bjørn, who added a comfortable 2 and 1 over Leonard and Faxon. Faldo, on his way towards setting a Ryder Cup points record with his eleventh appearance, again joined with Westwood to beat Woods and O'Meara in a match that saw Tiger actually putt into the water on the 17th. For Team USA, the only chink of light was a half for Mickelson/Lehman and Olazábal/Garrido, although even then, a 20-

foot putt from Olazábal at the 18th denied them victory.

The afternoon session was almost as convincing – more wins for Montgomerie/Langer and Olazábal/Rocca (in a convincing 5 and 4 triumph over Love/Couples) and a half for the unbeaten Parnevik and his partner Garrido against Leonard/ Woods. It was turning into a disaster for the Americans and only Hoch and Maggert's surprise win against Faldo/Westwood sweetened the pill. As Saturday finally closed, the sight of the scoreboard must have been a daunting one for all Americans, showing a 9-4 lead with matches still in play. Astonishingly, unthinkably, their dream team was taking a battering and only a minor miracle would turn it around.

Looking for exactly that, US captain Tom Kite pulled out all the stops to bring in a motivational speaker on the Saturday night to gee up his players. But this was no run-of-the-mill orator, but former President George Bush, who was staying in Cadiz after being invited to the opening ceremony. Who knows if his speech made a difference but the USA certainly came out fighting the following day and came so close towards achieving a miracle.

ABOVE: *Colin Montgomerie and Ignacio Garrido celebrate under an umbrella after an historic victory for Europe on Spanish soil.*

With no one giving the USA a hope of saving face in Valderrama, let alone winning, captain Tom Kite decided to go for broke in a bid to turn the situation around, packing his team with big-hitters at the front. Considering they were five points behind – the biggest lead Europe had ever taken into the final day – he believed the match might be over before his best players teed off, if he handled it any other way. The result proved how much the American team had underachieved in the opening two days because the quality of golf produced as they won the singles 8-4 was outstanding. It took them to within a point of doing the impossible until their comeback hit a brick wall when Colin Montgomerie, continuing his unbeaten record in Ryder Cup singles, earned a half against Scott Hoch, retaining the Cup for Europe.

In contrast to Kite's tactical team sheet, Seve Ballesteros democratically asked his players where they would like to play – not a scenario relished by his most senior golfers – and some reports suggest it was they who ensured the big four of Olazábal, Langer, Montgomerie and Faldo were placed close to the end in case anything went wrong. Whether or not it was Ballesteros' call proved important because things did go wrong, with the USA rampaging through the card, picking up points at will.

Ian Woosnam, who had seen little play over the weekend, was clearly rusty as he opened the order and was completely out-played by an impressive Fred Couples, losing 8 and 7. The result set the tone for a day of nerves and drama on the European side, during which they were steadied by the Swede Per-Ulrik Johansson beating Davis Love, 3 and 2, to make it four defeats in a row for the US team over the course of a frustrating week. Italian Costantino Rocca went one better in beating Tiger Woods, and now the home side needed just two more victories to retain the Ryder Cup trophy.

Things took a turn for the worse when Team USA suddenly came to life. Lehman crushed a worn-out Garrido, 7 and 6, while Maggert beat Westwood, 3 and 2. Even Faldo missed out, losing 3 and 2 to Furyk. When home-banker Olazábal (who had been two up) lost at the last to Janzen, the Europeans started to worry. With memories of his missed putt in 1991 well behind him, Langer seized one point in beating Brad Faxon - but where would the other come from? Thomas Bjørn might have seized it, but lost the 18th against Justin Leonard and was forced to settle for a half. And so it was all down to Monty at the last - so long as he didn't lose, Europe had overall victory.

" *I don't want to do that again – it wasn't fun out there.* "

Colin Montgomerie on the stress of going last in the Ryder Cup

It was tense, but the result was rarely in doubt. Hoch missed the fairway with his drive and was on the green in three, a good 15 feet from the hole. Montgomerie was on in two, with two putts for victory. But then, under instructions from Ballesteros, Monty conceded Hoch's putt and settled for a gentlemanly half to clinch the Ryder Cup for Europe by a single point. In some ways, this was a strange ending – but "oh so Seve!" And no one could say that Ballesteros – or Spain for that matter – had not delivered. Indeed, the first Ryder Cup to be held in Europe had proved a rip-roaring success. The rain (which returned during the presentation ceremony) made conditions more difficult than expected for spectators and players alike, but the 32nd Ryder Cup yet again provided incredible drama and a close result.

What a debt golf owed that day to Jack Nicklaus and his suggestion, almost 20 years earlier, to bring Europe into the competition – even if it left his beloved America wondering what they had to do to win again.

US captain Tom Kite blamed the weather and the course for his team's defeat in Spain. "It's a golf course that requires as much local knowledge as any I've seen, with the exception of the Augusta National," he insisted. "The only reason we got beat was they knew the golf course and the weather conditions better than us."

DAY THREE

FINAL DAY SINGLES

Ian Woosnam *lost to* **Fred Couples**, *8 and 7*

Per-Ulrik Johansson *beat* **Davis Love**, *3 and 2*

Jesper Parnevik *lost to* **Mark O'Meara**, *5 and 4*

Darren Clarke *lost to* **Phil Mickelson**, *2 and 1*

Costantino Rocca *beat* **Tiger Woods**, *4 and 2*

Thomas Bjørn *halved with* **Justin Leonard**

Ignacio Garrido *lost to* **Tom Lehman**, *7 and 6*

Bernhard Langer *beat* **Brad Faxon**, *2 and 1*

Lee Westwood *lost to* **Jeff Maggert**, *3 and 2*

José María Olazábal *lost to* **Lee Janzen** *by one hole*

Nick Faldo *lost to* **Jim Furyk**, *3 and 2*

Colin Montgomerie *halved with* **Scott Hoch**

Session Score: 4-8

Overall Score: Europe 14.5, USA 13.5

ABOVE: *Proud captain Seve Ballesteros holds the Ryder Cup aloft after a dramatic one-point victory over the USA in his home country.*

Ryder Cup legends
Bernhard LANGER

It takes a special kind of character to become a Ryder Cup legend but to follow up those successes by winning the trophy as captain needs something extra. But that's exactly what Europe's Bernhard Langer has achieved over the years and it marks him out as one of the greatest golfers the Ryder Cup has ever seen.

" In 1985... my life was pretty much 95 per cent golf and my wife was the rest. "

Bernhard Langer reveals the life of a golf pro

In an A-Z of the Ryder Cup, L would stand for Langer. The stylish German competed in 10 Ryder Cups and his performances were instrumental in helping Europe to win five, with a tied sixth enough to retain the trophy. The son of a German refugee who escaped from a Russian prisoner-of-war train bound for Siberia, perhaps it comes as no surprise that strength of character and mental agility have proved two of Langer's most important traits.

Legend has it that the young Bernhard - raised in Germany, where golf was not yet popular - was forced to trawl bookstores in his home town of Anhausen, Bavaria, for golfing magazines just to find out the latest Ryder Cup scores. By the time he reached his thirties, the name Langer was inextricably linked with the competition. His superb record of 24 points from 42 games is second only to Mr Ryder Cup himself, Nick Faldo, and his dramatic experience at the 1991 tournament must go down in folklore.

If L is for Langer, K is for Kiawah Island. The 1991 Ryder Cup, or "War on the Shore", went down to the final pairing and Langer was left with a six-foot putt to halve his match with Hale Irwin and retain the trophy for Europe. To everyone's disbelief, his putt shaved the hole, missing by mere millimetres, to hand the trophy to the USA. But there was pride in defeat, for Langer had contributed to quite a stunning spectacle. Indeed, he proved his mettle in winning a tournament in Germany the very next week and went on to compete in four more Ryder Cups.

Away from the Ryder Cup, Langer is a two-time Masters champion and was the world's first official No. 1 when the rankings were introduced in 1986. Famous for his use of the long broom-handle putter during long spells of his career, he also often overcame the "yips" (inexplicable jitters while putting), confirming his mental agility. Maybe for this reason, no one could quite believe that he missed "that putt" in 1991.

His Ryder Cup debut was made alongside Spain's Manuel Piñero in a Foursomes match of 1981, and he also formed excellent partnerships with players such as Sandy Lyle. Then, captaining Europe in 2004 at Oakland Hills, Langer led his team to one of the greatest victories of all - an 18.5-9.5 demolition of Tiger Woods & Co.

RYDER CUP RECORD

Ryder Cups: 1981, 1983, 1985 (winner), 1987 (winner), 1989 (tied but Europe retain trophy), 1991, 1993, 1995 (winner), 1997 (winner), 2002 (winner), 2004 (winner, non-playing captain)

Total wins: 6 (plus 1 tie to retain the trophy, 1989)

Matches: 42 (won 21, halved 6, lost 15)

Total points: 24

RIGHT: *German legend Bernhard Langer stares down the green at The Belfry in 1993.*

Paul **AZINGER**

If Bernhard Langer (opposite) was famous for his mental fortitude, then Paul Azinger must be made of similar stuff because his achievements as a player were barely interrupted by a personal battle with cancer, which he overcame with the same determination as he displayed on-course.

BELOW: *A typical pose from US star Paul Azinger as he blasts out of a bunker at the 1991 Ryder Cup at Kiawah Island.*

Shortly after the 1993 Ryder Cup, Azinger was diagnosed with non-Hodgkin's lymphoma in his right shoulder but he refused to give in and made an astonishing comeback, culminating in an emotional victory at the 2000 Sony Open in Hawaii. Anyone who witnessed him in action at The Belfry in 1993 could not possibly have guessed how ill he was because his singles battle against old foe Nick Faldo turned out to be one of the most competitive in Ryder Cup history. Even when Faldo holed-in-one, Azinger refused to give in and fought back to earn a half, playing his part in a 15-13 victory for the USA.

In other Ryder Cup appearances, Azinger experienced both highs and lows: tying in 1989, winning in 1991 (when he famously earned a key point against José María Olazábal in the singles) and losing in 2002. But perhaps his greatest moment of all came as captain in 2008. With Team USA desperate for a victory after years of European dominance, he led them to a 16.5-11.5 win in Valhalla. Azinger's style of captaincy, bringing in youthful, experienced players and changing the atmosphere around the US team, played a major part in the victory, confirming him a place in history as a Ryder Cup legend.

Azinger's other golfing achievements have been remarkable, too. He spent almost 300 consecutive weeks in golf's top 10 between 1988 and 1994 and won his first, and so far only, Major in 1993 when he lifted the PGA Championship, beating Greg Norman in a play-off. He also has 12 PGA Tour and two European Tour wins to his name.

But it is the drama of the Ryder Cup that seems to keep drawing him back. And even without a golf club in hand he was at Celtic Manor in 2010, this time as a television commentator.

> **❝** *I just want to say the greatest honour you can bestow on a professional golfer is to ask him to captain a Ryder Cup team and I'm awestruck by it.* **❞**
>
> *Paul Azinger on being named US captain for 2008*

RYDER CUP RECORD

Ryder Cups: 1989, 1991 (winner), 1993 (winner), 2002, 2008 (winner, non-playing captain)
Total wins: 3
Matches: 15 (won 5, halved 3, lost 7)
Total points: 6.5

ABOVE: *US players surge onto the 17th green after seeing Justin Leonard hole a massive putt against José María Olazábal.*

OPPOSITE: *Scenes of jubilation at the 17th hole as the US team continued its final day fightback in 1999.*

DAY THREE

FINAL DAY SINGLES

Tom Lehman beat **Lee Westwood**, *3 and 2*

Hal Sutton beat **Darren Clarke**, *4 and 2*

Phil Mickelson beat **Jarmo Sandelin**, *4 and 3*

Davis Love beat **Jean van de Velde**, *6 and 5*

Tiger Woods beat **Andrew Coltart**, *3 and 2*

David Duval beat **Jesper Parnevik**, *5 and 4*

Mark O'Meara lost to **Padraig Harrington** *by one hole*

Steve Pate beat **Miguel Angel Jiménez**, *2 and 1*

Justin Leonard halved with **José María Olazábal**

Payne Stewart lost to **Colin Montgomerie** *by one hole*

Jim Furyk beat **Sergio García**, *4 and 3*

Jeff Maggert lost to **Paul Lawrie**, *4 and 3*

Session Score: 8.5-3.5

Overall Score: USA 14.5, Europe 13.5

No team had ever won the Ryder Cup from more than two points adrift on the final day. But the USA won a stunning 56 holes to 33 to make history at Brookline. Of the pivotal first six matches, all of which were won, not a single one made it as far as the 17th. Europe's finest golfers were not just beaten, but demolished. "It was a mighty display of firepower," said Hal Sutton, who got it all started with a 4 and 2 victory over Darren Clarke.

The crowd were already on a high when Tom Lehman beat World No. 5 Lee Westwood. Lehman had not won on the PGA tour since 1996, while Westwood had won 14 tournaments in the same period, yet the American hit three birdies in a row to be two-up by the 6th and hit every single fairway before winning, 3 and 2. It soon became clear European captain James had made a fatal error of judgement. Having selected his senior players for all of the opening 16 matches, he was left with half a team that was worn-out, and another that hadn't played at all. Andrew Coltart, Jarmo Sandelin and Jean van de Velde had not even picked up a club in fury at this decision, yet they were expected to line up against America's best – and beat them. It just didn't add up.

Mickelson quickly demolished Sandelin, 4 and 3, while Love saw off van de Velde, 6 and 5, and Woods made short shrift of Coltart to make it five points for the USA and for the first time, the lead. The atmosphere at The Country Club was now truly explosive and the crowd, beginning to smell blood, turned up the volume with every putt that was holed – and every European putt missed.

David Duval earned the pivotal point of the day, beating an in-form Parnevik, 5 and 4 – a match that James must have expected to win after deliberately placing the Swede in the middle of the pack. But perhaps weary limbs were costing the Europeans dear... If Duval's display was crucial, the same might be said of Jim Furyk's victory over Sergio Garcia. Furyk had spotted that García – winning matches in tandem with Parnevik – hadn't been striking the ball well, and vowed to hit every fairway to keep his opponent under pressure. It worked, as he won 3 and 2.

Padraig Harrington's narrow victory over Mark O'Meara kept Europe in it, along with Paul Lawrie's confident win against Maggert but with only two matches left, the USA needed just a half to complete a memorable victory. With Leonard v Olazábal and Montgomerie v Stewart, the finale would be breathtaking. With so much at stake on the 17th, Leonard faced a huge 45-foot putt, while Olazábal was 25 feet from the hole. Pandemonium broke loose as Leonard's incredible effort rolled into the back of the cup to set off celebrations only seen once in a lifetime.

What the US players, wives, caddies and camera crew forgot, however, was that the match was still not over: Olazábal still had a putt to halve the hole. As the USA trampled all over the green, including a cameraman who ran across the line of the Spaniard's putt, both European players and management seethed at their opponent's ill-mannered display. We'll never know how much difference the unruly scenes made to Olazábal, but history shows he missed the putt and Team USA completed a remarkable victory.

In a show of sportsmanship, Stewart conceded to Montgomerie at the last, leaving the final score 14.5-13.5 for the second Ryder Cup in a row. In a sad addendum to the story, a few weeks later, Stewart was tragically killed in a plane crash. He did take part in the greatest Ryder Cup of all time, however, which is some legacy.

> **"*They got the momentum early on by holing a load of stuff. We didn't respond with our best play, and then the whole thing got out of hand.*"**
>
> *European captain Mark James explains what went wrong*

The new breed: Europe's Rory McIlroy (left) celebrates holing a putt on the 8th green with team-mate Graeme McDowell during the 2010 Ryder Cup at Celtic Manor.

The new breed: Europe's Rory McIlroy (left) celebrates holing a putt on the 8th green with team-mate Graeme McDowell during the 2010 Ryder Cup at Celtic Manor.

CHAPTER SEVEN

THE MODERN ERA

Following the Battle of Brookline in 1999, the Ryder Cup was bigger news than ever but needed to rediscover the sporting spirit envisaged by its founder. As the twenty-first century dawned, the competition entered a new era of intense but respectful competition, with Europe in the ascendancy.

2002

Europe 15.5
USA 12.5

The Belfry, Sutton Coldfield

September 27-29

THE COURSE

Brabazon Course
Location: The Belfry,
Sutton Coldfield,
England
Par: 72
Yards: 7,118
Par: 72
Yards: 7,356

Designed by Peter Alliss, The Belfry was hosting its fourth Ryder Cup. On its signature 10th hole, players must decide whether to drive and avoid the water – a part of Ryder Cup folklore.

After the bad feeling that lingered after the Battle of Brookline, the 2002 Ryder Cup was destined to be emotional, dramatic and compelling. Even so, the way Europe gained revenge on the USA, following a remarkable final day at The Belfry, was something truly special, whichever side you happened to be supporting.

THERE CANNOT, IN THE HISTORY of televised golf, have been many more engrossing days than September 29, 2002, when Europe and the USA went into the final day of the Ryder Cup locked at eight points all – and with the world's greatest golfers going head to head.

The 2002 Ryder Cup will be remembered for so many things: Paul McGinley's winning putt, Welsh rookie Phillip Price's amazing victory over World No. 2 Phil Mickelson, European captain Sam Torrance's tactical genius, Colin Montgomerie's consistency and the unfettered celebrations of the home team. But perhaps it should be remembered equally for the way in which the spirit of the Ryder Cup rose from the ashes.

There were still moments of tension – Sergio García kicking his golf bag in frustration at the American celebrations, for example – but after the Battle of Brookline in 1999, it was evident that the players on both teams had resolved to restore the competition's ideals of true sportsmanship and camaraderie. Given that this particular Ryder Cup was also postponed from 2001 due to the horrific 9/11 terrorist attack in New York, just 17 days before it was scheduled to take place – and with both captains agreeing to stick with the players originally selected for that year – golf needed this event to play its particular part in the overall healing process. "I was lucky in that their captain was Curtis Strange," explained Torrance. "We took about three seconds to agree there wasn't going to be a repeat of Brookline."

The drama didn't take long to unfold and by the end of the opening day, it was clear that the 2002 Ryder Cup was going to be something special for the Europeans, who led 4.5-3.5. The opening Fourballs saw Thomas Bjørn steal the limelight as he partnered Darren Clarke against Tiger Woods and Paul Azinger.

LEFT: *US captain Curtis Strange surveys the scene from his buggy during the morning Fourballs on the opening day of the 2002 Ryder Cup.*

OPPOSITE: *Colin Montgomerie (behind) and Bernhard Langer line up a putt during a Foursomes match against Scott Hoch and Jim Furyk.*

DAY ONE

CAPTAINS

Europe: Sam Torrance   **USA:** Curtis Strange

FRIDAY MORNING FOURBALLS

Clarke/Bjørn *beat* **Woods/Azinger** *by one hole*

García/Westwood *beat* **Duval/Love,** *4 and 3*

Montgomerie/Langer *beat* **Hoch/Furyk,** *4 and 3*

Harrington/Fasth *lost to* **Mickelson/Toms** *by one hole*

Session Score: 3-1

FRIDAY AFTERNOON FOURBALLS

Clarke/Bjørn *lost to* **Sutton/Verplank,** *2 and 1*

García/Westwood *beat* **Woods/Calcavecchia,** *2 and 1*

Montgomerie/Langer *halved with* **Mickelson/Toms**

Harrington/McGinley *lost to* **Cink/Furyk,** *3 and 21*

Session Score: 1.5-2.5

Overall Score: Europe 4.5, USA 3.5

> **"***The guys were really up for it and the way they performed was incredible. It's the best start we've made to a Ryder Cup for over 30 years.***"**
>
> *Sam Torrance, Europe's captain*

His sensational 20-foot putt on the 18th green halved the final hole, earning Europe the first point of the day. Just a hole earlier, it had seemed that Woods would turn out to be the headline-maker, providing a birdie to take the match to the last. But Bjørn's putt, his seventh birdie of the round, put the first block of blue on the scoreboard and saw Tiger lose for the seventh time in 11 Ryder Cup matches. "I'm so proud of the way Darren and Bjørn led from the front," said captain Sam Torrance.

Lee Westwood and Sergio García, who had never lost a Ryder Cup Fourballs or Foursomes, were next to contribute, beating David Duval and Davis Love, 4 and 3; Westwood's 18-foot putt on the 15th clinching victory. Colin Montgomerie then began what proved to be an almost exemplary weekend in partnering Bernhard Langer to beat Scott Hoch and Jim Furyk by the same score, with the Europeans contributing four birdies including a 20-foot putt from the German on the 14th. Suddenly it was beginning

to look like a European whitewash and so Phil Mickelson and David Toms' hard-fought one-up victory over Padraig Harrington and Niclas Fasth came as a welcome respite for the Americans.

The result must have given Curtis Strange's team renewed vigour for the afternoon Foursomes because Hal Sutton and Scott Verplank began a revival, beating Clarke and Bjørn, 2 and 1, having been two down at the 12th. Garcia and Westwood teamed up to beat Woods and Mark Calcavecchia, largely thanks to an impressive performance on the back nine, but the match was also notable for two terrible missed putts from Woods on consecutive holes. Could it be that the USA were about to capitulate? Not so, because Mickelson/Toms held on to halve with Montgomerie/Langer, clawing their way back from a three-shot deficit, while Cink/Furyk won, 3 and 2, against Harrington/McGinley, controlling the match from start to finish. The result left Europe one point ahead at the end of the day.

With so much to play for and only a point behind, there was a suspicion the Americans would prove highly dangerous on the Saturday and this was certainly the case. After a slow start, the holders were beginning to gain confidence and only the fact that Tiger Woods had failed to win a point seemed to be holding them back. By the end of Saturday, however, he was back on course and the match levelled. Suddenly what had looked to be a miserable defeat had the increasing potential to become a memorable victory.

As the atmosphere began to crackle, Mickelson/Toms continued their excellent form with a 2 and 1 victory over the inexperienced Pierre Fulke and Phillip Price. The European pair were surprisingly ahead after 10, but the match turned when Fulke missed a putt on the 12th that could have doubled their lead; Mickelson and Toms were ruthless as they won three in a row to turn the situation around. Then Mickelson's bunker shot at the 16th helped to secure an unlikely half, which finally broke their opponents' resolve.

Europe's reply saw García/Westwood beat Cink/Furyk, 2 and 1, to maintain their 100 per cent record, although the battling and scrambling nature of the victory summed up just how tight and desperate the match had become. Even veterans Montgomerie and Langer, in outstanding form, had to hold their nerve to beat Verplank/Hoch. In the end, they surrendered a two-hole lead to be level by the 15th and a nerve-jangling putt from Montgomerie on the 17th was needed to regain the lead. The relief on European faces was clear – and for Langer, this was yet another landmark as he secured a record eleventh victory in 18 Ryder Cup Foursomes. The morning was not over yet and when Woods/Love beat Bjørn/ Clarke, 4 and 3, Europe were just a point ahead and hanging on.

The afternoon matches proved even more dramatic, during which time nerves and tempers were tested in equal measure, but the big drama came during a match between García/Westwood and Woods/Love, bringing back bitter memories of three years earlier.

RIGHT: *Colin Montgomerie (left) and Padraig Harrington look relaxed on the 14th green during the Saturday afternoon matches.*

BELOW: *Tiger Woods and Davis Love celebrate winning their Fourballs match against Sergio García and Lee Westwood.*

DAY TWO

SATURDAY MORNING FOURSOMES

Fulke/Price *lost to* **Mickelson/Toms**, *2 and 1*

Westwood/García *beat* **Furyk/Cink**, *2 and 1*

Montgomerie/Langer *beat* **Verplank/Hoch** *by one hole*

Clarke/Bjørn *lost to* **Woods/Love**, *4 and 3*

Session Score: 1.5-2.5

SATURDAY AFTERNOON FOURBALLS

Fasth/Parnevik *lost to* **Calcavecchia/Duval** *by one hole*

Montgomerie/Harrington *beat* **Mickelson/Toms**, *2 and 1*

García/Westwood *lost to* **Woods/Love** *by one hole*

Clarke/McGinley *halved with* **Hoch/Furyk**

Session Score: 1.5-2.5

Overall Score: Europe 8, USA 8

García was furious when American team members, as well as a reporter and cameraman, rushed onto the 18th green as he and his partner lost their unbeaten record, with Westwood missing a five-foot putt that would have halved the match. The Spaniard hurled his ball into the lake and stormed off the green, kicking his golf bag as he left.

"It's his bag - he can do bloody well what he likes with it!" declared European captain Torrance as tempers frayed and memories of the way in which the American entourage celebrated Justin Leonard's putt by running onto the green, right in José María Olazábal's putting line in 1999 seeped to the surface. "He just lost a match, he felt he could have won," added Torrance, in explanation. "Good thing I wasn't there, he probably would have kicked me!" Fortunately, that injection of humour and a measured response from the Americans ensured García's moment of frustration had little impact on the overall spirit of the tournament. What the result of that Fourballs meant, however, was the Saturday games were completed with the scores level at 8-8, setting up the possibility of a classic final day's play at The Belfry.

Calcavecchia and Duval began the afternoon with a narrow victory over Fasth/Parnevik despite being three behind at one stage. The match hinged on an outstanding drive from Duval at the 10th, which found the green - something the Europeans were unable to match as both found water while attempting to follow suit. European dreams were reawakened by yet another victory for Montgomerie, this time teaming up with Harrington to beat Mickelson/Toms, 2 and 1. But Woods and Love's victory, together with a half for Hoch/Furyk, meant the day ended with the scores level and the USA feeling on the up. However, that doesn't tell the whole story because there was real drama in the final match, which left the Europeans on a high, too.

McGinley and Clarke showed the kind of battling spirit only the Ryder Cup engenders as they hung on against Hoch/Furyk, despite never being ahead. They were still one-down at the 17th following a Hoch birdie but somehow with the vociferous galleries now frantic, McGinley managed to find the concentration, skill and determination to birdie the 18th and therefore halve the match.

What a crucial putt it was - and there were more to come.

175

With the scores level and the eyes of the world on The Belfry for the final session of the 2002 Ryder Cup, there was everything to play for and what would follow goes down in history as one of the most engrossing days of sporting drama.

Team USA must have felt confident. As holders, they only needed to draw to retain the trophy and Europe had not secured an overall win in the singles since 1995. But perhaps they hadn't bargained on the tactical gamble that marks out Sam Torrance as one of the Ryder Cup's greatest ever captains. Going against tradition, he front-loaded his team, placing Europe's top eight players in the opening eight singles matches. By contrast, Strange saved his best players, including Woods and Mickelson, for later in the field. The idea, Torrance later revealed, was to whip the crowd into a frenzy by winning early points, a decision that proved inspired.

Montgomerie, so outstanding all weekend, got his team off to the perfect start in annihilating Hoch, 5 and 4, with a performance as fine as any seen at the Ryder Cup. As the crowd roared behind him, he crashed his first drive down the fairway and birdied from 18 feet to take an early lead. Hoch drew level at the 3rd, but Monty was three-up by the end of the first nine and never looked back, eventually admitting: "That's the best I can play. Scott is a great champion and a tough competitor, but I think I was eight-under and there's not much you can do about that."

Quite so, but the Americans were clearly not about to give up – far from it. Toms responded with a narrow victory over García, sealed at the 18th when the Spaniard thundered his tee-shot into the water. Clarke and Duval then halved before Langer, Harrington and Bjørn all won to put Europe 12.5-9.5 ahead and justify their captain's gamble. Only a stunning performance from Verplank, America's wild card rookie, against Westwood kept the USA in contention as he birdied the first and eagled the third to win, 2 and 1.

Paul Azinger, often the USA's most consistent performer, sensed the mood and produced a battling half against Fasth to maintain his unbeaten record in Ryder Cup singles; his remarkable bunker shot at the 18th, which found the hole to save him from defeat, was probably the shot of the day.

> **" The most important club used to win the Ryder Cup wasn't a putter or a drive, it was the pencil of European captain Sam Torrance. "**
>
> *USA Today*

SHOT OF THE DAY

It was a huge gamble to place Phillip Price so far down the order in the eleventh tie but what a pay-off Torrance received as the Welshman, ranked 119th in the world, produced the performance of his life against World No. 2 Phil Mickelson. Price was three-down by the 5th, but began a legendary comeback at the 6th when, with his feet almost in the water after driving close to the lake, he produced an inspired shot to the green and subsequently won the hole. That moment changed the whole balance of the game – and perhaps the Ryder Cup, too. An inspired Price was transformed as he won hole after hole, roared on by the home crowd.

OPPOSITE: *Paul McGinley of Ireland leaps in the air after sinking the putt at the 18th green that won the Ryder Cup for Europe.*

RIGHT: *Jubilant Europe captain Sam Torrance celebrates on the 18th after leading his team to victory at The Belfry.*

Perhaps the key for Torrance, though, was what happened in the match between Mickelson and Welsh rookie Phillip Price – a contest that in any context other than the Ryder Cup might have been a foregone conclusion. But Price won with three holes to spare, finishing with a nerveless 25-foot downhill putt at the 16th when the Cup was not yet won and pressure was heavy. "Tell 'em who I beat, go on, tell 'em who I beat!" Price was reported to shout in the post-match celebrations – and who can really blame him for such exuberance?

Remarkable as this performance was, it wasn't enough to clinch overall victory – Azinger's shot from the bunker had seen to that. So it was left to McGinley to complete the job against Furyk. The Irishman needed a half and tension was palpably in the air as he reached the 18th. He had trailed his opponent all the way from the second hole but drew level on the 17th with impeccable timing. Now everything was on McGinley's 10-foot putt after Furyk chipped close from a greenside bunker. Somehow McGinley held his nerve and when the ball finally dropped, it set off wild celebrations in the European camp.

Champagne flowed, Torrance was drenched and McGinley even ended up in the lake as the party began. "I'm very proud," said Torrance. "Apart from my marriage and the birth of my children, this is the proudest moment of my life." This is a common reaction from exhausted but elated captains on either winning team.

DAY THREE

FINAL DAY SINGLES

Colin Montgomerie *beat* **Scott Hoch,** *5 and 4*

Sergio García *lost to* **David Toms** *by one hole*

Darren Clarke *halved with* **David Duval**

Bernhard Langer *beat* **Hal Sutton,** *4 and 3*

Padraig Harrington *beat* **Mark Calcavecchia,** *5 and 4*

Thomas Bjørn *beat* **Stewart Cink,** *2 and 1*

Lee Westwood *lost to* **Scott Verplank,** *2 and 1*

Niclas Fasth *halved with* **Paul Azinger**

Paul McGinley *halved with* **Jim Furyk**

Pierre Fulke *halved with* **Davis Love**

Phillip Price *beat* **Phil Mickelson,** *3 and 2*

Jesper Parnevik *halved with* **Tiger Woods**

Session Score: 7.5-4.5

Overall Score: Europe 15.5, USA 12.5

Ryder Cup legends
Colin MONTGOMERIE

There can hardly be another golfer more immersed in the history of the Ryder Cup, or whose name is woven into the fabric of the contest than Colin Montgomerie. The great Scot has relished the drama of every European putt and every American drive for more than 20 years. His passion for Ryder Cup glory has led to many victories, both as player and captain.

So, where does one begin with an evaluation of Colin Montgomerie's contribution to golfing history? To put it bluntly, "Monty" is Ryder Cup royalty. Since making his debut in 1991, he has been at the heart of some of the most iconic episodes in the competition's history, not least the moment when he holed the winning putt at Oakland Hills Country Club, Michigan, in 2004 to give Europe a dramatic victory. There are those who will tell you that Ian Poulter's birdie on the 15th just three seconds earlier was mathematically the half-point guaranteeing a European win that day but in the hearts of European fans, it was Monty's day and certainly his face on the back of every British newspaper.

It was Montgomerie, too, who halved the last hole with Scott Hoch to clinch the half-point that secured Europe the Cup in 1997. Remarkably, in eight Ryder Cups he has never lost a singles match. Not everyone loves him - he hasn't always gone down well in the USA, unlike back home, but there is certainly something special about watching Monty play.

At first sight you might not necessarily place him as one of the world's greatest athletes - those rounded, sloping shoulders and a lumbering, almost lethargic gait are in complete contrast to the lean, super-fit youngsters now coming to the fore in world golf. But few can match the accuracy and natural ability of the Scotsman, who was born in Glasgow in 1963, but brought up in Yorkshire, England. Indeed, barely any can match the competitive spirit that has driven him thoughout his 24-year professional career. Monty has scored 23.5 points in eight Ryder Cups as a player, which places him only 1.5 points behind the all-time record holder, Nick Faldo, but perhaps his greatest moment came in 2010 - and without a club in hand.

As captain of the European team at Celtic Manor, Colin Montgomerie gave one of his most convincing performances, displaying true leadership as he inspirationally masterminded yet another remarkable victory for the home team. Later he described the experience as "the greatest moment of my golfing career." What really stood out was not just his meticulous preparation - although in itself impressive - but the big, generous, enthusiastic personality, which makes him such a legend.

There were times in his playing career, particularly in the USA, when he was labelled miserable or even grumpy as frustration with errant cameramen or noisy supporters in the gallery seemed to spill over and affect his concentration. But those who have met the great man will tell you that it's his enthusiasm, zest for life and sense of humour that really stand out - the qualities that made him such a successful captain.

He was willing to set aside differences to count players such as Darren Clarke and José María Olazábal among his vice-captains and employed passionate speeches - and a rallying phone call from Seve Ballesteros (who was fighting a brain tumour) - to prepare his troops for battle. "He was with every player, and every player was with him," explained Ireland's Padraig Harrington after the trophy was won. "We didn't want to let him down - we wanted to deliver for Monty."

What came across in those post-tournament interviews was that Colin Montgomerie trusted his players and they in turn responded to that trust - clearly his passion for the Ryder Cup rubbed off on everyone.

RYDER CUP RECORD

Ryder Cups: 1991, 1993, 1995 (winner), 1997 (winner), 1999, 2002 (winner), 2004 (winner), 2006 (winner), 2010 (winner, non-playing captain)
Total wins: 6
Matches: 36 (won 20, halved 7, lost 9)
Total points: 23.5

He has, of course, stepped down from the captaincy since 2010 and José Maíia Olazábal of Spain will take his place at the Medinah Country Club. Despite this, there's a possibility of seeing Monty somewhere in Chicago, such is his love for the Cup – "It would be nice to be involved in some individual capacity," he admits.

Away from the Ryder Cup, the Scotsman is famously known as probably the best golfer never to have won a Major although as you can see, the label doesn't do justice to an incredible career that includes a record eight Order of Merit titles – and an incredible character, too. Without him, the Ryder Cup just wouldn't be the same.

> "*Personally it means nothing.*
> *This is all about a team event.*"
>
> *Colin Montgomerie's teamwork ethic*

2004

Europe 18.5
USA 9.5

Oakland Hills CC, Michigan

September 17-19

THE COURSE

Oakland Hills Country Club
Location: Bloomfield
Township,
Michigan
Par: 70
Yards: 7,077

The South Course, designed by Donald Ross in 1918, is known by some as "The Monster". Ten Major championships had been held there before the 2004 Ryder Cup. The legendary Ben Hogan described it as "the greatest test of golf I have ever played."

If anyone still regarded Europe as perennial underdogs in the Ryder Cup, they were put firmly in their place in 2004, because that was the day when the Europeans underlined once and for all everything had changed. Not only did they travel to America and win, but they did so by an almost unthinkable record margin in Michigan, producing their best result of the modern era.

HOW COULD ANYONE HAVE PREDICTED what happened at Oakland Hills over a long weekend in September 2004? Suddenly, the US team, which had dominated the Ryder Cup, realized having the better-ranked players was no longer enough to guarantee victory. The Europeans, led by captain Bernhard Langer, took team play to a new level and in scoring 18.5 points, eclipsed every other side in history since the event was changed in 1979 to include players from continental Europe. The result was the USA's worst defeat, even more so than the 16.5-11.5 mauling at The Belfry in 1985, and set down a marker for Ryder Cups to come. As Colin Montgomerie reflected after victory was sealed, the European team would start off favourites for the first time ever in the next one.

Indeed, it was Monty who was destined to hit the winning putt and enhance his reputation as Europe's Mr Ryder Cup, but every

team member played their part as Europe took control in the first session, emerging from Friday's morning Fourballs with a 3.5-0.5 lead. After being given the honour of going out first, Montgomerie rewarded his captain with a typically focused and powerful display. He and Padraig Harrington were up against the formidable partnership of Tiger Woods and Phil Mickelson, who brushed aside rumours that the USA's so-called "dream team" didn't get along – and a titanic battle ensued.

Montgomerie set the tone by birdying the opening hole and the European pair picked up a total of seven birdies in the first eight on their way to an impressive 2 and 1 win. By that time, Darren Clarke and Miguel Angel Jiménez had already put Europe ahead after racing to a 5 and 4 victory over Davis Love and Chad Campbell, while Sergío Garcia and Lee Westwood were already on their way

RIGHT: *Colin Montgomerie hits from a fairway bunker on the 1st hole during a Fourballs match on the opening day.*

OPPOSITE: *Tiger Woods and Phil Mickelson awaiting action as the 2004 Ryder Cup prepares to get underway at Oakland Hills.*

to beating David Toms and Jim Furyk, 5 and 3. The USA's only half-point came in a classic tussle between Chris Riley and Stewart Cink against Paul McGinley and rookie Luke Donald, decided at the 18th. With a superb two-iron to the last green, Donald did his best to win it but Riley holed a crucial three-footer to save the USA from losing the session, 4-0. Even so, Langer had a right to be pleased, saying: "I'm thrilled, and so are the players – we wanted to make a fast start and it doesn't get much better than that."

Europe went on to dominate the afternoon Foursomes, too, winning three out of four to finish 6.5-1.5 ahead. Again, Montgomerie and Harrington led the way, making five birdies in the front nine to wipe out Love and Fred Funk, 4 and 2. The Mickelson/Woods partnership continued to be less than the sum of its parts, losing to Clarke/Westwood despite being three-up after five holes. It was all square going into the 18th but a poor tee shot by Mickelson, which veered badly left, resulted in Woods – whose body language revealed his frustration the whole day – having to take a penalty drop. In the end, a bogey five proved enough for Westwood and Clarke to claim their second point of the day, leaving the "dream team" pointless. "Who would have seen that coming?" US captain Sutton later admitted. "And also, who would have seen Davis Love, who played twice today and didn't win a point? You could have owned me today if you'd have wanted to take that bet because I'd bet it all – I'd bet the ranch!"

Everything was going Europe's way. García/Donald beat Perry/Cink, but it wasn't until DiMarco and Haas beat Jiménez/Levet, 3 and 2, that the Americans achieved a full point on the board.

DAY ONE

CAPTAINS

USA: Hal Sutton   **Europe:** Bernhard Langer

FRIDAY MORNING FOURBALLS

Mickelson/Woods *lost to* **Montgomerie/Harrington**, *2 and 1*

Campbell/Love *lost to* **Clarke/Jiménez**, *5 and 4*

Riley/Cink *halved with* **McGinley/Donald**

Toms/Furyk *lost to* **García/Westwood**, *5 and 3*

Session Score: USA 0.5, Europe 3.5

FRIDAY AFTERNOON FOURSOMES

DiMarco/Haas *beat* **Jiménez/Levet**, *3 and 2*

Love/Funk *lost to* **Montgomerie/Harrington**, *4 and 2*

Mickelson/Woods *lost to* **Clarke/Westwood** *by one hole*

Perry/Cink *lost to* **García/Donald**, *2 and 1*

Session Score: 1-3

Overall Score: USA 1.5, Europe 6.5

If the USA were to stand any chance of wiping out the bad memories of a miserable Friday, they knew everything must be put right 24 hours later in the second set of Fourballs and Foursomes. After a promising start, this proved a difficult task, though. Certainly, the morning was encouraging, particularly for Tiger Woods, who seemed a different character when partnered with Chris Riley. The pair romped to a convincing 4 and 3 over Darren Clarke and Ian Poulter. Suddenly, there was a glimmer of hope, which the crowd all too readily lapped up with chants of "USA, USA, USA!" reverberating round the course when the possibility of an American comeback looked at least feasible. There were even smiles from Tiger and at one stage it seemed as though a USA whitewash was possible with so much red on the board – especially when Cink and Love III inflicted a rare defeat on Montgomerie, partnered by Harrington.

Europe were not quite done, however for García/Westwood earned a half against Haas/DiMarco and then, crucially, the unheralded partnership of Paul Casey and David Howell came from a hole down, with two to play – and managed to win at the 18th against Furyk/Campbell. No two Europeans playing their first Ryder Cup had ever combined to win a full point since 1979, but that's exactly what Casey and Howell managed to do when the former holed the winning putt on the 18th green.

"Many of you probably thought I'm sacrificing a point when I sent them out, but deep down, I felt that they would be the surprise of the morning," said Langer. "And obviously, I'm very pleased that it happened, especially how it happened. To win the last two holes and gain a huge point for us, that gave us the momentum swing that we were hoping for." Indeed, that late point kept Europe in the driving seat and more importantly, morale was high as Lee Westwood later revealed when he reviewed the day's play. "We all owe David Howell and Paul Casey a beer," he said. "That was the biggest point of the week." US captain Sutton was also pleased with his team's response and at least he knew his players would fight for the trophy – something he may not have been quite so sure of, some 24 hours earlier. He had a quirky way of describing this, too, saying: "The guys played great – I felt their energy. And when I made the telephone call, I didn't get the

SHOT OF THE DAY

Sergio García's putt at the 18th in the morning Fourballs had to be seen to be believed, being all of 45 yards, with 25 feet of break (and a large swale in his line to add to the difficulty). Somehow he timed his shot to perfection as the ball rolled up, down and perfectly into the hole at the end of its momentum for the putt of a lifetime. Even if it was only for a bogey, he sealed a half for the Europeans.

ABOVE: *European players David Howell and Paul Casey look over the 18th green during their morning Fourballs match.*

DAY TWO

SATURDAY MORNING FOURBALLS

Haas/DiMarco *halved with* **García/Westwood**

Woods/Riley *beat* **Clarke/Poulter,** *4 and 3*

Furyk/Campbell *lost to* **Casey/Howell** *by one hole*

Cink/Love *beat* **Montgomerie/Harrington,** *3 and 2*

Session Score: 2.5-1.5

SATURDAY AFTERNOON FOURSOMES

Haas/DiMarco *lost to* **Clarke/Westwood,** *5 and 4*

Mickelson/Toms *beat* **Jiménez/Levet,** *4 and 3*

Furyk/Funk *lost to* **García/Donald** *by one hole*

Love/Woods *lost to* **Harrington/McGinley,** *4 and 3*

Session Score: 1-3

Overall Score: USA 5, Europe 11

answering machine: I got them." Unfortunately, when he rang again in the afternoon his players appeared to have gone fishing as Europe won the session, 3-1, to leave themselves 11-5 ahead, requiring only three more points to retain the trophy.

Europe's afternoon haul included three wins, notably a 3 and 2 victory for Irishmen Harrington and McGinley against Woods and Love III. Woods was unrecognizable from the morning, producing a string of errors that included missed putts on the 8th and 9th, as well as a scuffed chip on the 11th. "I basically missed some putts, hit a couple of bad shots and basically put us in a very difficult position to try and win a match," he admitted. "I just didn't have it – it was just not a good time to have that happen." The defeat was crucial because García and Donald won one-up against Furyk and Funk, while Westwood and Clarke cruised to a 5 and 4 victory over DiMarco and Haas. The only American point came from the partnership of Mickelson and Toms, who won 4 and 3 against Jiménez and Levet, but it wasn't enough. Afterwards, Langer again declared himself extremely happy and proud of his team. He also knew the Europeans were on the verge of glory, even if US hero Mickelson refused to admit defeat, insisting: "It would take something exceptional and it's very unlikely, but we won't give up."

" *We dug our hole deep, but we've got a powerful enough team that we can come out of this hole.* "

Hal Sutton attempts to rally the troops

Considering they were so far behind, it was all the US side could do on the final day at Oakland Hills to come out fighting and they found Bernhard Langer's team ready to do battle. With Tiger Woods scoring an early 3 and 2 victory over Paul Casey and Jim Furyk destroying David Howell, 6 and 4, there was a brief moment of hope for the home team when they gained the momentum. But Europe's team proved strong and ultimately, the talismanic Montgomerie (who had needed a wild card to join the fray after disappointing form in the previous year) was left to execute the winning putt and set up a record victory.

It was 1999 when the 41-year-old Scot last led the European Tour, but something about the Ryder Cup brings out the best in him. As he beat David Toms at the last, he was outstanding and displayed nerves of steel to convert the all-important putt. "Monty, Monty!" chanted the European fans as he strode purposefully up the final fairway in a very different scene to the Brookline of 1999, when a bitter battle with the American galleries left him furious. This time,

however, he had gained the respect – if not the affections, perhaps – of the American public as he proved his mettle just a week after the divorce from his wife Eimear came through and following a year in which his private life had been spread across the English tabloids. But any demons that remained, on or off the course, were swiftly banished as the crowd rose to acclaim him. "It has been a long four months for me personally," he said. "I don't want to talk about it but at the same time, it's quite well known. I have come a long way in those four months – I am proud of myself right now."

This moment of glory was hugely popular in the European ranks, with Paul Casey observing: "For him of all people to hole the putt, it was just perfect and you knew he wouldn't miss." Earlier, the visiting team had at least been made to fight for their victory as US captain Hal Sutton sent out his side in the order in which they had qualified, with Woods giving him a perfect start before former US Open champion Furyk took Howell apart. At one stage the USA were even up in five matches. Slowly but surely, Europe fought

DAY THREE

FINAL DAY SINGLES

Tiger Woods *beat* **Paul Casey**, *3 and 2*

Phil Mickelson *lost to* **Sergio García**, *3 and 2*

Davis Love *halved with* **Darren Clarke**

Jim Furyk *beat* **David Howell**, *6 and 4*

Kenny Perry *lost to* **Lee Westwood** *by one hole*

David Toms *lost to* **Colin Montgomerie** *by one hole*

Chad Campbell *beat* **Luke Donald**, *5 and 3*

Chris DiMarco *beat* **Miguel Angel Jiménez** *by one hole*

Fred Funk *lost to* **Thomas Levet** *by one hole*

Chris Riley *lost to* **Ian Poulter**, *3 and 2*

Jay Haas *lost to* **Padraig Harrington** *by one hole*

Stewart Cink *lost* to **Paul McGinley**, *3 and 2*

Session Score: 4.5-7.5

Overall Score: USA 9.5, Europe 18.5

back, with Sergio García providing the inspiration. His 3 and 2 victory over World No. 4 Mickelson was the turning point.

García, who had never won a singles match in two previous Cups, was two-down after eight holes with a fight on his hands, but the 24-year-old won three holes in a row to completely turn the match around. He won the 13th, too, and clinched an all-important point for his side at the 16th, when Mickelson found the water. "It's important to have that first point for our team," said García. "I was trying not to look at the leaderboards because we didn't start very well, but I really felt I could beat him."

With European spirits back up, the picture quickly transformed. Clarke earned a half against Love and when Westwood beat Perry, coming from two-down to win one-up, Team Europe already knew they would be keeping the trophy – leaving Montgomerie to put the icing on Langer's cake.

Further wins for Levet against Funk, Poulter against Riley, Harrington against Haas and McGinley against Cink made this a

record day: the 18.5-9.5 result was the USA's heaviest defeat in the 77-year history of the competition. "We just got outplayed," admitted a disconsolate Sutton. "I made mistakes and I take full responsibility." As for Langer, he was understandably jubilant. "We had so much fun as a team," he said. "I'm so proud of the guys. We were down early and came back strong – they have a lot of heart."

> **"** *We have beaten one of the strongest American teams ever assembled – a wonderful achievement for everybody involved.* **"**
>
> *Bernhard Langer, European captain*

LEFT: *Colin Montgomerie celebrates on the 18th green after a narrow victory over David Toms in their Sunday singles match.*

RIGHT: *Bernhard Langer is held aloft by team-mates Darren Clarke (left) and Lee Westwood as Team Europe wins in Michigan.*

BELOW: *The celebrations begin for the European team. France's Thomas Levet shares a congratulatory handshake with his captain.*

2006

Europe 18.5
USA 9.5

The K Club,
County Kildare

September 22-24

THE COURSE

The K Club
Location: County Kildare,
Ireland
Par: 72
Yards: 7,335

*Owned by Sir Michael Smurfit
and designed by Arnold
Palmer, the course, 20 miles
(32km) southwest of Dublin,
only opened in 1991 and
having been designed by an
American, was expected to
suit the US team.*

**The 36th Ryder Cup has its own place in history after Europe completed
a hat-trick of victories by winning at The K Club for the first time in an
emotional rollercoaster of a competition. It will be remembered for the
vociferous crowds in Ireland, Henrik Stenson's winning putt and for Ian
Woosnam's leadership, but most of all this was the story of Darren Clarke.**

OVER THE YEARS, there have been many Ryder Cup heroes, both European and American, but few have generated so much empathy and emotion as the man who symbolized the 2006 tournament at The K Club. Northern Irishman Clarke, 38, was a captain's pick for the European team, but arrived in County Kildare little more than a month after the death of his wife Heather from breast cancer, his emotions still raw.

"There was a time when I didn't think I would be able to play," he later admitted in a BBC interview, "but I sat down and deliberated, and weighed up the pros and cons and made my decision to play –

and I'm glad I stuck by it." The European team certainly benefited because Clarke won three out of three before finally breaking down in tears following a 3 and 2 singles victory over US rookie Zach Johnson on the final day, putting Europe 16-8 ahead and on their way to victory.

Right from the start he had been an inspiration to both his team and the crowd – and even his American opponents, who must have sensed his grief. Tiger Woods had lost his father Earl to cancer the same season and must have known just what his rival was going through. Woods had been equally emotional after winning

at Hoylake (near Liverpool), nine weeks earlier – his first Major without Earl by his side.

It was clear from the opening day that Clarke would receive tumultuous backing from the Irish crowd. "I'll never forget the reception I was given on the first tee," he said on the opening Friday, having teamed up with Westwood to win against Phil Mickelson and Chris DiMarco in the morning Fourballs. "It was a very, very special moment." He also combined with Westwood – another captain's pick, controversially chosen ahead of Thomas Bjørn – on the Saturday morning to beat Tiger Woods and Jim Furyk, 3 and 2. However, he saved the best until last by triumphing in the singles against Johnson. A birdie at the 5th, a 25-foot birdie putt at the 10th and a remarkable chip from 70 yards at 12 set up a victory to leave him collapsed in tears at the end, falling into the arms of father Godfrey, mother Hetty, sister Andrea and caddie Billy Foster. If it felt like the Darren Clarke Show in that moment, anyone would understand, but it wasn't the Northern Irishman who rolled in the putt to secure the Ryder Cup – that was left to Stenson – and there were plenty of other heroes to celebrate.

On the opening Friday, in a high-octane atmosphere, the action began with old-hand Colin Montgomerie, 43, combining with Harrington to take on Woods and Jim Furyk in a mouthwatering first of the morning Fourballs. But the European pair couldn't quite clinch the early victory they craved, with Woods/Furyk winning one-up to get the Americans off to an encouraging start. The response from the crowd hinted at the emotion and drama to come, however. "That is, without doubt, the noisiest and best reception I've ever had in all the years I've been involved in the Ryder Cup," observed Montgomerie.

In a fiercely and tightly contested opening day, matters improved for the Europeans after this, with Casey/Karlsson halving against Cink/Henry before Spaniards García and Olazábal combined for a hugely impressive 3 and 2 victory over Toms/Wetterich. Clarke and Westwood's narrow win against Mickelson/DiMarco followed to leave the crowd on a high for the afternoon Foursomes, which proved even tighter. The opening three matches were all halved – Irish heroes Harrington/McGinley against Campbell/Johnson; Howell/Stenson v Cink/Toms, with Westwood and Montgomerie against Mickelson/DiMarco. But it took a nerveless putt from Montgomerie – the last of the day – to rescue his pairing from defeat and he was grateful for an outstanding performance from Donald/García, who beat Woods/Furyk by two holes, to keep European spirits high as they ended the day ahead. "To be leading by two points is marvellous and I'm just happy and proud for my guys," said captain Woosnam.

> **" Darren being here was an inspiration in itself and his play was remarkable. "**
>
> *Tiger Woods compliments Darren Clarke's performance, following the recent death of Clarke's wife*

ABOVE: *Sergio García (left) consults with Luke Donald as they play Tiger Woods and Jim Furyk in the opening Foursomes.*

OPPOSITE: *Lee Westwood (right) hugs Darren Clarke after they beat Phil Mickelson and Chris DiMarco (front) in the opening Fourballs.*

DAY ONE

CAPTAINS

Europe: Ian Woosnam   **USA:** Tom Lehman

FRIDAY MORNING FOURBALLS

Harrington/Montgomerie *lost to* **Woods/Furyk** *by one hole*

Casey/Karlsson *halved with* **Cink/Henry**

García/Olazábal *beat* **Toms/Wetterich**, *3 and 2*

Clarke/Westwood *beat* **Mickelson/DiMarco** *by one hole*

Session Score: 2.5-1.5

FRIDAY AFTERNOON FOURSOMES

Harrington/McGinley *halved with* **Campbell/Johnson**

Howell/Stenson *halved with* **Cink/Toms**

Westwood/Montgomerie *halved with* **Mickelson/DiMarco**

Donald/Garcia *beat* **Woods/Furyk** *by two holes*

Session Score: 2.5-1.5

Overall Score: Europe 5, USA 3

> ❝*He might be a short man, but he's got a huge heart and he's just been awesome.*❞
>
> *Sergio García assesses captain*
> *Ian Woosnam's contribution*

All the galleries could talk about on Day Two of the 2006 Ryder Cup was Paul Casey's hole-in-one at the 14th but this turned out to be just one highlight in another excellent day's golf for the European side, who won both morning and afternoon sessions to go 10-6 ahead. Sergio García must take a large slice of the credit for having twice won on the opening day and repeated the trick to make it four from four by the end of Saturday.

The action commenced with Cink/Henry holding Casey/Karlsson to a very tight half (although perhaps rookie J.J. Henry deserved to win with an eagle at the par-five 16th). But Garcia's fluent display as he partnered Olazábal to a 3 and 2 victory over Mickelson/DiMarco set Europe on their way in a match that saw World No. 2 Mickelson appear worryingly off-colour. It was the same for World No. 1 Woods, who was particularly wayward as he partnered World No. 3 Furyk in a 3 and 2 defeat against Clarke/Westwood. True to the fairytale, it was Clarke who sealed victory with a chip at the 16th to add to Tiger's problems. The result left the American legend with a record of 13 defeats in 23 Ryder Cup matches and his performance was so disappointing that rumours began to circulate that the great man could even be dropped for the afternoon Foursomes.

In the event he went on to defy the critics in teaming up once more with Furyk to produce an excellent 3 and 2 victory over Harrington/McGinley. Meanwhile, US captain Lehman was adamant that he had never considered leaving his star man out of the team, admitting: "I don't know how you can sit down the best player in the world – that's impossible!" Whatever the truth, he was proved correct in his decision to stick by his man as Woods dramatically improved his driving and short game to post a crucial victory, even if Europe remained four points in the lead by the end

LEFT: *Paul Casey (right) celebrates his hole-in-one on the 14th hole with David Howell during the afternoon Foursomes.*

SHOT OF THE DAY

Paul Casey's sensational hole-in-one at the 14th was an easy pick for Shot of the Day, making its appearance during a 5 and 4 victory over Stewart Cink and Zach Johnson. The 29-year-old Englishman, only recently crowned World Match Play champion, sent his tee-shot 213 yards straight to the pin. To put this achievement into perspective, it was only the fifth hole-in-one in Ryder Cup history and the first since his fellow Englishman, Howard Clark, in 1995. Other Ryder Cup "aces" came from Costantino Rocca (1995), Nick Faldo (1993) and Peter Butler (1973). Twenty-four hours after Casey's effort, Scott Verplank became the first American to complete the same feat.

of play. As Furyk insisted, it was a long way for the side to come back but they had done it before and the point definitely helped.

It didn't look good for the Americans, though, and especially not after García/Donald beat Mickelson/Toms, 2 and 1. Casey – including that hole-in-one – joined forces with Howell to beat Cink/Johnson by a huge 5 and 4. With Montgomerie/Westwood earning a half against Campbell/Taylor, it was once again Europe and Woosnam's afternoon.

It did not go unnoticed, especially by the Americans, that every one of the 12 European players contributed to their points total during the first two days, which perhaps underlines the strength of Woosnam's team. "I'm delighted to have 10 points at this stage," he declared. "I think I played every single player again and as I said yesterday, everybody's added a half a point or a point. We came here playing as a team and we're still playing as a team – and that's what we intend tomorrow."

As far as Lehman was concerned, he knew the writing was on the wall but wasn't about to give up the ghost just yet, with the singles still to come. "There were a lot of tight matches and the difference was we didn't make a lot of putts," he insisted. "But we need to look at the positives because some of the guys played very well today. It's a pretty fine line between zero points, half a point or one point."

DAY TWO

SATURDAY MORNING FOURBALLS

Casey/Karlsson *halved with* **Cink/Henry**

García/Olazábal *beat* **Mickelson/DiMarco**, *3 and 2*

Clarke/Westwood *beat* **Woods/Furyk**, *3 and 2*

Stenson/Harrington *lost to* **Verplank/Johnson**, *2 and 1*

Session Score: 2.5-1.5

SATURDAY AFTERNOON FOURSOMES

García/Donald *beat* **Mickelson/Toms**, *2 and 1*

Montgomerie/Westwood *halved with* **Campbell/Taylor**

Casey/Howell *beat* **Cink/Johnson**, *5 and 4*

Harrington/McGinley *lost to* **Furyk/Woods**, *3 and 2*

Session Score: 2.5-1.5

Overall Score: Europe 10, USA 6

ABOVE: *Zach Johnson is congratulated on his putt on the 15th green by team-mate Scott Verplank (right) during Saturday's Fourballs.*

The final day of the 36th Ryder Cup dawned with Europe in a strong position, four points ahead. With home fans already dreaming of the prize, it came as no surprise when Colin Montgomerie was sent out first to seize the advantage. As so often the Scot did his job to perfection, producing a string of impressive iron shots to win one-up against David Toms. Wonderful approach shots to the 3rd and 4th holes gave him birdies and following this, he sealed victory with a nerve-racking up-and-down bunker shot on the 18th to extend his unbeaten run to eight singles matches. That stoic performance set the tone for Europe, who went on to complete a memorable victory.

The Americans did have a hero in Stewart Cink, however, who made four birdies in the first five against an in-form García – who had won six straight matches in the Ryder Cup. Cink crowned his performance in holing a 50-foot putt at the 12th before winning, 4 and 3, to keep US hopes alive. Woods then beat Robert Karlsson, 3 and 2, in his best display of the tournament, although Karlsson contributed to his own downfall in driving into the lake at the 15th; also sending his second shot in the water at the 16th. While Woods had won three points – his best total in Ryder Cup golf in five attempts – for him, this was no celebration. "I'm not real happy," he declared. "I'm 1-4 in Ryder Cups and it doesn't sit well, nor should it! They just outplayed us." Indeed, his performance was one of few positives for the USA as Europe continued their inexorable drive to glory, with Casey winning 2 and 1 against Furyk, and Howell beating Brett Wetterich, 5 and 4.

In the Singles, Tiger Woods managed to beat Robert Karlsson, 3 and 2, despite seeing his nine-iron dropped in a lake! Woods had asked caddie Steve Williams to clean the club alongside the 7th green, but he stumbled and dropped it in the water. "The

DAY THREE

FINAL DAY SINGLES

Colin Montgomerie *beat* **David Toms** *by one hole*

Sergio García *lost to* **Stewart Cink,** *4 and 3*

Paul Casey *beat* **Jim Furyk,** *2 and 1*

Robert Karlsson *lost to* **Tiger Woods,** *3 and 2*

Luke Donald *beat* **Chad Campbell,** *2 and 1*

Paul McGinley *halved with* **J.J. Henry**

Darren Clarke *beat* **Zach Johnson,** *3 and 2*

Henrik Stenson *beat* **Vaughn Taylor,** *4 and 3*

David Howell *beat* **Brett Wetterich,** *5 and 4*

José María Olazábal *beat* **Phil Mickelson,** *2 and 1*

Lee Westwood *beat* **Chris DiMarco** *by two holes*

Padraig Harrington *lost to* **Scott Verplank,** *4 and 3*

Session Score: 8.5-3.5

Overall Score: Europe 18.5, USA 9.5

ball got muddy," explained Woods. "I handed it to Stevie and he was going to rinse the nine-iron as well. He was dipping the towel and slipped on a rock. It was either him or the nine-iron – and he chose the nine-iron!"

It was England's Luke Donald, in the fifth singles tie, who would ensure the trophy was retained after beating Chad Campbell, 2 and 1, on the 17th green. With so many players still on course, a European victory was assured – and the fairytale was for Clarke to make the winning putt. It nearly came true but as the people's hero played his approach shot on the 16th, Swede Henrik Stenson was holing from seven feet on the 15th against to seize the glory moment for himself. Not that it mattered, of course – the victory was as sweet as it could possibly be for Europe and Clarke still received a thunderous reception after his match ended at the 16th when his putt fell just short. Generously, Johnson lifted his marker to concede, 3 and 2. The celebrations that followed were vivid, frenetic and deafening.

Almost inevitably as the adrenalin seeped away, Clarke broke down in tears and players from both teams rushed in to console him – US captain Lehman and Tiger Woods among them as thousands of fans ran up the fairway to join the party. "Darren, you hurt us so bad, but we're so glad you're on this team!" Lehman told him later. A record-equalling winning margin was

completed as McGinley halved with J.J. Henry, Olazábal beat Mickelson, 2 and 1; Westwood, despite complaining of feeling ill, beat DiMarco by two holes.

For the USA, the only consolation was a mesmerizing display from Verplank as he beat Harrington, 4 and 3, including a hole-in-one at the 14th. But the celebrations were all about Europe – and Clarke. Towards the end, Woosnam lifted his hero's arm into the air like a victorious boxer and it must be said, Clarke had fought harder than most for that special moment. As to be expected of a Ryder Cup in Ireland, the post-match celebrations were something to behold, with Clarke downing a pint of Guinness on the balcony. He was swiftly followed – and matched – by Woosnam. US captain Lehman was fulsome in his praise for such impressive opponents, saying: "I don't think there's ever been a European team which has played better."

> **"***Our team came ready, but maybe we weren't quite ready enough.***"**
>
> *US captain Tom Lehman reflects on defeat*

191

Henrik Stenson celebrates holing his putt on the 15th green to beat Vaughn Taylor and win the 2006 Ryder Cup for Europe.

MATCH	HOLE	EUROPE
1		MONTGOMER
2		GARCIA
3		CASEY
4		KARLSSON
5	16	DONALD
6	15	McGINLEY
	15	CLARKE
	14	STENSON
	13	HOWELL
	12	OLAZABAL
	12	WESTWOOD
	10	HARRINGT
	10	

BELOW: *A show of unity as Tiger Woods and Phil Mickelson walk off the 18th green following a match in 2004.*

Ryder Cup legends
Tiger **WOODS** and Phil **MICKELSON**

Quite simply, Tiger Woods is one of the greatest golfers ever to have lived, while Phil Mickelson is the player who has challenged him hardest, yet it is one of sport's great mysteries why neither has been able to dominate the Ryder Cup in the same way as every other competition.

Woods remains one of the biggest draws of the Ryder Cup. But his record in the competition is at best mixed and at worst, hugely disappointing: 14 points from 29. In turn, Mickelson has lost more Ryder Cup matches - 17 out of 34 - than any other American in history. Woods has won 71 times, including 14 Majors, on the PGA Tour and Mickelson has secured four Majors and a total of 39 events on tour, so the pair must be regarded as the heavyweights of Team USA, having spent much of the modern era as the World's No. 1 and 2. So, what happens when they pull on a Ryder Cup shirt?

Perhaps Woods, 10 times PGA Player of the Year, is so driven to concentrate on his own game that when playing in pairs, he loses a little of his edge. And whisper it, but maybe he prefers playing in individual tournaments than for Team USA. He once infuriated team-mates in suggesting he had "a million reasons" (first-prize money) to prefer the WGC-American Express tournament to the Ryder Cup. But one story ahead of the 2010 event suggested Woods took the team's rookie players aside, lecturing them on just how special the Ryder Cup is. It's obvious he cares and as he grows older, his record appears only to improve.

Maybe he has simply been unlucky over the years. In only his second year as a pro, he was part of the US team of 1997. He has played in six tournaments, losing five. Mickelson has had similar difficulties. A veteran of eight Ryder Cups, "Lefty" (a moniker borne out of his distinctive swing) has won the trophy just twice.

In 1997, the pair endured mixed fortunes as Mickelson and Davis Love lost to José María Olazábal and Costantino Rocca in the morning Fourballs, while Mark O'Meara and Woods lost to the indomitable duo of Bernhard Langer and Colin Montgomerie in the afternoon Foursomes. Woods lost again to Rocca in the singles, but Mickelson at least kept the USA in it after beating the dangerous Darren Clarke. Two years later, they enjoyed success when both scored victories in the singles to help the USA win 14.5 to 13.5, but the all-time low must be 2004, when the duo first played together for the USA and were billed a "dream team". It didn't prove that way for they barely talked as they lost in both the Friday Foursomes - Clarke and Westwood reigning supreme - as well as the Fourballs (where they went down, 2 and 1, to Montgomerie/Harrington). Stony faces all round - and they have never since been paired.

Mickelson can at least claim to have played a large part in the victory of 2008, when he became the highest-ranked player in the US side. Playing with Anthony Kim, the pair beat Harrington and McDowell in the Friday afternoon Fourballs, having claimed a half in the Foursomes against Harrington/Karlsson. But he was off-colour at Celtic Manor in 2010, losing the first three matches before sealing his first point in the singles against Peter Hanson. There were signs, though, that Tiger was coming to terms with the format, finishing top points-scorer for the USA and ending with a singles win over Francesco Molinari. Has Woods at last found a way to love the Ryder Cup? Maybe we'll find out in Illinois. One thing is for certain: the crowds will still be chanting his name.

> **"***It's just so neat to be a part of a team and quite frankly, we don't get to do it very often.***"**
>
> *Tiger Woods on the Ryder Cup*

RYDER CUP RECORD

Tiger WOODS
Ryder Cups: 1997, 1999 (winner), 2002, 2004, 2006, 2008 (winner), 2010, 2012
Total wins: 2
Matches: 33 (won 13, halved 3, lost 17)
Total points: 14.5

Phil MICKELSON
Ryder Cups: 1995, 1997, 1999 (winner), 2002, 2004, 2006, 2008 (winner), 2010, 2012, 2014
Total wins: 2
Matches: 41 (won 16, halved 6, lost 20)
Total points: 19

AS A PAIR:
Matches: 2 (won 0, halved 0, lost 2)
Points: 0

2008

USA 16.5
Europe 11.5

Valhalla Golf Club, Kentucky

September 19-21

Valhalla will be remembered – after three successive defeats – as the time when the USA fought back to reassert their authority by recording their biggest victory since 1981. Perhaps just as importantly, under the leadership of captain Paul Azinger and with the introduction of a collection of enthusiastic rookies, it was the moment when America finally rediscovered the joy of the Ryder Cup.

IF THE RYDER CUP WAS BEGINNING to fill some Americans with a sense of foreboding by 2008, then it was perhaps understandable. Three European victories in a row, the last two by record margins, had seen them lose the sense of excitement and child-like enthusiasm that seemed to grip their opponents every two years. But Paul Azinger changed all that in leading his team to a 16.5-11.5 victory during which, for the first time ever, the US led after every session. This was no fluke: it came down to a desire to completely alter the atmosphere surrounding the Team USA.

Azinger wanted his side to enjoy playing Ryder Cup golf and he was also keen for the crowd to get involved. Having campaigned for the right to be given four captain's picks instead of two, he made a point of choosing local boy J.B. Holmes, who joined another Kentucky golfer, Kenny Perry, in the team. Following this, he began his genius "13th man" campaign, even having T-shirts printed up with the slogan.

LEFT: *Rival captains Paul Azinger (left) of the USA and Nick Faldo of Europe pose with the Ryder Cup trophy in Kentucky in 2008.*

OPPOSITE: *Justin Leonard celebrates after chipping in to beat Sergio García and Miguel Angel Jiménez on the opening day.*

"The fans in Kentucky can be the 13th man," Azinger said. "They're rabid fans, they understand rivalries – they serve alcohol there so anything is possible. But my message really will be simply that I want the crowd to be completely into it." His campaign proved remarkable. The players threw 10,000 lapel pins into the galleries when the team arrived to play practice rounds on Tuesday; they also fired T-shirts out of a cannon in downtown Louisville and attended a Ryder Cup pep rally on the Thursday.

Azinger was unable to pick Tiger Woods, who was still recovering from knee surgery, but he was helped by the high-spirited Boo Weekley, who was adopted by Kentucky fans as one of their own – especially as, at the very first hole he galloped down the fairway using his driver as a toy horse, whipping his butt as he went! The gallery roared their approval and continued to do so from then on.

Kentucky boy Perry, who at 48 had dedicated his season to qualifying for a "home" Ryder Cup, also shone, but the selection of Holmes, ranked 56th in the world, proved an inspiration as he remained unbeaten – winning twice and halving his other match. Despite such focused preparation, it was Europe who started faster, taking the lead in all four matches in Friday's morning Foursomes. Azinger's side, along with the home crowd, however, were not ready to back down and by the end of the morning held a 3-1 lead.

Leonard and Mahan were unplayable in their 3 and 2 victory over Stenson/Casey, while Cink/Campbell clinched the narrowest of victories over Rose/Poulter before Perry/Furyk halved against Westwood/García. But the session was symbolized by the performance of Phil Mickelson and Anthony Kim, a veteran-and-rookie combination typifying the way Azinger wanted the game played. They were three-down against Harrington/Karlsson, but rescued a half at the last. Mickelson's verdict on his new partner was fascinating, saying: "His youthfulness, his excitement, exuberance is infectious and I was very fortunate to be able to spend the day with him. We had a lot of fun playing together."

Fun? Things were certainly looking up for the US side as the afternoon Fourballs proved. Europe might have been ahead in three out of four matches after the first nine, but were unable to hole-out and won just one. And so it was that the Americans took their largest lead on the first day since Europe joined the fray in 1979.

As well as Mickelson/Kim, who won an astonishing match, 2 and 1 against Harrington/McDowell, there were victories for Leonard/Mahan and a half for Holmes/Weekley to leave the score 5.5-2.5 in the home team's favour. This particular Ryder Cup was not going to be like the last three.

> ❝*My cheeks are sore from smiling all day.*❞
>
> Justin Leonard sums up the spirit in the US camp

DAY ONE

CAPTAINS

USA: Paul Azinger   **Europe:** Nick Faldo

FRIDAY MORNING FOURSOMES

Mickelson/Kim *halved* **Harrington/Karlsson**

Leonard/Mahan *beat* **Stenson/Casey**, *3 and 2*

Cink/Campbell *beat* **Rose/Poulter** *by one hole*

Perry/Furyk *halved* **Westwood/García**

Session Score: 3-1

FRIDAY AFTERNOON FOURBALLS

Mickelson/Kim *beat* **Harrington/McDowell** *by two holes*

Stricker/Curtis *lost to* **Poulter/Rose**, *4 and 2*

Leonard/Mahan *beat* **García/Jiménez**, *4 and 3*

Holmes/Weekley *halved* **Westwood/Hansen**

Session Score: 2.5-1.5

Overall Score: USA 5.5, Europe 2.5

ABOVE: *Nick Faldo (left) stands behind the USA's Stewart Cink and Chad Campbell (right) during Saturday's Foursomes.*

Europe knew they must do something special on the second day at Valhalla to force their way back into the match – but no one expected captain Nick Faldo to rest his biggest names, Lee Westwood and Sergio García, in order to achieve this. Both men were stood down for the morning Foursomes, raising eyebrows either side of the Atlantic. Westwood (unbeaten in 12 Ryder Cup matches) was said to be suffering from blisters and García (who had previously never lost a Foursomes match) was fatigued, but if Faldo was bracing himself for criticism, then he was saved by the performance of the players he did select. They were led by Ryder Cup debutant Oliver Wilson, who teamed up with Henrik Stenson for a remarkable victory over Mickelson/Kim.

After six holes, the European pairing were four-down but came back to win 2 and 1, going ahead for the first time at the 15th, when Mickelson drove into the trees and Kim fired his approach into the water. And Wilson sealed the point in some style, converting a 20-foot birdie putt at the 17th.

Faldo was further justified when his captain's pick, Ian Poulter – a choice that had caused great controversy back home – shone alongside Justin Rose in a 4 and 3 victory over Cink/Campbell. Meanwhile, Jiménez and Graeme McDowell managed to claim a half against Leonard/Mahan. Kenny Perry and Jim Furyk were the only US pair to win: 3 and 1 victors over the out-of-touch Harrington (subsequently rested for the afternoon Fourballs) and Karlsson. "It was a much better morning," said Faldo. "The United States had their day but we are here in good spirits. This is a physical and mental battle and I believe with what we have seen that you need to give guys a rest. We came off the road a bit and now we're back on it."

The afternoon session would prove even more dramatic and even tighter – in fact, three of the four Fourballs matches went to the 18th as both sides battled to claim two points each, eventually leaving the US just 9-7 ahead. Indeed, the Europeans were so impressive that the fact that Azinger's side were still able to

DAY TWO

SATURDAY MORNING FOURSOMES

Cink/Campbell *lost to* **Poulter/Rose,** *4 and 3*

Leonard/Mahan *halved with* **Jiménez/McDowell**

Mickelson/Kim *lost to* **Stenson/Wilson,** *2 and 1*

Furyk/Perry *beat* **Harrington/Karlsson,** *3 and 1*

Session Score: 1.5-2.5

SATURDAY AFTERNOON FOURBALLS

Weekley/Holmes *beat* **Westwood/Hansen,** *2 and 1*

Curtis/Stricker *halved with* **García/Casey**

Perry/Furyk *lost to* **Poulter/McDowell** *by one hole*

Mickelson/Mahan *halved with* **Stenson/Karlsson**

Session Score: 2-2

Overall Score: USA 9, Europe 7

ABOVE: *Europe's Ian Poulter looks ecstatic after holing a birdie putt on the 18th green during the afternoon Fourballs.*

take one-and-a-half points from the session was an achievement, eventually setting up the opportunity for overall victory. Just as in the morning, it was controversial wild card Poulter who led the charge. Paired with debutant Graeme McDowell, he posted a victory at the last over hometown heroes, Perry and Furyk. The European duo were never behind, although McDowell had to sink two pressure putts at 15 and 16 to preserve the lead and when Poulter drained a 14-footer for a birdie at the 17th before knocking in the decisive putt to win the match at the last, he was naturally elated. "Sinking that putt at the last was a special moment," he said. "What a day! G-Mac [Graeme McDowell] played awesome. To play as well as I have played, I'm speechless. I am so proud to be here as one of Nick's picks – I felt I had to do something this week."

He would end the weekend as the top points scorer on either side, which says a lot about his character and determination. However, Poulter's run would not end with a trophy; this was partly down to Boo Weekley and J.B. Holmes edging Westwood and Dane Hansen, 2 and 1 in the opening match of the afternoon. It was a result that kept the US ahead and ended Westwood's long unbeaten record in the Ryder Cup, stretching back 12 matches.

Sweden's Robert Karlsson paired with compatriot Henrik Stenson and hit four birdies in the closing seven holes to secure a half against Phil Mickelson and Hunter Mahan, but perhaps the key result in terms of overall score was Steve Stricker and Ben Curtis battling to halve against Casey/García. The match was so close – 16 out of the 18 holes were halved – and inevitably culminated in dramatic scenes at the last. Europe must have believed they were set for victory when the US found the rough with their approach but Stricker's up-and-down 18-foot birdie putt turned that assumption around – in fact, Casey had to hole a nervy 10-footer to secure a half. "They played really well and never gave us anything," said Casey afterwards. "We would have wanted a full point, but we did well to get a half from a fantastic match."

SHOT OF THE DAY

Boo Weekley conjured up an amazing shot from halfway down the 15th to leave his ball within 2 feet of the pin in an afternoon Fourballs battle against Westwood and Hansen. When later asked if this was his best-ever shot, Weekley replied: "I'd have to say number nine because I've had eight holes-in-one." Team Europe didn't seem quite so impressed, though. Westwood refused to concede the putt, to which Kentucky fans responded with a chorus of boos. That's Ryder Cup rivalry for you.

As if to underline patriotic fervour, the US team – who had worn white on the Friday and blue on the Saturday – announced they would be sporting red on Sunday. Captain Paul Azinger urged their supporters to strengthen the atmosphere as the US attempted to win back the Ryder Cup for the first time since 1999. They certainly responded, although not everyone was pleased by the response, with Lee Westwood saying: "Some people don't know the difference between supporting their team and abusing the opposition – I have been abused from start to finish." But in the end, the US victory was so convincing and so compelling any criticism became lost in the celebrations.

As holders, Europe needed seven points to retain the trophy and the US 5.5 to claim it back. In this, they were helped by a controversial decision from Faldo, who put his star men Harrington, Westwood and Poulter in the final three singles pairings, but found the result was over before they could make an impact. Setting the tone, Anthony Kim thrashed García, 5 and 4, in the first match, and the US won seven of the 12 singles matches on a remarkable day of American celebrations. Perry, Weekley, J.B. Holmes, Furyk, Curtis and Campbell were the other victors, while debutant Mahan halved with Casey. For Europe, the only bright spots were the wins for Karlsson, Rose, McDowell and Poulter.

It was Europe's worse defeat since Walton Heath in 1981, when they were beaten 18.5-9.5, and Faldo was bound to receive criticism although his players were quick to respond, with Westwood saying: "We hold the golf clubs, we hit the shots, not the captain." Rookie Kim, 23, summed up why the Americans had performed so well. Decked in a glitzy, gaudy belt, with USA in red, white and blue letters on the buckle, he displayed confidence bordering on cockiness as he beat García, 5 and 4.

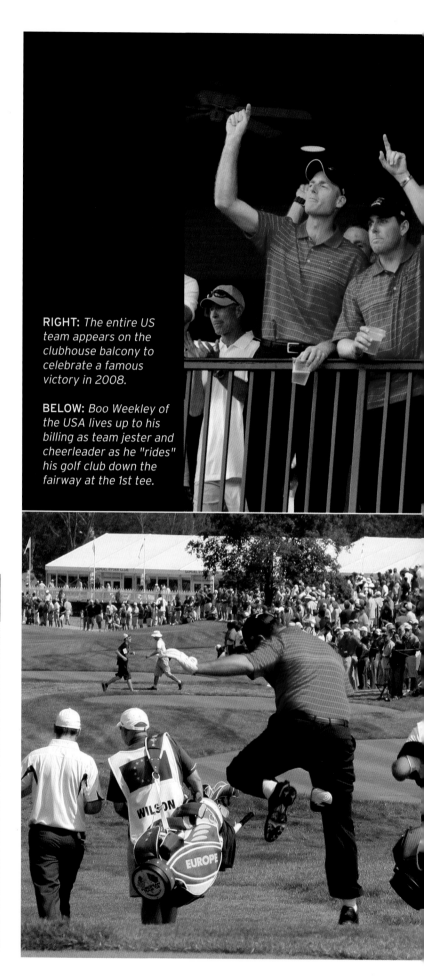

RIGHT: *The entire US team appears on the clubhouse balcony to celebrate a famous victory in 2008.*

BELOW: *Boo Weekley of the USA lives up to his billing as team jester and cheerleader as he "rides" his golf club down the fairway at the 1st tee.*

DAY THREE

FINAL DAY SINGLES

Anthony Kim *beat* **Sergio García,** *5 and 4*

Hunter Mahan *halved with* **Paul Casey**

Justin Leonard *lost to* **Robert Karlsson,** *5 and 3*

Phil Mickelson *lost to* **Justin Rose,** *3 and 2*

Kenny Perry *beat* **Henrik Stenson,** *3 and 2*

Boo Weekley *beat* **Oliver Wilson,** *4 and 2*

J.B. Holmes *beat* **Søren Hansen,** *2 and 1*

Jim Furyk *beat* **Miguel Angel Jiménez,** *2 and 1*

Stewart Cink *lost to* **Graeme McDowell,** *2 and 1*

Steve Stricker *lost to* **Ian Poulter,** *3 and 2*

Ben Curtis *beat* **Lee Westwood,** *2 and 1*

Chad Campbell *beat* **Padraig Harrington,** *2 and 1*

Session Score: 7.5-4.5

Overall Score: USA 16.5, Europe 11.5

Ryder Cup legends
Rory **McILROY**
and Graeme **McDOWELL**

The Northern Irish pairing of Graeme McDowell and Rory McIlroy – 'G-Mac' and 'Little-Mac' as they were originally known – are Ryder Cup heroes in European eyes. They were paired for six matches in their first two Ryder Cups together, winning in 2010 and 2012. They were given different roles for the 2014 victory in Gleneagles, but still had a major say in the destiny of the Samuel Ryder trophy.

Whenever Europe needs a hero, it seems an Irishman steps up. Darren Clarke's emotional and inspirational performance of 2006 springs to mind, as does the match-winning performances of Eamonn Darcy at Muirfield Village (1987), Christy O'Connor Jnr. at The Belfry (1989), Philip Walton at Oak Hill (1995) and Paul McGinley at The Belfry (2002). Now there are two more heroes on board in the shape of the young prodigy McIlroy and McDowell, senior of the two by 10 years.

McDowell already had a reputation for being a man with nerves of steel before he linked up with his fellow countryman at Celtic Manor. He had made one previous Ryder Cup appearance (2008), winning 2.5 points, and going into the 2010 tournament, he was the reigning US Open champion. Significantly, he had also won the Welsh Open at Celtic Manor in June, shortly before his US Open win at Pebble Beach, where he became the first Northern Irishman to win the title and the first European to win since Tony Jacklin in 1970. He was also the first UK winner of a Major in 11 years, holding his nerve in difficult conditions to secure the title. Following this, he immediately promised McIlroy that they would make a great Ryder Cup pairing – and he was proved right.

McDowell and McIlroy were chosen by captain Colin Montgomerie as the second of his four Fourball pairings on the opening Friday of the 2010 Ryder Cup when they were up against Stewart Cink and Matt Kuchar. In sodden conditions, play had to be suspended after just four holes and the day ended with the Americans two-up after 11. When the match resumed early the next morning, the Europeans stormed back to salvage a crucial half. Though the friends lost to the same pair in the Foursomes, they returned to beat Zach Johnson and Hunter Mahan later that day, winning the first hole and never looking back as they won, 3 and 1.

The effervescent McIlroy was now revelling in the atmosphere, geeing up the crowd at every opportunity and playing the showman. Indeed, the only shame with Europe three points ahead going into the singles was that he and his friend now had to be split up! McIlroy faced Stewart Cink in the second singles game, while McDowell was given responsibility for closing out the match. This proved a wise decision: already McDowell had shown the composure needed to handle the pressure of winning just a few months earlier, overtaking final-day leader Dustin Johnson to seize the US Open.

Perhaps he was always destined for Ryder Cup action. Having won Ulster schoolboy titles, McDowell went on to a golf scholarship at the University of Alabama, Birmingham, USA. As a teenager, he won numerous college events. He also represented Great Britain and Ireland in the successful 2001 Walker Cup side and when he turned professional in 2002, he divided his time between the US and European tours. With this experience under his belt, he already knew how to beat the Americans and was in control from the start against Mahan.

McIlroy had to settle for a half with Cink but it was still a satisfactory debut for the youngster from Holywood (Ireland, rather than California), who had been tipped for stardom since his father Gerry introduced him to the rudiments of golf as a toddler. In many ways, McIlroy resembled a British Tiger Woods. Schooled from a young age by his father, with his prodigious talent he was soon winning tournaments. He represented Europe in the Junior Ryder Cup and also played against America in the amateur Walker Cup, so he understood what team play was all about. He had also made his mark on the European Tour – starting at 16, turning pro at 17 and winning his first event at 19. By the time he was 20, he was in the world's Top 10 (reaching No. 1 in March 2012 as the reigning US Open champion) and so it came as no surprise that he ended his first Ryder Cup with a commendable two out of four points.

It was McDowell who was to steal the limelight, though, winning the point that secured the Ryder Cup, thanks to a stunning birdie putt at the 16th and Mahan's ultimate concession on the 17th green, leaving Europe to claim a glorious victory. It seems highly likely this will not be the last time that McDowell and McIlroy celebrate together for the Irish legacy appears to be in good hands.

> **"*I'm going to miss him tomorrow.*"**
>
> *Graeme McDowell muses on playing the 2010 singles without his partner Rory McIlroy*

2012

USA 13.5
Europe 14.5

Medinah Country Club, Illinois

September 28-30

THE COURSE

Medinah Country Club, Course No. 3
Location: Medinah, Illinois, USA
Par: 72
Yards: 7,657

This historic club was established in 1924, but Course 3 is the most highly regarded of the three Tom Bendelow courses at Medinah. One of the longest on the US tour, it had hosted five major championships before welcoming the Ryder Cup in 2012.

American captain Davis Love III was right to feel confident on home turf. He had adapted the master plan from the time the Europeans last visited America in 2008 and had everything set up to help his players avenge their agonizing one-point defeat at Celtic Manor two years before. Team USA started so well too, only to succumb ultimately to the "Miracle of Medinah".

DAVIS LOVE HAD A 5-3 LEAD to take into the second morning of the Ryder Cup after dominating the afternoon Fourballs at the Medinah Country Club. It had been a thrilling first day of the 39th Ryder Cup and it all pointed towards an overall home victory. Everyone agreed it was only going to end one way. Everyone, that is, bar a few stubborn European golfers, who happened to believe in sporting miracles. The most stubborn of all was possibly Europe's Spanish captain José-María Olazábal, who invoked the spirit of his late friend and Ryder Cup partner Seve Ballesteros, a renowned miracle-worker on a golf course. But would the spirit of Seve be enough against an in-form American side, packed with Major winners?

Either way, Day One (and Day Two, for that matter), would belong to the home team. After a stalemate two points each from the morning Foursomes, the Americans showed their class and ability from all areas of the course to take three of the four points on offer after lunch.

The American captain had called on the Chicago crowd to get behind his team just as they had when Paul Azinger led them to victory on home soil at Valhalla four years before. And Love's team certainly gave them something to shout about. He was also keen to give his rookies as much support as possible; Love had three new faces to Ryder Cup action on his crew, compared to Europe's one.

It was clear to see after the first day's play why some saw Ryder Cup inexperience as a possible advantage. Former winning

> *"There are no tools you can use out there. You've just got to go with what you have in your pants."*
>
> *European rookie Nicolas Colsaerts, on his debut*

LEFT: *US team captain Davis Love III (left) plots Europe's opening day demise with his brother Mark during the afternoon Fourballs matches.*

ABOVE: *Rory McIlroy splashes out of the sand on the 10th to help Europe win their first point of the morning Foursomes and the 2012 Ryder Cup.*

European captain and player Bernard Gallacher explained: "The US might have most rookies, but there are rookies of different sorts. One is a US PGA champion and another is a US Open champion. While they are new to the Ryder Cup, they are hardly inexperienced or unproven." Dave Stockton, the US captain and survivor of Kiawah Island's 1991 "War on the Shore", pointed out: "A lot of the veterans have scar tissue, particularly in the American team. The rookies don't have the negative feelings."

Yet all four American teams had briefly been behind before the sun had even fully risen over Medinah's Course 3. The formidable European pair of Sergio García and Luke Donald, for example, had won all four of their previous Ryder Cup matches in this alternate shot format and were one up against rookie Keegan Bradley, the 2011 PGA Championship winner, and multiple Major-winning veteran Phil Mickelson after winning the fifth and sixth holes.

But it was Bradley, not his more illustrious partner, who led the fight back with a smart eight-foot birdie putt on the ninth. The Europeans then faltered on the back nine before the Americans both holed birdie putts on the 13th and 15th to secure four successive holes and take the first point of the event and secure an impressive 4 and 3 win.

The new American duo would team up to win again later in the day and it was almost too much for Mickelson to take, despite this being his ninth consecutive Ryder Cup appearance. "Lefty" said: "It's awesome. It feels spectacular. This is one of the most emotional days of playing in the Ryder Cup we will ever have. I love playing with Keegan, it's kept me up. He's been awesome."

DAY ONE

CAPTAINS

USA: Davis Love III   **Europe:** José María Olazábal

FRIDAY MORNING FOURSOMES

Furyk/Snedeker *lost to* **McIlroy/McDowell** *1 up*

Mickelson/Bradley *beat* **Donald/García**, *4 and 3*

Dufner/Z Johnson *beat* **Westwood/Molinari**, *3 and 2*

Woods/Stricker *lost to* **Poulter/Rose**, *2 and 1*

Session Score: 2-2

FRIDAY AFTERNOON FOURBALLS

Watson/Simpson *beat* **Lawrie/Hanson**, *5 and 4*

Mickelson/Bradley *beat* **McIlroy/McDowell**, *2 and 1*

Woods/Stricker *lost to* **Westwood/Colsaerts** *1 up*

D Johnson/Kuchar *beat* **Rose/Kaymer**, *3 and 2*

Session Score: 3-1

Overall Score: USA 5, Europe 3

The Europeans then wobbled with their Irish heavyweight pair of Rory McIlroy and Graeme McDowell, who were also one up after six holes and even three up after 11 before Jim Furyk and another rookie, Brandt Snedeker, came back hard with a succession of birdies from hole 13. But they struggled to maintain their form and a crucial loose drive from the in-form Snedeker on the 18th and final hole gave the Europeans a chance to win the match as McDowell sealed Europe's first notch on the scoreboard with an ice-cool nine-footer.

Elsewhere, it was nip and tuck all over the course. Tiger Woods, for example, appeared a touch out of sorts alongside Steve Stricker as they trailed Justin Rose and his fellow English countryman Ian Poulter by two after six. Poulter would emerge as Europe's key player at Medinah and he showed a flash of what was to come when he holed from a greenside bunker on the 11th before sinking a putt on the 12th to put the Europeans three up. Woods and Stricker fought back over the next two holes but they were forced to concede on the 17th after Rose hit an approach to within six inches and secure a 2 and 1 win.

Perhaps Woods and Stricker were guilty of trying too hard. Either way, this was not their finest hour; Woods' play included a fluffed chip, and a series of drives that tested Love's generous course set-up. He hit a portable toilet with one wayward effort, while another knocked a spectator to the ground and drew blood. More impressive was the American duo of Jason Dufner, yet another rookie in opening morning action, and Zack Johnson who

dispatched Lee Westwood and Francesco Molinari in a relatively comfortable 3 and 2 win.

So, all square after four matches and plenty for the two captains to ponder before sending out their players for the afternoon Fourballs. The big surprise came from Olazábal, who decided to stick with the struggling Westwood and omit both Donald and Poulter from his pairings. Only time would tell how crucial a decision that would be in the destiny of the Samuel Ryder trophy.

Poulter himself insisted that he had no problem with sitting out the afternoon. "I would have loved to have played five matches, but we are a team, and that team is very, very strong this year," he said. "Ollie really wanted to get everyone playing on Friday, so four guys have to change from the morning round, and that's going to be difficult. He said he would like to keep me fresh."

Westwood remains one of Europe's greatest ever Ryder Cup players, but this was not his day and Olazábal's decision initially looked a poor call as the momentum turned decisively towards America in the afternoon. The USA won three of the four points on offer and very nearly took half a point in the only match they did not win. Mickelson and Bradley led the way defeating McIlroy and McDowell, and Bubba Watson and Webb Simpson were inspired golfers in their 5 and 4 win over Peter Hanson and Paul Lawrie. Martin Kaymer came in for Poulter to partner Rose and there was little they could do to resist Dustin Johnson and Matt Kuchar, who won 3 and 2.

ABOVE: *Phil Mickelson and Keegan Bradley betray joy and relief after a second opening day win – a 2 and 1 Fourballs triumph over McIlroy/McDowell at the 17th.*

It was not so much the Europeans were capitulating, it was largely the Americans were playing the game as they liked it, with the crowd, weather and the course all seemingly in their favour. "Just everybody played real well and hung in there and had a lot of fun. Seemed like as the sun came out, we just got better and better," Love explained that evening.

Spaniard Olazábal did his best to put a brave face on the state of play and said: "We're only two points behind with eight to play for on Saturday so we're still in a decent position. We're pretty strong on Foursomes so if we get a good start in the morning and even things up that would be great. "The atmosphere is incredible. You can feed off the energy but when people are cheering for the other guys you've just got to stay focused. It's definitely nothing like Celtic Manor was a couple of years ago."

In reality, the only glimmer of hope for Olazábal came in his brave selection of rookie Nicolas Colsaerts that afternoon. The Belgian was outside the world's top 1,000 three years before Medinah so his mere participation in the Ryder Cup seemed almost absurd, but he answered his critics by letting his clubs do the talking, partnering a faltering Westwood to a one-up win over Woods and Stricker. The point would prove to be absolutely crucial.

Colsaerts virtually won on his own, scoring eight birdies and an eagle to post a remarkable 10-under for the day on his debut. Westwood said: "You can see he handles pressure well. He hit it fantastic that day and putted great. I didn't play my best but Nicolas was brilliant to watch. I tried to support him whenever I could but it was one of those amazing days."

The defeated Stricker agreed and added: "He hit it longer than any guy I've ever seen. He made every putt that he looked at. He's got a lot of offence. I was pretty impressed with what he has." Woods, who lost his first two matches for the fourth time in his Ryder Cup career, said: "Nicolas probably had one of the greatest putting rounds I've ever seen." A relieved Olazábal commented: "He was amazing. I've heard that's a record score for a rookie in the history of the Ryder Cup so it shows how special his round was. The afternoon was tough. That last point from Nicolas Colsaerts and Lee Westwood was very important." Colsaert's take on his day? "That was a lot of fun. I have never had that much fun and I want to have more fun. You've got to go with what's in your pants," he explained.

It was that round and a statistical omen that was all the Europeans had to cling to as the sun set on Friday's action: America had led 5-3 after the first day, at the same stage in the 1985, 1995 and 2010 Ryder Cups, ultimately losing all three.

ABOVE: *His US team was winning but Tiger Woods still struggled to find his touch on the Medinah greens.*

"*I'm going to make it clear to the boys that they need to step it up. There are no secrets to this game. You have to make more birdies than your opponent. And if you don't do that, you are going to struggle.*"

Olazábal rues a first day dominated by the USA

DAY TWO

SATURDAY MORNING FOURSOMES

Simpson/Watson *lost to* **Poulter/Rose** *1 up*

Bradley/Mickelson *beat* **Westwood/Donald,** *7 and 6*

Dufner/Z Johnson *beat* **Colsaerts/García,** *2 and 1*

Furyk/Snedeker *beat* **McIlroy/McDowell** *1 up*

Session Score: 3-1

SATURDAY AFTERNOON FOURBALLS

Simpson/Watson *beat* **Rose/Molinari,** *5 and 4*

D Johnson/Kuchar *beat* **Colsaerts/Lawrie** *1 up*

Woods/Stricker *lost to* **García/Donald** *1 up*

Dufner/Z Johnson *lost to* **McIlroy/Poulter** *1 up*

Session Score: 2-2

Overall Score: USA 10, Europe 6

If the USA just about dominated the first day of the 39th Ryder Cup, they virtually annihilated Europe when play resumed on Saturday, leaving many experts declaring the competition over as a contest as they opened up a 10-6 lead. A boxing trainer might have thrown in the towel.

Davis Love's players were in devastating form in the morning, winning three of the Foursomes ties, and they were inspired once again by the impressive new pairing of Keegan Bradley and Phil Mickelson. The Americans looked like sweeping through the afternoon matches too, until Europe finally found a reason to turn up on Sunday by winning dramatic late points through Luke Donald and Sergio García, Rory McIlroy and the insatiable Ian Poulter.

Coming into the second day, the Europeans needed to dominate both sessions to claim a stake in the tournament. They were given some encouragement when Tiger Woods and partner Steve Stricker were rested for the morning Foursomes matches, but that was about the only good news of the day.

Despite this, early on, it looked like the Europeans would have a chance to succeed as Ian Poulter and Justin Rose's 1-up defeat of Americans Bubba Watson and Webb Simpson gave them an opening win and the opportunity to make an impact on the second day. Playing in a fiercely contested match, Poulter and Rose won by virtue of some outstanding putting under pressure, something their American opposition just could not match, for once. Simpson, in particular, struggled with his putter, missing a critical attempt at the 18th hole to give Europe a victory. Poulter was now emerging as the man of the moment as this victory took him to a career Ryder Cup record of 11-3 and he showed the emotion of what it meant to him after virtually every decent strike of the ball.

The Englishman would later in the day partner Northern Irishman McIlroy to a stunning comeback victory in the Fourballs,

recovering from two holes down with six to play to win a point. He then summed up what it was like to be out on the course that sunny Saturday and said: "That was unbelievable... we had to get something going. From then on (with six holes to play) my putter warmed up nicely, having been pretty cold for the first 13 holes. Then it just went crazy. It was tough out there. We're in Chicago, they've had a few drinks today and they weren't making it easy for us. I will be honest - it was brutal."

And brutal was a good word to describe the way Europe were deconstructed in the other morning matches by Love's confident teams. As stated, Mickelson and Bradley were the US figureheads as they equalled the biggest Foursomes win in Ryder Cup history as America played their way into an 8-4 lead.

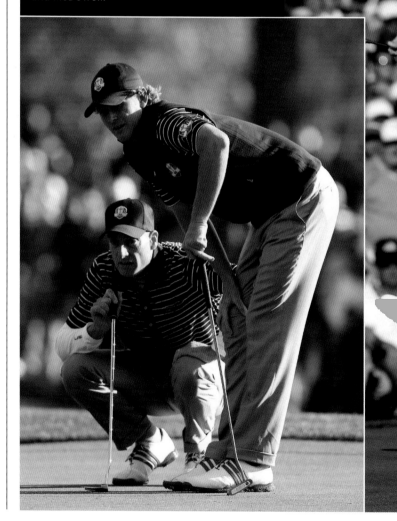

RIGHT: *Webb Simpson (right) and Bubba Watson dance their way to victory after Simpson's birdie on the 13th in the Day Two afternoon Fourballs.*

BELOW: *Jim Furyk and Brandt Snedeker line up a putt on their way to a Day Two Foursomes win over Europe's McIlroy and McDowell.*

The American pairing had won both their Foursomes and Fourballs matches on Friday and were even more impressive in action against Luke Donald and Lee Westwood, smiling and fist-pumping their way to a 7 and 6 victory. The European duo was supposed to be one of Olazábal's top pairs, having beaten Woods and Stricker 6 and 5 the last time they played in a Foursomes match. But this time out their humbling was reminiscent of previous Ryder Cup anguishes suffered by the likes of Nick Faldo and David Gilford in 1991 and Ken Brown and Des Smyth in 1979.

But as poorly as the Europeans played, the Americans were equally impressive as Mickelson and Bradley cemented their reputation with golf that left them on six-under for the 12 holes they needed for victory. The Europeans' three-putting on the

> *"It was tough out there. We're in Chicago, they've had a few drinks today and they weren't making it easy for us. I will be honest – it was brutal."*
>
> *Ian Poulter*

Matt Kuchar also seemed to have events at Brookline on his mind from 13 years ago. He cautioned: "There's a lot of memories from '99, and I think we have to know that that [10-6] deficit is overcomable. We have to go out and still play some really good golf and make sure that we don't let a comeback like that happen to us."

But there had been little evidence on the first two days' play that Europe would suddenly find their touch on the Medinah greens that would give them the slimmest hope and belief that a comeback just might be possible. After an exemplary display of Ryder Cup golf on Day Two, America needed only 4.5 points from the 12 on offer to reclaim the trophy. Europe's task was obvious too: they needed 7.5 points to retain the Cup with a draw, and eight to win it outright.

> **"***We're excited about our position but we know, as Ollie said, it's not over yet.***"**
>
> *American captain, Davis Love*

ABOVE: *Inspirational Ian Poulter celebrates with his caddie Terry Mundy after making birdie on the 16th during Day Two of the afternoon Fourballs.*

DAY THREE

FINAL DAY SINGLES

Bubba Watson *lost to* **Luke Donald,** *2 and 1*

Webb Simpson *lost to* **Ian Poulter,** *2 up*

Keegan Bradley *lost to* **Rory McIlroy,** *2 and 1*

Phil Mickelson *lost to* **Justin Rose,** *1 up*

Brandt Snedeker *lost to* **Paul Lawrie,** *5 and 3*

Dustin Johnson *beat* **Nicolas Colsaerts,** *3 and 2*

Zach Johnson *beat* **Graeme McDowell,** *2 and 1*

Jim Furyk *lost to* **Sergio García,** *1 up*

Jason Dufner *beat* **Peter Hanson,** *2 up*

Matt Kuchar *lost to* **Lee Westwood,** *3 and 2*

Steve Stricker *lost to* **Martin Kaymer,** *1 up*

Tiger Woods *halved with* **Francesco Molinari**

Session Score: 3.5-8.5

Overall Score: USA 13.5, Europe 14.5

So, all Europe needed was a miracle. A sporting one, of course, but a miracle all the same. In the final day of the Ryder Cup at Medinah Country Club, Luke Donald was sent out to play Bubba Watson in the opening Singles match as Europe set about their long-haul fight back and America reached the short distance for shore.

In fact, Olazábal put four of his most experienced players at the top of the order with Ian Poulter second out against Webb Simpson. Rory McIlroy faced Keegan Bradley, and Justin Rose lined up against the other in-form American, Phil Mickelson. World number two Tiger Woods was the last man out for the USA, bidding to emulate his 4 and 3 win over Italian Francesco Molinari two years before at Celtic Manor.

Paul Lawrie, who was fifth out against Brandt Snedeker, played in the same team as Olazábal when the USA produced the biggest comeback in Ryder Cup history, overturning a 10-6 deficit to win at Brookline in 1999. Significantly, the Scot was one of only three Europeans to win on that final day when America won 8.5 points. So perhaps he did not sound too foolhardy when he proclaimed on Sunday at Medinah: "There's still 12 Singles matches. We can all win and why not? It's certainly not over. It would be nice to make a big comeback, so we'll see what happens. It's always possible. Until it's impossible to do it, then you fight on, certainly for José María this week. No one is going to be giving up."

ABOVE: *All eyes on Europe's Luke Donald as he hits his tee shot on the first hole during the Singles of the 39th Ryder Cup.*

Olazábal and his fellow European compatriots also had the inspiration of playing in the blue and white colours favoured by the late Seve Ballesteros, who died in May 2011 after a long battle with a brain tumour. No one was closer in golf to Seve than fellow Spaniard Olazábal, who was his partner for much of his Ryder Cup career, and the players had the image of Ballesteros on their bags as well as his silhouette on their shirts. Poulter commented: "We have Seve's blue and white, Seve on the bag and his right-hand man as our captain hopefully seeing us home."

But Europe would need more than lucky omens to turn the tide against an American team now moving with the momentum of a runaway train. To reclaim the trophy they lost at Celtic Manor in 2010, Love's men would need just 4.5 points from the 12 on offer. Europe had only once before recovered from a losing position going into Sunday's Singles matches to win this event. And that 1995 turnaround at Oak Hill came when they had trailed by only two points.

So, they set about taming America's finest golfers and a vociferous home crowd with some sense of belief, but surely hope more than faith. But for the first time in this Ryder Cup battle, the Europeans started the day well and, for the first time, the American players showed they had frailties too. Donald started turning the scoreboard blue by going into an early two-hole lead over Bubba Watson – if nothing else, it kept the crowd a bit quieter. Rose was then two up on Mickelson, McIlroy was

SHOT OF THE DAY

Rose's twisting downhill 30-foot putt on the 17th for birdie was the difference between winning and losing.

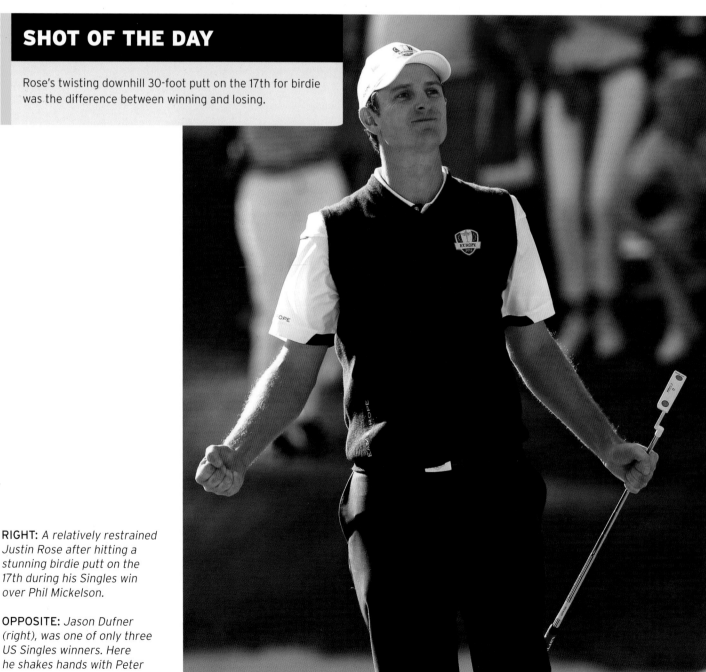

RIGHT: *A relatively restrained Justin Rose after hitting a stunning birdie putt on the 17th during his Singles win over Phil Mickelson.*

OPPOSITE: *Jason Dufner (right), was one of only three US Singles winners. Here he shakes hands with Peter Hanson on the 18th green.*

coping well with the irrepressible Bradley, and the unassuming, unlikely hero Lawrie took an early lead against Snedeker. Donald's role was key in that his task was to win the first point of the day and send out a message of confidence to his fellow Europeans. And the Englishman faced up to his task by winning on the 17th despite a gallant comeback attempt by Watson.

McIlroy's win was far less straightforward as he almost missed his match entirely. He was still in the team hotel just 25 minutes before he was due to tee off, due to a misunderstanding over the start time, and needed a police escort to scramble to the first hole – just on time. What followed was an epic battle of wits and talent with Bradley, but McIlroy persevered and took the lead on the 14th before going two up on the 15th, finally finishing his opponent off with a long putt on the 17th. Would the result have been the same had McIlroy not made it to the first tee on time, thereby conceding the first hole? Had a police outrider unwittingly emerged as Europe's saviour?

Poulter, almost inevitably, secured his fourth win from his fourth match in a cracking match against Webb Simpson. The Englishman trailed by two holes early on in the clash and only went in front for the first time on the par-three 17th when Simpson finally wilted by hitting a tee-shot into a left-hand bunker. Simpson faltered again at the final hole, while Poulter rose to the occasion and fired an iron from the oak trees to 13 feet. The American had a final shot at a putt but did not really threaten, and the first three points of the day had gone against the home side.

Snedeker had won a mouthwatering £6m at the Fed-Ex Cup before the Ryder Cup. But money cannot buy Ryder Cup points and he was duly dismissed 5 and 3 by Lawrie.

Rose's triumph over the previously unbeaten Mickelson was perhaps even more impressive. Their match will go down as a true Ryder Cup classic. Rose also had to battle the less savoury elements of the Medinah crowd. He was repeatedly heckled by spectators, trying to put him off his game, and Mickelson assisted in calling security to have some of the worst offenders removed from the arena. Rose showed great composure to keep his cool, while Mickelson displayed the sportsmanship both he and the Ryder Cup are famed for. Rose said: "As long as the Ryder Cup stays wholesome inside the ropes, golf is in a great place."

But he might not have been feeling so sanguine had he not stared down a 10-footer at 16 to save himself from going two down with two to play. He sunk the putt, of course, but saved something really special at the 17th when he putted out from 30 feet after Mickelson had chipped to gimme range. It was widely agreed to be the shot of the day, on a day when there were a few candidates for the honour. Mickelson remained favourite going to the 18th, but that monster putt from Rose had clearly knocked his concentration and he hit his approach through the green. Rose, who had been heckled again on the fairway, hit his ball to 15 feet before curling in yet another stunning putt for birdie and the match.

There was no stopping Europe now and the Medinah course crowd had a very different tone from the domineering chants of the first two days. Jim Furyk imploded against Sergio García, missing two six-foot putts to the right. Zach Johnson restored a modicum of pride and kept US hopes alive by beating Graeme McDowell, but Lee Westwood regained some of his trademark Ryder Cup confidence to beat Matt Kuchar 3 and 2. Westwood's point put Europe 13-12 up, and after Jason Dufner held his nerve to see off Peter Hanson two up on the 18th, the score was level again at 13-13, with just two matches, both all-square, left on the course.

Something was going to have to give because none of the remaining four players – Kaymer, Stricker, Molinari and Woods –

"An unbelievable week. Seve has been trying hard for us."

Ian Poulter

THE 39TH RYDER CUP

ABOVE: *Europe's Martin Kaymer celebrates his putt that won the 39th Ryder Cup as caddie Craig Connelly watches on.*

ABOVE: *Nicolas Colsaerts (left) and Graeme McDowell rush to congratulate Martin Kaymer as Europe retain the Ryder Cup.*

had won a single point between them all week. First to crack was Stricker, handing Kaymer a one-hole lead when he three-putted at the 17th. The German then benefited from a stunning approach shot from a bunker on the 18th green. Kaymer had been playing way below his best all summer, which is why Olazábal left him out of three of the first four sessions, and now the Ryder Cup was all on his shoulders, just as it had been for his fellow German Bernard Langer 21 years before. Langer, of course, missed his six-footer at Kiawah, but Kaymer was able to make up for that in style with a five-foot putt to get his team to the 14 points they needed to retain the trophy. He later revealed: "José María told me: 'We need your point. I don't care how you do it, just deliver.' But I like those [putts], it was straightforward. That is the way we Germans are. Fortunately, I could handle it and I made the last putt."

Then all eyes, cameras and attention turned to Woods and his Italian opponent Molinari. The European's half a point, gained at the death by Woods missing two putts from inside eight feet, gifted Olazábal's side overall victory. Molinari said afterwards: "When I knew I was coming out last, I was really happy because I knew the guys would do a great job and it would come down to the last matches. Martin [Kaymer] did a great job and I just fought as hard as I could to get that last point."

So, from almost nowhere, the Europeans produced a stunning final-day performance, dropping only three matches all day, ultimately winning 14.5 to 13.5.

Olazabal shifted between tears of joy, sadness and relief as he celebrated victory in memory of his late friend Ballesteros. He memorably said: "To the 12 men of Europe, what you did out there was outstanding. All men die but not all men live and you

made me feel alive again this week. I don't know how heaven feels, but it must be close to this. Seve will always be present with this team. He was a big factor for this event, for the European side." American captain Love remained composed enough to accept defeat with grace, but admitted: "We know what it feels like now. It's a little bit shocking. We were playing so well."

BBC commentator Peter Alliss thought he had seen it all before, but he said: "It was a magnificent performance from the whole European team and I have never seen a more exciting end to a Ryder Cup – and I've seen plenty." Ultimately, it came down to a battle of nerves with five of those Sunday Singles matches reaching the 18th green. America won just one of those five ties.

After being written off going into the final day, it was understandable how heartily the Europeans celebrated with their Ryder Cup trophy. Many of them, Olazábal included, re-enacted the Spaniard's famous cheesy celebration dance of 1987.

They laughed, they cried, while the feeling in the American camp was one of disbelief. But if ever three days of play summed up the enduring magic, mystery and raw unpredictable entertainment of the Ryder Cup, it was the golf played by the 24 men of the USA and Europe in September 2012.

RIGHT: *European team captain José Marìa Olazábal enjoys his press conference, explaining how he miraculously managed to retain the Ryder Cup.*

LEFT: *Poulter's emotional celebration on the 11th hole during the 2012 Ryder Cup shows what the competition means to him.*

Ryder Cup legends
Ian **POULTER**

The eyes have it. Just a look at the intense stare of Ian Poulter in Ryder Cup action tells the tale of how much the competition means to him. So pivotal was his involvement in Europe's emergence as the dominant Ryder Cup force, team-mate Lee Westwood claimed there should be a permanent Poulter wildcard. No wonder the Americans love to hate him and he has already been tipped as a future captain.

Ironically, Poulter loves all things American and lives with his wife and four children in Florida. It's just that he loves beating them at golf even more.

The Englishman has occasionally threatened in the Majors – he finished third at the PGA and is an Open runner-up – but the big one will always be the Samuel Ryder trophy.

His love affair with the competition began when he watched Nick Faldo's hole-in-one against arch-rival Paul Azinger at The Belfry in 1993. "That Ryder Cup changed my opinion on golf," Poulter recalled. "It gave me the drive to be the best player I could. That's where I set myself the goals. To come from being outside those ropes to playing Ryder Cup golf is more than a dream come true. But for that year at The Belfry, I might not have chased down any of my golf dreams."

Little did the teenaged Poulter know he would be one of the few European players to emerge with credit when he played under Faldo against Azinger's winning American team at Valhalla 15 years later.

His 80 per cent winning percentage in Ryder Cup play ranks as the best from players with more than 15 matches played, and his performances in four Ryder Cups are the stuff of legend.

It started when he made his debut in the 35th staging of the event in 2004 at the South Course of Oakland Hills Country Club in Bloomfield Township, Michigan. The European team won 18.5 to 9.5 – their largest margin in the history of the event.

Poulter's own debut was a defeat, partnering Darren Clarke to a 4 and 3 loss to Americans Tiger Woods and Chris Riley. The European team were already 6.5 to 1.5 ahead going into the Saturday morning session – the pressure was off. But ever the steely competitor, Poulter made his mark 24 hours later when he faced Riley again in the Singles and triumphed 3 and 2. A star was born.

Poulter really started to take hold in the public's consciousness at Celtic Manor in 2010. The strength of the Americans and the unprecedented rainfall dampened European spirits on and off the course, forcing play into a fourth day. After suffering an opening defeat in the Fourball he recovered to win two Foursomes and an emphatic 5 and 4 Singles win over Matt Kuchar, to help Europe defy an excellent US performance to win by one point: 14.5 to 13.5.

Tiger Woods is the only man who has had the measure of Poulter in Ryder Cup play. Of the three games he has lost in 15 matches, Woods has been responsible for two. But even Tiger could not tame him when Europe fought to retain the trophy in 2012, at Medinah Country Club. Poulter won four-from-four, including a Foursomes triumph over Woods and a miraculous comeback win alongside Rory McIlroy, inspired by his five-hole birdie spree against Jason Dufner and Zach Johnson, which just about kept Europe in the match.

Still, many believed Europe had no chance in 2012, trailing by four points going into the final day Singles at Medinah. Poulter had other ideas. Reflecting after the miraculous comeback win, he said: "There was a buzz in the team room that didn't feel like we had a four-point deficit. We felt we had that tiny little chance and the boys proved it and made history.

"These [Ryder Cup matches] might be my Majors. If this is it, I'm a happy man. I've got more pride and passion to give in the Ryder Cup than a Major. I want to win one, don't get me wrong. I've been close and, who knows, this might be the changing factor to get me over that line, but if I don't win another tournament, this will go down as the highlight of my golfing career."

The Arsenal-supporting petrol-head, with a fleet of rare cars, credits his success to his matchplay prowess – he has won both versions of the world matchplay tournaments – and his nerves of steel when he has a putter in his hand.

Team-mate Luke Donald commented: "He's the heartbeat. He gets so up for it that you feed off his energy. He doesn't want to lose and he's going to do whatever he can to motivate the team."

The final tribute to this Ryder Cup legend comes from one of its finest-ever representatives as a player and captain, José María Olazábal, who declared: "I think the Ryder Cup should build a statue for him."

> *"This is my Major. Nothing comes close to getting me up for it like the Ryder Cup – not even remotely."*

Ian Poulter

2014

Europe 16.5
USA 11.5

Gleneagles Hotel, Gleneagles

September 26-28

THE COURSE

PGA Centenary Course,
Gleneagles Hotel
Location: Perthshire, Scotland
Par: 72
Yards: 7,262

Gleneagles, covering 850 acres near Edinburgh, was the scene for the first international match between America and Great Britain in 1920, but there was no hotel then. The Centenary Course, one of three at Gleneagles, was designed by American Ryder Cup legend Jack Nicklaus

Europe hosted the 40th edition of the Ryder Cup and were favourites to defend the trophy they won in Medinah. America reappointed captain Tom Watson, undefeated as player and leader, to face Irishman Paul McGinley, also always a winner in the five Cups he had been involved in. Something had to give.

THE TASK FOR TEAM EUROPE CAPTAIN Paul McGinley, a three-time winner as a Ryder Cup player and twice as vice-captain, was to ward his men away from complacency and prepare them to defeat an American side high on talent, desperate for "redemption".

Returning American captain Tom Watson, back in the Ryder Cup after a 21-year absence at the age of 65, was the man who relentlessly referred to redemption. The sporting great, who won four of his five Open championships on Scottish soil, was desperate to regain the Samuel Ryder trophy in the country he regards the home of golf and erase the nightmare of what Europeans fans called the "Miracle of Medinah" but Americans dubbed "The Meltdown."

Captain Watson was and is McGinley's golfing hero and despite the Irishman's standing in the game, few can stand club-to-club

with the genial giant of the sport from Kansas City. But maybe that is where America went wrong. Did they under-estimate McGinley, a man who also only knew success in this great old competition and had been unanimously campaigned for to lead the team by Europe's leading golfers?

Despite it ending in a comfortable European win, a match in which, ultimately, the better team won, the outcome was far from certain until midway through the last day's Singles matches. And all indicators pointed towards a US victory after the first morning's Fourballs had returned to the Gleneagles clubhouse.

The great American sporting crowd at Chicago's Medinah had been unprecedented in its size and sound, but Gleneagles took the volumes and colour to new heights. Some 40,000-plus spectators were already on the course at 7.30am when the players made their way to the first tee on a fresh autumnal Friday morning.

ABOVE *The United States' Bubba Watson hits his opening tee shot during the morning Fourballs matches as the 2014 Ryder Cup gets under way.*

Patrick Reed (front) and Jordan Spieth had a combined age of 45 and were the United States' youngest pairing in Ryder Cup history.

Never before have golfers received such acclaim and fanfare before teeing off, with the majority of the good-natured support naturally for the home side.

It was spine-tingling stuff and there were even first hole nerves for veteran announcer Ivor Robson, who briefly got Bubba Watson and Webb Simpson confused before the latter proceeded to sky his drive no further than an 18-handicap Sunday afternoon golfer would have been happy with. Masters winner Watson then found the rough before experienced Europeans Henrik Stenson and Justin Rose drilled their drives down the fairway. The crowd went wild and the tone was set for European domination, or was it?

The imperious English Rose, the world's sixth-highest ranked player and in-form Swede Stenson, rated fifth on the planet going into Gleneagles, proceeded to win their match 5 and 4, but it would prove to be the only victory for Captain McGinley on the opening morning.

Americans Rickie Fowler and Jimmy Walker fought back with style and determination from two holes down against Great Dane Thomas Bjorn and Germany's finest Martin Kaymer to earn an impressive half point, but the shiniest visiting stars were the third American pair out, Jordan Spieth and Patrick Reed.

The unabashed new boys were soon dubbed the "Super Rookies." The pair had played together many times coming through the ranks and Spieth was a Junior Ryder Cup winner at Gleneagles in 2010, but even that could not have prepared them for this. The Spieth/Reed pairing had a combined age of 45, compared to the previous youngest American pairing which had been the 46 of Justin Leonard and Tiger Woods in 1997. The Ryder Cup's all-time youngsters are Mark James and Ken Brown, who boasted a mere 43 years between them when they teamed up in 1977.

Captain Watson clearly fancied his dynamic duo, however, sending them out in the opening session against European Ryder Cup stalwart Ian Poulter, who McGinley paired with local hero and one of his three captain's picks Stephen Gallacher. So much for reputations, as Spieth and Watson humiliated their European opponents 5 and 4. It could have been an even wider margin of victory as the Americans had led by six at one stage and the result ended a seven-match winning streak for Poulter.

Spieth revealed afterwards how important it had been to beat Poulter in a bid to dampen home support. He admitted: "It feels incredible. It was very quiet around our group today. It was a goal we had to achieve. It was nice to have a partner that was

> **"***It was very, very quiet out there compared to what I think Patrick and I expected in the first round of a Ryder Cup over here, and that's the goal.***"**

American rookie Jordan Spieth

DAY ONE

CAPTAINS

Europe: Paul McGinley **USA:** Tom Watson

FRIDAY MORNING FOURSOMES

Rose/Stenson *beat* **Watson/Simpson** *5 and 4*

Bjorn/Kaymer *halved with* **Fowler/Walker**

Gallacher/Poulter *lost to* **Spieth/Reed** *5 and 4*

Garcia/McIlroy *lost to* **Bradley/Mickelson** *1 down*

Session Score: 1.5-2.5

FRIDAY AFTERNOON FOURBALLS

Donaldson/Westwood *beat* **Furyk/Kuchar** *2 up*

Rose/Stenson *beat* **Mahan/Johnson** *2 and 1*

McIlroy/Garcia *halved with* **Walker/Fowler**

Dubuisson/McDowell *beat* **Mickelson/Bradley** *3 and 2*

Session Score: 3.5-.5

Overall Score: Europe 5, USA 3

making everything he looks at." His red-hot partner Reed added: "Coming out and playing with Jordan, who I've played a lot of golf with, and have him play with me was great."

The heavyweight clash of the morning pitted world No. 1 Rory McIlroy and the No. 3 Sergio Garcia against America's bankers Phil Mickelson and Keegan Bradley, who had won all three of their matches at Medinah. It was an absorbing match of the highest quality from which the Americans emerged with a 1 up victory and a clear one point overall lead after the morning's play.

Tom Watson commented afterwards: "There was a lot of ebb at the beginning and some flow later on in the matches. That is

ABOVE: *Victor Dubuisson of France (right) and Northern Ireland's Graeme McDowell formed an impressive partnership for Europe and overcame Phil Mickelson and Keegan Bradley in the afternoon Foursomes.*

what you expect in the Ryder Cup and it was a key way to go into the afternoon. It's a marathon, not a race, and we are a few paces ahead but it has been exciting and very, very special."

Watson's next move, and perhaps a mistake on his behalf, was to rest his wonder rookies for the afternoon Foursomes as the match proceeded to swing back in favour of McGinley's men. Watson had stated in advance every member of his team would play on the opening day and he was good to his word, but was it to the detriment of his team's chances of winning, or were Europe simply too good?

The Garcia/McIlroy versus Mickelson/Bradley match was still out on the course when the afternoon Foursomes teed off and both captains sprung surprises with their selections.

Captain McGinley led with Welsh debutant Jamie Donaldson and one of his three picks, the mightily experienced Lee Westwood, making his ninth appearance. World No. 4 Jim Furyk, partnering the affable Matt Kuchar, was also teeing off for the ninth time in the Ryder Cup and the old foes did not disappoint with some entertaining and classy matchplay golf.

However it was Donaldson, Westwood's sixth partner in the competition, who particularly impressed as the Europeans won 2 up. Westwood said afterwards: "Jamie's right up there [with anyone else I've partnered] and he took to the Ryder Cup like a duck to water. I was very impressed, making his debut like that in Foursomes as it is not the easiest format to play."

A beaming Donaldson, who would emerge as one of the stars of the European team, added: "That first tee is like a sudden death play-off in a major – it feels like there's 20,000 people on one hole. It's incredible. It's an awesome event to play in. I thoroughly enjoyed it. Lee told me what to expect as we went out and how par golf wins Foursomes. We were four under and only just won it on the last, so it was a really tough game."

Rose, in the form of his life, and Stenson showed more winning skills to defeat Hunter Mahan and Masters winner Zach Johnson 2 and 1 to make it two blue points on the scoreboard with the two remaining Foursomes to finish.

Now Captain Watson's decision to bench Spieth and Reed was beginning to look questionable, as was his continued faith in Bradley and Mickelson. At 44 and in his tenth Ryder Cup, Mickelson, who had worn two gloves in the morning chill, seemed to tire in the latter stages following his drawn out win from the morning.

They were up against the redoubtable Graeme McDowell, a stalwart of the Cup himself now, and the enigmatic debutant from France, Victor Dubuisson.

SHOT OF THE DAY

Sergio Garcia and Rory McIlroy were facing their second defeat of the opening day after the Northern Irishman's wayward tee-shot to the 18th in the afternoon Foursomes. Garcia's five-wood from 229 yards into a difficult wind from the left put them perfectly on the green and set up to win the hole and a crucial half point against Jimmy Walker and Rickie Fowler.

The Frenchman, who secured his place after finishing third in the European Tour's points list for 2014, was paired on the opening day alongside the experienced McDowell. This proved a master-stroke as the Americans were vanquished 3 and 2.

Dubuisson, in particular struck some fine shots under pressure, moving McDowell to comment: "I was very fortunate to be playing alongside a player who I think really is Europe's next superstar, I really believe that."

Last to finish yet again, were McIlroy and Garcia, the Spaniard hitting the shot of the day with a five-wood to the green from some nasty rough to help salvage half a point for the Europeans just as USA had looked set to win.

That meant America had won only half a point after lunch and Team Europe were 5-3 ahead at the close. McIlroy said his half felt like a win and McGinley agreed. "We've seen how important momentum is over the years," he said. "The US had that this morning and for our guys to react so well shows real strength of character."

Watson retorted: "I'm disappointed with the result, but not the attitude. I told them in the locker room it is 5-3. You win two matches, you're back in it."

Coincidentally, just as Europe were leading now, USA had led 5-3 at Medinah after the first day. Was history about to reinvent itself and another miraculous Ryder Cup about to unfold?

ABOVE: *Lee Westwood (left) and Jamie Donaldson celebrate victory in the afternoon Foursomes, much to the delight of the Europe team captain Paul McGinley.*

DAY TWO

SATURDAY MORNING FOURBALLS

Rose/Stenson *beat* **Watson/Kuchar** *3 and 2*

Donaldson/Westwood *lost to* **Furyk/Mahan** *4 and 3*

Bjorn/Kaymer *lost to* **Spieth/Reed** *5 and 3*

McIlroy/Poulter *halved with* **Walker/Fowler**

Session Score: 1.5-2.5

SATURDAY AFTERNOON FOURSOMES

Donaldson/Westwood *beat* **Johnson/Kuchar** *2 and 1*

Kaymer/Rose *halved with* **Spieth/Reed**

Garcia/McIlroy *beat* **Furyk/Mahan** *3 and 2*

Dubuisson/McDowell *beat* **Walker/Fowler** *5 and 4*

Session Score: 3.5 -.5

Overall Score: Europe 10, USA 6

> ❝*My job as captain is I'm half a day ahead of everyone else.*❞
>
> *Europe Captain Paul McGinley*

Another topsy-turvy day of outstanding golf in stunning Gleneagles sunshine featured some record-breaking scores, an American comeback and another display of European Foursomes that put them in an almost unassailable lead by the end of the second afternoon's play.

Bubba Watson led the Americans out on a mission to close the two-point gap from Friday's tense play. "Just two wins is all we need," had been Captain Tom Watson's message in the team room. But after encouraging the massed ranks of supporters, some of whom had been at the course since before 4:00am, to create a wall of sound throughout his tee shot, Watson and partner Matt Kuchar were hit by a hurricane force storm in the form of Justin Rose and Henrik Stenson.

The Europeans, who had played so well on Friday too, finished with 10 straight birdies to get the first blue point of the day on

RIGHT: *Team Europe's Justin Rose (right) and playing partner Henrik Stenson discuss their options on the 16th hole on their way to victory over Bubba Watson and Matt Kuchar in Saturday's Fourball matches.*

OPPOSITE: *Europe's Ryder Cup talisman Ian Poulter celebrates chipping in on the 15th hole during the morning Fourballs. Partnered by Rory McIlroy, they halved their match against Jimmy Walker and Rickie Fowler.*

the board. America hit back impressively in the three remaining matches, winning two and halving one to bring them within a point of Europe's overall lead by the morning session's close.

Rose and Stenson won 3 and 2 against an American duo who notched up nine birdies themselves; form which would normally be enough to win. But the European 12-under score was a Fourballs Ryder Cup record, as was the combined 21-under total for the two teams.

The Americans were in front after seven holes and playing more than well enough to win. Bubba Watson, as ever, captured the whole spirit of the Ryder Cup when he said: "That was wild. We would like to go to a few more holes, just so we could watch some great golf again."

Kuchar admitted: "They were unstoppable." And Stenson seemed almost stunned by his own feat when he modestly reflected afterwards: "It might be a highlight to put on the big screen with the grandkids one day.

"It was one half Stenson, one-and-a-half parts Rose because Justin played phenomenally well and I was there to back him up on a couple of occasions."

Rose, who hit seven of the record-breaking birdies, added: "I really got into reading the greens well and I just had the feeling of the anticipation of what it's going to feel like to make putts. You see the ball going in the hole and you sort of get those positive vibes. It was a day when it all happened for me."

SHOT OF THE DAY

Even some Americans were beginning to feel a bit for Ian Poulter as he struggled his way through his second match of the weekend without firing. Then, out of nowhere, or from 40-odd yards and over a bunker on the 15th to be precise, he chipped in to win the hole and help secure a crucial half point.

Stenson also revealed that a back problem would keep him out of the next session of Foursomes, but while the skippers plotted their next set of pairings, this was no time for Captain Watson's men to think further ahead than where their next point was coming from.

And they did not have to wait too long to find it as Jim Furyk and Hunter Mahan took out Lee Westwood and Jamie Donaldson 4 and 3 in a devastating display of matchplay golf.

Jordan Spieth and Patrick Reed continued where they left off on day one with an emphatic 5 and 3 win in their match against Thomas Bjorn and Martin Kaymer, before Rickie Fowler and Jimmy Walker halved with European heavyweights Rory McIlroy and Ian Poulter.

America were right back in the mix, where Watson wanted them, and they could so easily have been closer with Poulter finally finding some form to help prevent Fowler and Walker taking all the glory in their match.

The Foursomes would follow and other intriguing team selections were there to be discussed with the absence of Phil Mickelson a talking point around the golfing globe.

The most experienced player in the US team had looked weary on Friday afternoon, but was itching to get back into the action come Saturday afternoon, reportedly even texting his captain with a plea to play. But Watson had made up his mind and he was going with his younger guns now.

McGinley, meanwhile, with the Fourballs still in swing, had already sent out one of his old hands in the morning as Poulter returned to the fray to partner McIlroy against the highly-rated Walker and Fowler.

Poulter, who had lost his first Ryder Cup match in eight outings the morning before, seemed destined for another defeat as he trailed again approaching the 15th green and had hardly hit a decent ball all day.

This time, faced with a chip over a bunker, a good 40 yards from the pin, he ran it in for a birdie and the man who sparked the Medinah comeback with a Saturday run of five birdies briefly

ABOVE: *Jim Furyk (right) and Hunter Mahan of the United States shake hands after their victory on the 15th hole during the morning Fourballs against European pairing Jamie Donaldson and Lee Westwood.*

LEFT: *Europe's Sergio Garcia and Rory McIlroy line up a putt on the 12th green during the afternoon Foursomes. They eventually defeated Jim Furyk and Hunter Mahan 3 and 2.*

BELOW: *Victor Dubuisson and Graeme McDowell celebrate on the 3rd green during the afternoon Foursomes, much to the delight of the European supporters at Gleneagles.*

reappeared as he pumped the European crest on his jumper like a footballer who had scored a goal in a cup final.

Poulter was indeed "back" as he managed to channel his adrenaline to sink a long birdie putt at the 16th too. As it was, they went down the 18th all square and both teams had chances to win it, Fowler with the ultimate opportunity from an 18-foot eagle putt.

America were back in it, but the ensuing half meant Europe had once again lost the morning session by just one point when the margin could have been greater. The experienced Ryder Cup players really know how to graft out a half and just how important it can be – the score now standing at Europe's 6.5 to America's 5.5.

That factor still did not earn a Mickelson a recall for the afternoon's Foursomes. But Captain Watson could have put out a team of eight Tiger Woods at his peak and Europe might still have won. The Europeans seem to relish the Foursomes format, where the players strike alternate shots, and for the second day in a row they dropped only half a point in the four matches.

Westwood resumed his partnership with rookie Donaldson to score the first point of the afternoon with a 2 and 1 victory over Zach Johnson and Kuchar. The point took Westwood ahead of Seve Ballesteros' all-time Ryder Cup record, but still two short of Nick Faldo's European best of 25.

And he confirmed afterwards he has not yet finished scoring points for Europe. He said: "Hopefully I have one or two more Ryder Cups to play in before I get to the captaincy stage. I am still relatively young at 41 so I'd like to concentrate on playing for the time being and think about the captaincy in six to eight years."

Next into the clubhouse with a blue point were Graeme McDowell and Victor Dubuisson, who was rapidly becoming a hero of the packed Scottish galleries. The seemingly nerveless Frenchman once again played a key role in winning another point to increase Europe's lead to three overall as they dispatched Rickie Fowler and Jimmy Walker 5 and 4.

It meant the new dynamic duo had won 12 of the 30 holes they had contested. The modest Dubuisson said little more than how "incredible and amazing" everything was, leaving to McDowell to sum it all up.

The Irishman, known as "G-Mac", reported: "I said to Victor going out yesterday. Every one of these fans will be cheering and they will be cheering loud and they will be cheering for us. We have to use them to our advantage. This is such a big piece of land, you forget how many people there are out here and how passionate they are and how much they love this tournament. It's a special, special golf tournament. We're very proud to be part of it."

Spieth birdied the second to win the hole and put the first red marker on the scoreboard as McDowell looked edgy – just what Captain Tom had ordered. McIlroy hit straight back by going one up after the first hole with a peerless birdie at the first. Honours even.

Reed, initially, was struggling against Stenson and the so-called Super Rookie seemed to betray nerves and fallibility for the first time in the three days of competition when he lost the second hole with a bogey. There were two blues on the board and two more would mean the Ryder Cup was retained.

All of a sudden, Spieth took a three-hole lead over McDowell through the first five holes to put America in a commanding position to take the first point of the day. But with Europe leading in two of the other four first games out, McIlroy threatening to tear Fowler apart after playing the first six holes in six under par and leading five up, it was not really going well enough for Watson's men.

Fifth out were a fired-up Phil Mickelson and rookie Stephen Gallacher, who had not played since his opening morning Fourballs defeat. He looked a bit nervous, and understandably so, as he missed a close putt on the first hole, but then he took the second to place another blue on the board and settle the nerves. That

also made the projected scores 14-9 and Europe would have retained the Ryder Cup if time had been frozen then.

But with Spieth playing so well, and the hugely pumped up Reed leading against Stenson and Mahan and Mickelson in front too, the Americans were soon leading four of the opening five singles, building the momentum Watson had insisted they could get going to win the day.

Once all 12 singles matches had completed at least hole, the dashing Victor Dubuisson teeing off the final game against America's Zach Johnson, the projected final result was 15.5-12.5. There was, of course still a lot more golf to play.

Just as Ferguson had warned, there was certainly no room for complacency in Team Europe, a factor world No. 1 McIlroy was fully aware of. The Irishman claimed just winning this latest chapter of the Ryder Cup would not be enough; he wanted to overtake America's life-time lead which stood at 25-12 going into the 2014 showdown.

McIlroy also revealed an inspirational image in the European locker-room was a massive all-time Ryder Cup scoreboard which had been strategically placed there by McGinley. McIlroy said: "We see so many American flags on that record and know we still have a long way to catch up and this would just be another step in the right direction to achieving that."

ABOVE: *World Number One and a four-time major champion Rory McIlory overcame Rickie Fowler 5 and 4 in their last day Singles match.*

Indeed, with America threatening to dominate the singles as the day progressed, they were soon up in six of the 12 matches, down in only two, there was every chance the match could all come down to debutant Dubuisson and his match against the more experienced Johnson. The Frenchman, already one of Europe's star players of the match having won two points in Foursomes tandem with McDowell, had the faith of his captain and all his team-mates.

But his colleagues were doing everything they could to take the pressure off. McDowell, for example, went from three down at the turn against Spieth to be one up after 13 holes. Rose, who had trailed by four after six holes, was level after winning eight through 11 with a devastating return to form. Devastating to Mahan that is, or at least it should have been as the American hit back to ultimately lead going onto the 18th and then halve the match.

McIlroy was the main man for Europe, though, seeing off Fowler 5 and 4 to get their first point. He struck seven birdies and an eagle in 12 holes with golf widely agreed to be best in the world for many a year. The world No. 1 said: "I knew what was expected of me and I was more up for this than the two final days in majors I won this year. I had no option but to win and played my best golf of the week."

McDowell, also celebrating his first wedding anniversary, brought in the second point with a 2 and 1 win over Spieth in one of the Ryder Cup's great comeback wins. G-Mac said: "I was given a big role [to lead the team out first] and I'm so happy I was able to deliver. It was hard out there because I wanted it so badly and I had to remind myself when I was three down just to try and win the next hole, get the crowd on my side and try to extend the match. Thankfully it was enough in the end."

The American player now making the biggest statements, with his clubs and his actions, was Spieth's friend and fellow rookie Reed. The big, confident 24-year-old was fist-pumping in the extreme and even tried to hush the crowd by putting his fingers to his lips after one super putt on the seventh. It had the opposite effect of course, but Reed was relishing it and proceeded to beat the in-form Swede.

Matt Kuchar beat Thomas Bjorn 4 and 3 to make the overall score 12-9 to Europe, only for US Open champion Martin Kaymer to quickly dampen US spirits by sinking a chip from off the green to secure a comprehensive 4 and 2 win against Bubba Watson.

> **"** *I took a pill for my headache before I started because I knew what the noise would be like and I think this has to be the best Ryder Cup I have ever played in. I had goosebumps on every tee.* **"**
>
> *Martin Kaymer*

Kaymer explained: "I thought I needed to get the match won before the par fives because I know how good Bubba is over the long holes, but to chip the ball in was amazing. It was a big rush and you feel emotions you don't normally experience in golf in the Ryder Cup – every single hole I had goosebumps walking on to the tee."

Rose's half with Mahan left Europe within half a point of retaining the Cup once again. The only two questions being asked now were "could America stage the comeback of all comebacks," or "where would the winning European point come from?"

With chips, drives and mega putts flying into the holes from outrageous distances and angles, nothing was predictable on a day of remarkably high quality golf.

ABOVE: *Matt Kuchar gestures to the crowd on his way to a 4 and 3 victory over Europe's Thomas Bjorn in the Singles matches.*

ABOVE: *Fighting to the end, Phil Mickelson plays out of a tricky bunker on the 17th hole in his Singles match. Alas, his 3 and 1 victory over Stephen Gallacher wasn't enough to reduce Europe's impressive lead.*

RIGHT: *Jamie Donaldson's delightful approach shot to the 15th hole set up his victory over Keegan Bradley and retained the Ryder Cup for Europe.*

SHOT OF THE DAY

Jamie Donaldson's stone-dead wedge to the 15th to win the Ryder Cup. "I hit the wedge shot of my life," he said afterwards. And what a time to do it!

And few were playing better than European rookie Jamie Donaldson. The Welshman had performed very well claiming two points from his first three matches, and was up against one of America's better players in Keegan Bradley, but produced a faultless and seemingly nerveless display.

Neither player dropped a shot until Bradley bogeyed the ninth, just before Donaldson went on a run of birdies to lead 4 up by the 13th hole. It proved to be an insurmountable lead for the American especially when Donaldson hit one of the shots of the weekend; to within a foot from 146 yards at the 15th. It was such a good shot it forced the honourable Bradley to concede the hole, the match and the Ryder Cup.

The celebrations started straight away and continued long into the next day. McGinley was lauded as Europe's greatest ever captain while there was some stiff criticism for Tom Watson, but nothing to damage the long-term reputation of one of golf's genuine greats.

Watson graciously conceded that the better team had won. He will be back and so will the Ryder Cup, when the best golfers of America and Europe go club-to-club again at the Hazeltine National Golf Course in Minnesota in 2016.

From left, Europe's Sergio Garcia, Lee Westwood, Rory McIlroy and Ian Poulter celebrate their well-deserved victory in the 2014 Ryder Cup.

RYDER CUP
2014

GLENEAGLES
SCOTLAND 2014

Europe team captain Paul McGinley celebrates with his team. Their 16.5-11.5 victory ensured they won the Cup for the third successive time.

RYDER CUP

OFFICIAL
SOUVENIR PROGRAMME

PRICE 1/-

THE FOURTH INTERNATIONAL GOLF MATCH

GREAT BRITAIN *versus* THE UNITED STATES OF AMERICA

TO BE PLAYED ON THE SOUTHPORT AND AINSDALE COURSE,
SOUTHPORT

ON MONDAY AND TUESDAY, JUNE 26-27, 1933

This Official Programme is published by the Professional Golfers' Association and the proceeds will be devoted
to the British Ryder Cup Fund.

Ryder Cup Records
Complete Ryder Cup Listings

2014, September 26-28
Gleneagles Golf Resort, The PGA Centenary Course, Scotland.
Captains: Tom Watson (USA), Paul McGinley (Europe)
Europe 16.5 - USA 11.5

2012, September 28-30
Medinah Country Club, Course No. 3, Medinah, Illinois.
Captains: Davis Love III (USA), José María Olazábal (Europe)
USA 13.5 - Europe 14.5

2010, October 1-4
Celtic Manor Resort, Newport, Wales.
Captains: Colin Montgomerie (Europe), Corey Pavin (USA)
Europe 14.5 - USA 13.5

2008, September 19-21
Valhalla Golf Club, Louisville, Kentucky, USA.
Captains: Paul Azinger (USA), Nick Faldo (Europe)
USA 16.5 - Europe 11.5

2006, September 22-24
The K Club, Straffan, County Kildare, Ireland.
Captains: Ian Woosnam (Europe), Tom Lehman (USA)
Europe 18.5 - USA 9.5

2004, September 17-19
Oakland Hills Country Club, Bloomfield Township, Michigan, USA.
Captains: Hal Sutton (USA), Bernhard Langer (Europe)
USA 9.5 - Europe 18.5

2002, September 27-29
The Belfry, Wishaw, Warwickshire, England.
Captains: Sam Torrance (Europe), Curtis Strange (USA)
Europe 15.5 - USA 12.5

1999, September 24-26
The Country Club, Brookline, Massachusetts, USA.
Captains: Ben Crenshaw (USA), Mark James (Europe)
USA 14.5 - Europe 13.5

1997, September 26-28
Valderrama Golf Club, Sotogrande, Spain.
Captains: Severiano Ballesteros (Europe), Tom Kite (USA)
Europe 14.5 - USA 13.5

1995, September 22-24
Oak Hill Country Club, Pittsford, New York, USA.
Captains: Lanny Wadkins (USA), Bernard Gallacher (Europe)
USA 13.5 - Europe 14.5

1993, September 24-26
The Belfry, Wishaw, Warwickshire, England.
Captains: Bernard Gallacher (Europe), Tom Watson (USA)
Europe 13 - USA 15

1991, September 27-29
Kiawah Island Golf Resort, Kiawah Island, South Carolina, USA.
Captains: Dave Stockton (USA), Bernard Gallacher (Europe)
USA 14.5 - Europe 13.5

1989, September 22-24
The Belfry, Wishaw, Warwickshire, England.
Captains: Tony Jacklin (Europe), Raymond Floyd (USA)
Europe 14 - USA 14

1987, September 25-27
Muirfield Village, Dublin, Ohio, USA.
Captains: Jack Nicklaus (USA), Tony Jacklin (Europe)
USA 13 - Europe 15

1985, September 13-15
The Belfry, Wishaw, Warwickshire, England.
Captains: Tony Jacklin (Europe), Lee Trevino (USA)
Europe 16.5 - USA 11.5

1983, October 14-16
PGA National Golf Club, Palm Beach Gardens, Florida, USA.
Captains: Jack Nicklaus (USA), Tony Jacklin (Europe)
USA 14.5 - Europe 13.5

1981, September 18-20
Walton Heath Golf Club, Surrey, England.
Captains: John Jacobs (Europe), Dave Marr (USA)
Europe 9.5 - USA 18.5

1979, September 14-16
The Greenbrier Course, White Sulphur Springs, West Virginia, USA.
Captains: Billy Casper (USA), John Jacobs (Europe)
USA 17 - Europe 11

1977, September 15-17
Royal Lytham & St Annes Golf Club, Lytham St Annes, England.
Captains: Brian Huggett (GB&I), Dow Finsterwald (USA)
Great Britain & Ireland 7.5 - USA 12.5

1975, September 19-21
Laurel Valley Golf Club, Ligonier, Pennsylvania, USA.
Captains: Arnold Palmer (USA), Bernard Hunt (GB&I)
USA 21 - Great Britain & Ireland 11

1973, September 20-22
Muirfield, East Lothian, Scotland.
Captains: Bernard Hunt (GB&I), Jack Burke Jnr. (USA)
Great Britain & Ireland 13 - USA 19

1971, September 16-18
Old Warson Country Club, St. Louis, Missouri, USA.
Captains: Jay Hebert (USA), Eric Brown (GB&I)
USA 18.5 - Great Britain 13.5

Ryder Cup Records

1969, September 18-20
Royal Birkdale Golf Club, Southport, England.
Captains: Eric Brown (Great Britain), Sam Snead (USA)
Great Britain 16 - USA 16

1967, October 20-22
Champions Golf Club, Houston, Texas, USA.
Captains: Ben Hogan (USA), Dai Rees (Great Britain)
USA 23.5 - Great Britain 8.5

1965, October 7-9
Royal Birkdale Golf Club, Southport, England.
Captains: Harry Weetman (Great Britain), Byron Nelson (USA)
Great Britain 12.5 - USA 19.5

1963, October 11-13
Atlanta Athletic Club, Atlanta, Georgia, USA.
Captains: Arnold Palmer (USA), John Fallon (Great Britain)
USA 23 - Great Britain 9

1961, October 13-14
Royal Lytham & St Annes Golf Club, Lytham St Annes, England.
Captains: Dai Rees (Great Britain), Jerry Barber (USA)
Great Britain 9.5 - USA 14.5

1959, November 6-7
Eldorado Golf Club, Indian Wells, California, USA.
Captains: Sam Snead (USA), Dai Rees (Great Britain)
USA 8.5 - Great Britain 3.5

1957, October 4-5
Lindrick Golf Club, Rotherham, South Yorkshire, England.
Captains: Dai Rees (Great Britain), Jack Burke Jnr. (USA)
Great Britain 7.5 - USA 4.5

1955, November 5-6
Thunderbird Country Club, Rancho Mirage, California, USA.
Captains: Chick Harbert (USA), Dai Rees (Great Britain)
USA 8 - Great Britain 4

1953, October 2-3
Wentworth Golf Club, Surrey, England.
Captains: Henry Cotton (Great Britain), Lloyd Mangrum (USA)
Great Britain 5.5 - USA 6.5

1951, November 2-4
Pinehurst Resort, Pinehurst, North Carolina, USA.
Captains: Sam Snead (USA), Arthur Lacey (Great Britain)
USA 9.5 - Great Britain 2.5

1949, September 16-17
Ganton Golf Club, Scarborough, North Yorkshire, England.
Captains: Charles Whitcombe (Great Britain), Ben Hogan (USA)
Great Britain 5 - USA 7

1947, November 1-2
Portland Golf Club, Portland, Oregon, USA.
Captains: Ben Hogan (USA), Henry Cotton (Great Britain)
USA 11 - Great Britain 1

1937, June 29-30
Southport & Ainsdale Golf Club, Southport, England.
Captains: Charles Whitcombe (Great Britain), Walter Hagen (USA)
Great Britain 4 - USA 8

1935, September 28-29
Ridgewood Country Club, Paramus, New Jersey, USA.
Captains: Walter Hagen (USA), Charles Whitcombe (Great Britain)
USA 9 - Great Britain 3

1933, June 26-27
Southport & Ainsdale Golf Club, Southport, England.
Captains: John Henry Taylor (Great Britain), Walter Hagen (USA)
Great Britain 6.5 - USA 5.5

1931, June 26-27
Scioto Country Club, Columbus, Ohio, USA.
Captains: Walter Hagen (USA), Charles Whitcombe (Great Britain)
USA 9 - Great Britain 3

1929, April 26-27
Moortown Golf Club, Leeds, West Yorkshire, England.
Captains: George Duncan (Great Britain), Walter Hagen (USA)
Great Britain 7 - USA 5

1927, June 3-4
Worcester Country Club, Worcester, Massachusetts, USA.
Captains: Walter Hagen (USA), Ted Ray (Great Britain)
USA 9.5 - Great Britain 2.5

Ryder Cup Points

Total Ryder Cup points (1927-2014) - USA and GB&I/Europe
USA - 514.5
GB&I/Europe - 413.5

Total Ryder Cup points (1927-1977) - USA and GB&I
USA - 268.5
GB&I - 155.5

Total Ryder Cup points (1979-2014) - USA and Europe
USA - 246
Europe - 258

Wins Records

Number of Ryder Cup matches won
USA - 25 wins
Europe - 13 wins (10 as Europe, 3 as GB&I)
Tied - 2

Largest Ryder Cup winning margins
USA
15 -   23.5-8.5 in 1967 (Champions GC, USA)
14 -   23-9 in 1963 (Atlanta Athletic Club, USA)
10 -   11-1 in 1947 (Portland GC, USA);
        21-11 in 1975 (Laurel Valley GC, USA)

GB&I/Europe

9 - 18.5-9.5 in 2004 (Oakland Hills CC, USA);
18.5-9.5 in 2006 (The K Club, Ireland)

5 - 16.5-11.5 in 1985 (The Belfry, England)
16.5-11.5 in 2014 (Gleneagles, Scotland)

3 - 7.5-4.5 in 1957 (Lindrick GC, England);
15.5-12.5 in 2002 (The Belfry, England)

Most consecutive Ryder Cup victories

USA - 7 - 1935-1955
Europe - 3 - 2002-2006 & 2010-2014

Ryder Cup Singles Results 1979-2012

Year	USA	Europe
1979	8.5	3.5
1981	8	4
1983	6.5	5.5
1985	4.5	7.5
1987	7.5	4.5
1989	7	5
1991	6.5	5.5
1993	7.5	4.5
1995	4.5	7.5
1997	8	4
1999	8	3.5
2002	4.5	7.5
2004	4.5	7.5
2006	3.5	8.5
2008	7.5	4.5
2010	7	5
2012	3.5	8.5
2014	5.5	6.5

PLAYER STATISTICS

Most appearances

Sir Nick Faldo - 11 (GB&I/Europe)
Bernhard Langer - 10 (GB&I/Europe)
Phil Mickelson - 10 (USA)
Christy O'Connor Snr. - 10 (GB&I/Europe)
Jim Furyk - 9 (USA)
Dai Rees - 9 (GB&I/Europe)
Lee Westwood - 9 (GB&I/Europe)
Peter Alliss - 8 (GB&I/Europe)
Severiano Ballesteros - 8 (GB&I/Europe)
Billy Casper - 8 (USA)
Neil Coles - 8 (GB&I/Europe)
Raymond Floyd - 8 (USA)
Bernard Gallacher - 8 (GB&I/Europe)
Bernard Hunt - 8 (GB&I/Europe)
Colin Montgomerie - 8 (GB&I/Europe)
Sam Torrance - 8 (GB&I/Europe)
Lanny Wadkins - 8 (USA)
Ian Woosnam - 8 (GB&I/Europe)

Most overall matches played

Sir Nick Faldo - 46 (GB&I/Europe)
Bernhard Langer - 42 (GB&I/Europe)
Phil Mickelson - 41 (USA)
Lee Westwood - 41 (GB&I/Europe)

Neil Coles - 40 (GB&I/Europe)
Severiano Ballesteros - 37 (GB&I/Europe)
Billy Casper - 37 (USA)
Christy O'Connor Snr. - 36 (GB&I/Europe)
Colin Montgomerie - 36 (GB&I/Europe)
Tony Jacklin - 35 (GB&I/Europe)
Jim Furyk - 34 (USA)
Lanny Wadkins - 34 (USA)

Most overall matches won

Sir Nick Faldo - 23 (GB&I/Europe)
Arnold Palmer - 22 (USA)
Bernhard Langer - 21 (GB&I/Europe)
Severiano Ballesteros - 20 (GB&I/Europe)
Billy Casper - 20 (USA)
Colin Montgomerie - 20 (GB&I/Europe)
Lanny Wadkins - 20 (USA)
Lee Westwood - 20 (GB&I/Europe)
Sergio Garcia - 18 (GB&I/Europe)
José María Olazábal - 18 (GB&I/Europe)
Jack Nicklaus - 17 (USA)
Lee Trevino - 17 (USA)

Most overall matches halved

Gene Littler - 8 (USA)
Tony Jacklin - 8 (GB&I/Europe)
Billy Casper - 7 (USA)
Stewart Cink - 7 (USA)
Neil Coles - 7 (GB&I/Europe)
Colin Montgomerie - 7 (GB&I/Europe)

Eight players who have halved six matches overall:

Brian Huggett - 6 (GB&I/Europe)
Bernard Hunt - 6 (GB&I/Europe)
Bernhard Langer - 6 (GB&I/Europe)
Justin Leonard - 6 (USA)
Phil Mickelson - 6 (USA)
Sam Torrance - 6 (GB&I/Europe)
Lee Trevino - 6 (USA)
Lee Westwood - 6 (GB&I/Europe)

Most overall points won

Sir Nick Faldo - 25 (GB&I/Europe)
Bernhard Langer - 24 (GB&I/Europe)
Billy Casper - 23.5 (USA)
Colin Montgomerie - 23.5 (GB&I/Europe)
Arnold Palmer - 23 (USA)
Lee Westwood - 23 (GB&I/Europe)
Severiano Ballesteros - 22.5 (GB&I/Europe)
Lanny Wadkins - 21.5 (USA)
José María Olazábal - 20.5 (GB&I/Europe)
Sergio Garcia - 20 (GB&I/Europe)
Lee Trevino - 20 (USA)

Most Singles matches played

Neil Coles - 15 (GB&I/Europe)
Christy O'Connor - 14 (GB&I/Europe)
Peter Alliss - 12 (GB&I/Europe)
Sir Nick Faldo - 11 (GB&I/Europe)
Bernard Gallacher - 11 (GB&I/Europe)
Arnold Palmer - 11 (USA)
Tony Jacklin - 11 (GB&I/Europe)

Eight players who have played 10 Singles matches:

Brian Barnes - 10 (GB&I/Europe)

Index

Aaron, Tommy 86, 87
Adams, Jimmy
  1947 Ryder Cup 49
  1949 Ryder Cup 51
  1951 Ryder Cup 54, 55
  1953 Ryder Cup 57
Ainsdale Golf Club 38-9, 44-5
Alexander, Skip 55
Alliss, Percy
  1931 Ryder Cup 34
  1933 Ryder Cup 38, 39
  1935 Ryder Cup 41
  1937 Ryder Cup 45
Alliss, Peter 88-9
  1953 Ryder Cup 56, 57
  1955 Ryder Cup 60
  1957 Ryder Cup 62, 63
  1959 Ryder Cup 67
  1961 Ryder Cup 69
  1963 Ryder Cup 72, 73
  1965 Ryder Cup 74, 75
  1967 Ryder Cup 78, 79
  1969 Ryder Cup 81
Armour, Tommy 22
Atlanta Athletic Club 72-3
Azinger, Paul 163
  1989 Ryder Cup 126, 127, 128-9
  1991 Ryder Cup 133, 134, 135, 136, 137
  1993 Ryder Cup 141, 142, 143, 144, 145
  2002 Ryder Cup 172, 173, 176, 177
  2008 Ryder Cup 196, 197
Baker, Peter 141, 142, 143, 144, 145
Ballantine, Jock 50
Ballesteros, Severiano 9, 112-13, 146-7
  1979 Ryder Cup 98, 99, 100, 101
  1981 Ryder Cup 102-3, 105
  1983 Ryder Cup 108, 109, 110, 111
  1985 Ryder Cup 115, 116, 117
  1987 Ryder Cup 120, 121, 122, 123
  1989 Ryder Cup 126, 127, 128, 129
  1991 Ryder Cup 133, 134, 135, 136, 137
  1993 Ryder Cup 141, 142, 144, 145
  1995 Ryder Cup 149, 151, 152, 153
  1997 Ryder Cup 156, 157, 160, 233
Bannerman, Harry 84, 85
Barber, Jerry
  1955 Ryder Cup 61
  1961 Ryder Cup 68, 69
Barber, Miller
  1969 Ryder Cup 80, 81
  1971 Ryder Cup 84, 85
Barnes, Brian
  1969 Ryder Cup 81
  1971 Ryder Cup 85
  1973 Ryder Cup 86, 87
  1975 Ryder Cup 90, 91
  1977 Ryder Cup 95
  1979 Ryder Cup 100, 101
Barnes, Jim 22
Barron, Herman 48, 49
Bean, Andy
  1979 Ryder Cup 99, 100, 101
  1987 Ryder Cup 121, 122, 123
Beard, Frank
  1969 Ryder Cup 80, 81
  1971 Ryder Cup 84, 85
Beck, Chip
  1989 Ryder Cup 127, 129
  1991 Ryder Cup 133, 136, 137
  1993 Ryder Cup 142, 143-4, 145

Belfry, The 114-17, 126-9, 140-5, 172-7
Bembridge, Maurice
  1969 Ryder Cup 80, 81
  1971 Ryder Cup 84
  1973 Ryder Cup 86, 87
  1975 Ryder Cup 90, 91
Bird, Robert 50, 87
Bjorn, Thomas
  1997 Ryder Cup 158, 159, 160, 161
  2002 Ryder Cup 172-3, 174, 176, 177
  2010 Ryder Cup 204
  2014 Ryder Cup 229, 232, 235, 237
Blancas, Homero 86
Bolt, Tommy
  1955 Ryder Cup 61
  1957 Ryder Cup 62, 63
Boomer, Aubrey
  1926 competition 22
  1927 Ryder Cup 27, 28, 29
  1929 Ryder Cup 33
  1931 Ryder Cup 34
Boros, Julius
  1957 Ryder Cup 62
  1959 Ryder Cup 67
  1963 Ryder Cup 72, 73
  1965 Ryder Cup 74, 75
  1967 Ryder Cup 78, 79
Bousfield, Ken
  1949 Ryder Cup 51
  1951 Ryder Cup 55
  1957 Ryder Cup 62, 63
  1959 Ryder Cup 67
  1961 Ryder Cup 69
Boyle, Hugh 79
Bradley, Keegan
  2012 Ryder Cup 213, 214, 216, 217, 218, 221, 223
  2014 Ryder Cup 229, 230, 232, 238
Bradshaw, Harry
  1953 Ryder Cup 56, 57
  1955 Ryder Cup 61
  1957 Ryder Cup 63
Braid, James 14, 19, 50
Brand, Gordon J.
  1983 Ryder Cup 110, 111
  1987 Ryder Cup 121, 122
  1989 Ryder Cup 126, 127, 129
Brewer, Gay
  1967 Ryder Cup 78, 79
  1973 Ryder Cup 86, 87
Broadhurst, Paul 135, 136, 137
Brookline 236, 237
Brown, Eric
  1953 Ryder Cup 56, 57
  1955 Ryder Cup 61
  1957 Ryder Cup 62, 63
  1959 Ryder Cup 67
  1969 Ryder Cup 80
  1971 Ryder Cup 84
  1977 Ryder Cup 95
Brown, Ken
  1977 Ryder Cup 229
  1979 Ryder Cup 99, 101
  1983 Ryder Cup 109, 110, 111
  1985 Ryder Cup 115, 116
  1987 Ryder Cup 121, 122
Burke, Billy
  1931 Ryder Cup 35
  1933 Ryder Cup 38, 39
Burke Jnr., Jack
  1951 Ryder Cup 54, 55

  1953 Ryder Cup 57
  1955 Ryder Cup 61
  1957 Ryder Cup 62, 63
  1973 Ryder Cup 86
Burkemo, Walter 56, 57
Burton, Dick
  1935 Ryder Cup 41
  1937 Ryder Cup 45
  1949 Ryder Cup 51
Busson, Jack 40, 41
Butler, Peter
  1965 Ryder Cup 74, 75
  1969 Ryder Cup 80, 81
  1971 Ryder Cup 84
  1973 Ryder Cup 87
  1979 Ryder Cup 98
Calcavecchia, Mark
  1987 Ryder Cup 121, 122, 123
  1989 Ryder Cup 126, 127, 128, 129
  1991 Ryder Cup 133, 134, 135, 136, 137
  2002 Ryder Cup 173, 174, 175, 177
Campbell, Chad
  2004 Ryder Cup 180, 181, 182, 183, 184
  2006 Ryder Cup 189, 191, 192, 193
  2008 Ryder Cup 197, 198, 199, 200
Cañizares, José Maria
  1981 Ryder Cup 103, 104
  1983 Ryder Cup 109, 111
  1985 Ryder Cup 115, 116, 117
  1989 Ryder Cup 129
Casey, Paul
  2004 Ryder Cup 182, 183, 184
  2006 Ryder Cup 189, 190, 191, 192
  2008 Ryder Cup 197, 199, 200, 201
Casper, Billy 69, 70-1, 92-3
  1963 Ryder Cup 72, 73
  1965 Ryder Cup 74, 75
  1967 Ryder Cup 78, 79
  1969 Ryder Cup 80, 81
  1971 Ryder Cup 84
  1973 Ryder Cup 86, 87
  1975 Ryder Cup 90, 91
  1979 Ryder Cup 99
Caygill, Alex 81
Celtic Manor 14, 204-9
Champions Golf Club 78-9
Chisholm, Tom 50
Cink, Stewart
  2002 Ryder Cup 173, 174, 177
  2004 Ryder Cup 181, 182, 183, 184, 185
  2006 Ryder Cup 189, 190, 191, 192
  2008 Ryder Cup 197, 198, 199, 200
  2010 Ryder Cup 205, 206, 207, 208, 209
Clark, Howard
  1977 Ryder Cup 95
  1981 Ryder Cup 103, 104
  1985 Ryder Cup 116, 117
  1987 Ryder Cup 121, 122, 123
  1989 Ryder Cup 126, 127, 128, 129
  1995 Ryder Cup 149, 152, 153
Clarke, Darren 202-3
  1997 Ryder Cup 158, 159, 161
  1999 Ryder Cup 165, 166, 167, 169
  2002 Ryder Cup 172, 173, 174, 175, 176, 177
  2004 Ryder Cup 180, 181, 182, 183, 184, 185
  2006 Ryder Cup 188, 189, 190, 191, 192, 193
  2010 Ryder Cup 204
Coles, Neil
  1961 Ryder Cup 69
  1963 Ryder Cup 72, 73

1965 Ryder Cup 74, 75
1967 Ryder Cup 79
1969 Ryder Cup 80
1971 Ryder Cup 84, 85
1973 Ryder Cup 86, 87
1977 Ryder Cup 95
Collins, Bill 69
Colsaerts, Nicolas
   2012 Ryder Cup 212, 213, 215, 216, 218, 221
Coltart, Andrew 169
Compston, Archie 43
   1926 competition 22
   1927 Ryder Cup 27, 28, 29
   1929 Ryder Cup 33
   1931 Ryder Cup 35
Coody, Charles 84, 85
Cook, John 142, 143-4, 145
Cotton, Henry
   1929 Ryder Cup 32, 33
   1931 Ryder Cup 34
   1933 Ryder Cup 38
   1935 Ryder Cup 40, 41
   1937 Ryder Cup 44-5
   1947 Ryder Cup 48-9
   1949 Ryder Cup 50
   1953 Ryder Cup 56, 57
   1955 Ryder Cup 61
Country Club 164-9
Couples, Fred
   1989 Ryder Cup 126, 127, 129
   1991 Ryder Cup 133, 134, 135, 136, 137
   1993 Ryder Cup 141, 142, 144, 145
   1995 Ryder Cup 149, 150, 151, 153
   1997 Ryder Cup 157, 158, 159, 160, 161
Cox, Bill
   1935 Ryder Cup 41
   1937 Ryder Cup 45
Cox, Wiffy 35
Crenshaw, Ben
   1981 Ryder Cup 103, 104
   1983 Ryder Cup 109, 110, 111
   1987 Ryder Cup 121, 122, 123
   1995 Ryder Cup 149, 151, 153
   1999 Ryder Cup 165, 167
Curtis, Ben 197, 199, 200
Daly, Fred
   1947 Ryder Cup 49
   1949 Ryder Cup 51
   1951 Ryder Cup 55
   1953 Ryder Cup 57
Darcy, Eamonn
   1975 Ryder Cup 90, 91
   1977 Ryder Cup 95
   1981 Ryder Cup 103, 104
   1987 Ryder Cup 122, 123
Darwin, Bernard 50
Davies, William
   1931 Ryder Cup 35
   1933 Ryder Cup 38, 39
Dawson, John 60
Dawson, Peter 95
Demaret, Jimmy
   1947 Ryder Cup 48, 49
   1949 Ryder Cup 51
   1951 Ryder Cup 54-5
Derby, Lord 98
Dickinson, Gardner 76-7
   1967 Ryder Cup 78, 79
   1971 Ryder Cup 84, 85
Diegel, Leo
   1927 Ryder Cup 27, 28, 29
   1929 Ryder Cup 33
   1931 Ryder Cup 35

1933 Ryder Cup 39
DiMarco, Chris
   2004 Ryder Cup 181, 182, 183, 184
   2006 Ryder Cup 189, 190, 191, 192, 193
Dobson, Fred 33
Donald, Luke
   2004 Ryder Cup 181, 183, 184
   2006 Ryder Cup 189, 191, 192, 193
   2010 Ryder Cup 205, 206, 207, 208, 209
   2012 Ryder Cup 213, 214, 216, 217, 218, 219,
      221, 222, 223
Donaldson, Jamie
   2014 Ryder Cup 229, 230, 231, 232, 233,
      238
Douglas, Dale 56, 57
Douglass, Dale 81
Drew, Norman 67
Dubuisson, Victor
   2014 Ryder Cup 229, 230, 231, 232, 234, 235,
      236, 237
Dudley, Ed
   1929 Ryder Cup 33
   1933 Ryder Cup 38, 39
   1937 Ryder Cup 44, 45
Dufner, Jason
   2012 Ryder Cup 213, 214, 216, 218, 219, 221,
      222, 223
Duncan, George 10, 14, 15, 16, 24-5
   1926 competition 19, 22
   1927 Ryder Cup 27, 28, 29
   1929 Ryder Cup 30-1, 32, 33
   1931 Ryder Cup 34, 35
Dutra, Olin
   1933 Ryder Cup 39
   1935 Ryder Cup 41
Duval, David
   1999 Ryder Cup 165, 167, 169
   2002 Ryder Cup 173, 174, 175, 176, 177
Dye, Pete 132
Easterbrook, Syd
   1931 Ryder Cup 35
   1933 Ryder Cup 38-9
Elder, Lee 99, 100, 101
Eldorado Golf Club 66-7
Erath, Paul 90
Espinosa, Al
   1929 Ryder Cup 33
   1931 Ryder Cup 35
Faldo, Nick 106-7, 233
   1977 Ryder Cup 94-5
   1979 Ryder Cup 99, 100, 101
   1981 Ryder Cup 103, 104
   1983 Ryder Cup 109, 110, 111
   1985 Ryder Cup 115, 116
   1987 Ryder Cup 120, 121, 122-3
   1989 Ryder Cup 126, 127, 129
   1991 Ryder Cup 132, 133, 134, 135, 136, 137
   1993 Ryder Cup 141, 142, 143, 144, 145
   1995 Ryder Cup 148, 149, 150, 151, 152, 153
   1997 Ryder Cup 156-7, 158, 159, 160, 161
   2008 Ryder Cup 197, 198, 200, 235
Fallon, Johnny
   1955 Ryder Cup 61
   1963 Ryder Cup 72, 73
Farrell, Johnny
   1927 Ryder Cup 27, 28, 29
   1929 Ryder Cup 33
   1931 Ryder Cup 35
Fasth, Niclas 173, 174, 175, 176, 177
Faulkner, Max
   1947 Ryder Cup 49
   1949 Ryder Cup 51
   1951 Ryder Cup 54, 55

1953 Ryder Cup 57
1957 Ryder Cup 62-3
Faxon, Brad
   1995 Ryder Cup 149, 150, 151, 152, 153
   1997 Ryder Cup 157, 158, 159, 160, 161
Fazio, George 108
Fazio, Tom 108
Feherty, David 133, 134, 135, 136, 137
Ferguson, Sir Alex 235, 236
Finsterwald, Dow
   1957 Ryder Cup 62, 63
   1959 Ryder Cup 66, 67
   1961 Ryder Cup 69
   1963 Ryder Cup 72, 73
Fisher, Ross 205, 206, 207, 208, 209
Floyd, Ray
   1969 Ryder Cup 80, 81
   1975 Ryder Cup 90, 91
   1977 Ryder Cup 94, 95
   1981 Ryder Cup 103, 104
   1983 Ryder Cup 109, 111
   1985 Ryder Cup 115, 116, 117
   1989 Ryder Cup 126, 127
   1991 Ryder Cup 133, 134, 135, 136, 137
   1993 Ryder Cup 140, 141, 142, 143, 144, 145
Forbes, Sir Charles 57
Ford, Doug
   1955 Ryder Cup 61
   1957 Ryder Cup 62, 63
   1959 Ryder Cup 67
   1961 Ryder Cup 68, 69
Fowler, Rickie 204, 206-7
   2014 Ryder Cup 229, 230, 232, 233, 234, 235,
      236, 237
French, Emmett 15
Fulke, Pierre 174, 177
Funk, Fred 181, 183, 184, 185
Furgol, Marty
   1955 Ryder Cup 61
   1957 Ryder Cup 63
Furyk, Jim
   1997 Ryder Cup 157, 158, 159, 160, 161
   1999 Ryder Cup 165, 166, 167, 169
   2002 Ryder Cup 173, 174, 175, 177
   2004 Ryder Cup 181, 182, 183, 184
   2006 Ryder Cup 189, 190, 191, 192
   2008 Ryder Cup 197, 198, 199, 200, 201
   2010 Ryder Cup 206-7, 208, 209
   2012 Ryder Cup 213, 214, 216, 218, 221, 223
   2014 Ryder Cup 229, 230, 232, 234, 235
Gadd, George
   1926 competition 22
   1927 Ryder Cup 29
Gallacher, Bernard 124-5
   1969 Ryder Cup 80, 81
   1971 Ryder Cup 85
   1973 Ryder Cup 86, 87
   1975 Ryder Cup 90, 91
   1977 Ryder Cup 95
   1979 Ryder Cup 99, 100, 101
   1981 Ryder Cup 103, 104
   1983 Ryder Cup 108, 109, 111
   1991 Ryder Cup 133, 134, 136
   1993 Ryder Cup 140, 141, 142
   1995 Ryder Cup 148, 149, 150, 151
Gallacher, Stephen
   2014 Ryder Cup 229, 235, 236, 238
Gallacher, Tony 91
Gallagher, Jim 141, 142, 144, 145
Ganton Golf Club 50-1
García, Sergio
   1999 Ryder Cup 165, 167, 169
   2002 Ryder Cup 172, 173, 174, 175, 176, 177, 177

2004 Ryder Cup 180-1, 182, 183, 184, 185
2006 Ryder Cup 189, 190, 191, 192
2008 Ryder Cup 197, 198, 199, 200
2012 Ryder Cup 213, 216, 218, 219, 221, 223
2014 Ryder Cup 229, 230, 231, 232, 234, 235, 239
Garrido, Antonio 99, 100, 101
Garrido, Ignacio 158, 159, 160, 161
Geiberger, Al
    1967 Ryder Cup 78, 79
    1975 Ryder Cup 90, 91
Gilder, Bob 109, 110, 111
Gilford, David
    1991 Ryder Cup 133, 134, 135, 136, 137
    1995 Ryder Cup 149, 150, 151, 153
Gleneagles Hotel 228, 232, 235
Goalby, Bob 72, 73
Golden, Johnny
    1927 Ryder Cup 27, 28, 29
    1929 Ryder Cup 33
Goodwin, Sir Stuart 62
Graham, Lou
    1973 Ryder Cup 86, 87
    1975 Ryder Cup 90, 91
    1977 Ryder Cup 95
Green, Hubert
    1977 Ryder Cup 95
    1979 Ryder Cup 99, 101
    1985 Ryder Cup 114, 115, 116
Green, Ken 126, 127, 129
Greenbrier Course 98-101
Gregson, Malcolm 78, 79
Guidahl, Ralph 45
Haas, Fred 56, 57
Haas, Jay
    1983 Ryder Cup 109, 110, 111
    1995 Ryder Cup 150, 151, 152, 153
    2004 Ryder Cup 181, 182, 183, 184, 185
Hackney, Clarence 15
Haeggman, Joakim 141, 142, 144, 145
Hagen, Walter 11, 13, 14, 15, 36-7
    1926 competition 20-1, 22
    1927 Ryder Cup 26-9
    1929 Ryder Cup 32, 33
    1931 Ryder Cup 34-5
    1933 Ryder Cup 38, 39
    1935 Ryder Cup 40, 41
    1937 Ryder Cup 44, 45
Haliburton, Tom
    1961 Ryder Cup 69
    1963 Ryder Cup 72, 73
Hamilton, Bob 51
Hansen, Søren 197, 200, 201
Hanson, Peter
    1999 Ryder Cup 206, 207, 208, 209
    2012 Ryder Cup 213, 214, 221, 222, 223
Harbert, Chick
    1949 Ryder Cup 51
    1955 Ryder Cup 61
Harnett, James 13, 15
Harper, Chandler 61
Harrington, Padraig
    1999 Ryder Cup 165, 166, 167, 169
    2002 Ryder Cup 173, 174, 175, 176, 177
    2004 Ryder Cup 180, 181, 182, 183, 184, 185
    2006 Ryder Cup 189, 191, 192, 193
    2008 Ryder Cup 197, 198, 199, 200
    2010 Ryder Cup 205, 206, 207, 208, 209
Harrison, E. J.
    1947 Ryder Cup 49
    1949 Ryder Cup 51
Havers, Arthur 14
    1926 competition 19, 22

1927 Ryder Cup 27, 28, 29
1931 Ryder Cup 35
1933 Ryder Cup 38, 39
Hawkins, Fred 62, 63
Hayes, Mark 100, 101
Heafner, Clayton
    1949 Ryder Cup 51
    1951 Ryder Cup 55
Hebert, Jay
    1959 Ryder Cup 67
    1961 Ryder Cup 69
    1971 Ryder Cup 84
Henry, J. J. 189, 190, 191, 192, 193
Herbert, Lionel 63
Herd, Alex 19
Hill, Dave
    1969 Ryder Cup 80, 81
    1973 Ryder Cup 87
    1977 Ryder Cup 95
Hill, John 18
Hitchcock, Jimmy 74, 75
Hoch, Scott
    1997 Ryder Cup 158, 159, 160, 161
    2002 Ryder Cup 173, 174, 175, 176, 177
Hodson, Bert 35
Hogan, Ben 52-3
    1947 Ryder Cup 48, 49
    1949 Ryder Cup 50, 51
    1951 Ryder Cup 55
    1953 Ryder Cup 56
    1957 Ryder Cup 62
    1967 Ryder Cup 78
Holmes, J. B. 196, 197, 199, 200, 201
Horton, Tommy
    1975 Ryder Cup 90, 91
    1977 Ryder Cup 95
Howell, David
    2004 Ryder Cup 182, 183, 184
    2006 Ryder Cup 189, 191, 192
Hudson, Robert 48, 50
Huggett, Brian
    1963 Ryder Cup 72, 73
    1967 Ryder Cup 78, 79
    1969 Ryder Cup 80, 81
    1971 Ryder Cup 84, 85
    1973 Ryder Cup 86, 87
    1975 Ryder Cup 91
    1977 Ryder Cup 94, 95
    1979 Ryder Cup 98
Hughes, Larry 60
Hunt, Bernard
    1953 Ryder Cup 56, 57
    1955 Ryder Cup 60
    1957 Ryder Cup 62, 63
    1959 Ryder Cup 67
    1961 Ryder Cup 69
    1963 Ryder Cup 72, 73
    1965 Ryder Cup 74, 75
    1967 Ryder Cup 79
    1969 Ryder Cup 80, 81
    1973 Ryder Cup 86
    1975 Ryder Cup 90
Hunt, Geoff 72, 73
Hunt, Guy 90, 91
Hutchinson, Jock 15
Irwin, Hale
    1975 Ryder Cup 90, 91
    1977 Ryder Cup 95
    1979 Ryder Cup 99, 100, 101
    1981 Ryder Cup 103, 104
    1991 Ryder Cup 133, 134, 135, 136-7
Jacklin, Tony 124-5
    1967 Ryder Cup 78, 79

1969 Ryder Cup 80, 81, 82-3
1971 Ryder Cup 84, 85
1973 Ryder Cup 86, 87
1975 Ryder Cup 90, 91
1977 Ryder Cup 95
1979 Ryder Cup 99, 100, 101
1981 Ryder Cup 103, 105
1983 Ryder Cup 108, 109, 110
1985 Ryder Cup 114, 115
1987 Ryder Cup 121, 123
1989 Ryder Cup 126-7
Jacobs, John
    1955 Ryder Cup 61
    1979 Ryder Cup 99
    1981 Ryder Cup 103, 105
Jacobs, Tommy 75
Jacobsen, Peter
    1985 Ryder Cup 114, 115, 116, 117
    1995 Ryder Cup 149, 150, 151, 152, 153
James, Mark
    1977 Ryder Cup 95, 229
    1979 Ryder Cup 99, 100
    1981 Ryder Cup 103, 104
    1989 Ryder Cup 126, 127, 128, 129
    1991 Ryder Cup 133, 134, 135, 136, 137
    1993 Ryder Cup 141, 142, 144, 145
    1995 Ryder Cup 149, 153
    1999 Ryder Cup 164, 165, 169
January, Don
    1965 Ryder Cup 74, 75
    1977 Ryder Cup 95
Janzen, Lee
    1993 Ryder Cup 141, 145
    1995 Ryder Cup 150
    1997 Ryder Cup 157, 158, 159, 160, 161
Jarman, Edward 41
Jermain, Sylvanus P. 12, 13
Jiménez, Miguel Angel
    1999 Ryder Cup 165, 166, 167, 169
    2004 Ryder Cup 180, 181, 183, 184
    2008 Ryder Cup 197, 198, 199, 200, 201
    2010 Ryder Cup 206, 207, 208, 209
Johansson, Per-Ulrik
    1995 Ryder Cup 148, 149, 153
    1997 Ryder Cup 157, 160, 161
Johnson, Dustin
    2010 Ryder Cup 205, 206, 207, 208, 209
    2012 Ryder Cup 213, 214, 216, 218, 221
Johnson, Zach
    2006 Ryder Cup 188, 189, 191, 192, 193
    2010 Ryder Cup 206, 207, 208, 209
    2012 Ryder Cup 213, 214, 216, 218, 219, 221, 223
    2014 Ryder Cup 229, 230, 232, 233, 235, 236, 237
Jolly, Herbert 22, 26-7, 28, 29
K Club 188-93
Karlsson, Robert
    2006 Ryder Cup 189, 190, 191, 192-3
    2008 Ryder Cup 197, 198, 199, 200, 201
Kaymer, Martin
    2010 Ryder Cup 205, 206, 207, 208, 209
    2012 Ryder Cup 213, 214, 221, 223-4
    2014 Ryder Cup 229, 232, 234, 237
Keiser, Herman 48, 49
Kiawah Island 132-7
Kim, Anthony 197, 198, 199, 200
King, Michael 101
King, Sam
    1937 Ryder Cup 44, 45
    1947 Ryder Cup 48, 49
    1949 Ryder Cup 51
King's Course, Gleneagles 12, 13
Kirkwood, Joe 22

Kite, Tom 154-5
    1979 Ryder Cup 99, 100, 101
    1981 Ryder Cup 103, 104, 105
    1983 Ryder Cup 111
    1985 Ryder Cup 115, 116, 117
    1987 Ryder Cup 121, 122-3
    1989 Ryder Cup 127, 128, 129
    1993 Ryder Cup 141, 142, 145
    1997 Ryder Cup 159, 160, 161
Kroll, Ted
    1953 Ryder Cup 56, 57
    1955 Ryder Cup 61
    1957 Ryder Cup 62, 63
Kuchar, Matt
    2010 Ryder Cup 205, 206, 207, 208, 209
    2012 Ryder Cup 213, 214, 216, 218, 220, 221, 223
    2014 Ryder Cup 229, 230, 232, 237
Lacey, Arthur
    1933 Ryder Cup 39
    1937 Ryder Cup 45
    1951 Ryder Cup 54, 55
Laffoon, Ky 41
Lane, Barry 141, 142, 143, 144, 145
Langer, Bernhard 96-7, 162
    1981 Ryder Cup 103, 104
    1983 Ryder Cup 109, 110, 111
    1985 Ryder Cup 114, 115, 116, 117
    1987 Ryder Cup 120, 121, 122, 123
    1989 Ryder Cup 126, 127, 128, 129
    1991 Ryder Cup 132, 133, 134, 135, 136-7
    1993 Ryder Cup 141, 142, 145
    1995 Ryder Cup 149, 150, 151, 153
    1997 Ryder Cup 158, 159, 160, 161
    2002 Ryder Cup 173, 174, 176, 177
    2004 Ryder Cup 180, 181, 182, 185
Laurel Valley Golf Club 90-1
Lawrie, Paul
    1999 Ryder Cup 165, 166, 167, 169
    2012 Ryder Cup 213, 214, 216, 218, 221, 223
Lees, Arthur
    1947 Ryder Cup 49
    1949 Ryder Cup 51
    1951 Ryder Cup 54, 55
    1955 Ryder Cup 61
Lehman, Tom
    1995 Ryder Cup 149, 150, 151, 152, 153
    1997 Ryder Cup 158, 159, 160, 161
    1999 Ryder Cup 165, 167, 169
    2006 Ryder Cup 189, 190, 191, 193
    2010 Ryder Cup 204
Lema, Tony
    1963 Ryder Cup 72, 73
    1965 Ryder Cup 74, 75
Leonard, Justin
    1997 Ryder Cup 157, 158, 159, 160, 161, 229
    1999 Ryder Cup 164, 165, 166, 167, 169
    2008 Ryder Cup 197, 198, 199, 200, 201
Levet, Thomas 181, 183, 184, 185
Levi, Wayne 135, 136, 137
Lietzke, Bruce 103, 104
Lindrick Golf Club 62-3
Littler, Gene
    1961 Ryder Cup 69
    1963 Ryder Cup 72, 73
    1965 Ryder Cup 74, 75
    1967 Ryder Cup 78, 79
    1969 Ryder Cup 80, 81
    1971 Ryder Cup 85
    1975 Ryder Cup 90, 91
Love, Davis
    1993 Ryder Cup 141, 142, 144, 145
    1995 Ryder Cup 149, 150, 151, 153
    1997 Ryder Cup 157, 158, 159, 160, 161
    1999 Ryder Cup 165, 166, 167, 169

    2002 Ryder Cup 173, 174-5, 177
    2004 Ryder Cup 180, 181, 182, 183, 184, 185
    2010 Ryder Cup 204
    2012 Ryder Cup 212-16, 218-20, 222, 224
Lyle, Sandy
    1979 Ryder Cup 99, 100, 101
    1981 Ryder Cup 103, 104, 105
    1983 Ryder Cup 109, 110, 111
    1983 Ryder Cup 114, 115
    1985 Ryder Cup 116, 117
    1987 Ryder Cup 120, 121, 122, 123
    1989 Ryder Cup 127
McCumber, Mark 126, 127, 129
McDowell, Graeme 210-11
    2008 Ryder Cup 197, 198, 199, 200
    2010 Ryder Cup 204, 205, 206, 207, 208-9
    2012 Ryder Cup 213, 214, 216, 218, 221, 223
    2014 Ryder Cup 229, 230, 231, 232, 235, 237, 238, 239
Mackenzie, Alister 32
Mackie, John 13
McGee, Jerry 95
McGinley, Paul
    2002 Ryder Cup 172, 173, 174, 175, 177
    2004 Ryder Cup 181, 184, 185
    2006 Ryder Cup 189, 191, 192, 193
    2010 Ryder Cup 204
    2014 Ryder Cup 228, 230, 231, 233, 232, 234, 235, 236, 237
McIlroy, Rory
    2010 Ryder Cup 205, 206, 207, 208, 209, 210-11
    2012 Ryder Cup 213, 214, 216, 218, 221, 222, 223
    2014 Ryder Cup 229, 230, 231, 232, 234, 235, 236, 237, 239
McLeod, Fred 15, 22
Maggert, Jeff
    1995 Ryder Cup 149, 150, 151, 152
    1997 Ryder Cup 158, 159, 160, 161
    1999 Ryder Cup 165, 166, 167, 169
Mahaffey, John 99, 100, 101
Mahan, Hunter
    2008 Ryder Cup 197, 198, 199, 200, 201
    2010 Ryder Cup 204, 206, 207, 208-9
    2014 Ryder Cup 229, 230, 232, 234, 235, 237
Manero, Tony 44, 45
Mangrum, Lloyd 64-5
    1947 Ryder Cup 48, 49
    1949 Ryder Cup 51
    1951 Ryder Cup 54, 55
    1953 Ryder Cup 56, 57
Marr, Dave
    1965 Ryder Cup 74, 75
    1981 Ryder Cup 103, 105
Martin, Jimmy 74
Martín, Miguel 156
Mayer, Dick 62, 63
Medinah Country Club 212-25, 228, 231
Maxwell, Billy 72, 73
Mehlhorn, Bill 15
Mickelson, Phil 9, 194-5
    1995 Ryder Cup 149, 150, 151, 153
    1997 Ryder Cup 157, 158, 159, 161
    1999 Ryder Cup 165, 167, 169
    2002 Ryder Cup 172, 173, 174, 175, 176, 177
    2004 Ryder Cup 180, 181, 183, 184, 185
    2006 Ryder Cup 189, 190, 191, 192, 193
    2008 Ryder Cup 197, 198, 199, 200, 201
    2010 Ryder Cup 14, 205, 206, 207, 208, 209
    2012 Ryder Cup 213, 214, 216, 217, 218, 221, 222, 223
    2014 Ryder Cup 229, 230, 233, 236, 238
Middlecoff, Cary
    1949 Ryder Cup 50
    1953 Ryder Cup 56, 57

    1955 Ryder Cup 61
    1957 Ryder Cup 62
    1959 Ryder Cup 67
Miller, Johnny
    1975 Ryder Cup, 90, 91
    1981 Ryder Cup 103, 104
Mills, Peter 63
Mitchell, Abe 8, 14, 16
    1926 competition 18, 19, 22
    1927 Ryder Cup 26
    1929 Ryder Cup 33
    1931 Ryder Cup 35
    1933 Ryder Cup 39, 39
    on Ryder Cup Trophy 23
Mize, Larry 121, 122
Moffitt, Ralph 69
Molinari, Eduardo 206, 207, 208, 209
Molinari, Francesco
    2010 Ryder Cup 206, 207, 208, 209
    2012 Ryder Cup 213, 214, 216, 218, 221, 223-4
Montgomerie, Colin 178-9
    1991 Ryder Cup 133, 134, 135, 136, 137
    1993 Ryder Cup 141, 142, 143, 145
    1995 Ryder Cup 149, 150, 151, 153
    1997 Ryder Cup 157, 158, 159, 160, 161
    1999 Ryder Cup 165, 166, 167, 169
    2002 Ryder Cup 172, 173, 174, 175, 176, 177
    2004 Ryder Cup 180, 181, 182, 183, 184, 185
    2006 Ryder Cup 189, 191, 192
    2010 Ryder Cup 204, 205, 207, 208, 209
Moortown Golf Club 32-3
Morgan, Gil
    1979 Ryder Cup 99, 101
    1983 Ryder Cup 109, 110, 111
Muirfield 86-7
Muirfield Village 120-3
Murphy, Bob 90, 91
Nelson, Byron
    1937 Ryder Cup 44, 45
    1947 Ryder Cup 48, 49
    1949 Ryder Cup 50
    1965 Ryder Cup 74
Nelson, Larry
    1979 Ryder Cup 99, 100, 101
    1981 Ryder Cup 103, 104
    1987 Ryder Cup 121, 122, 123
Nichols, Bobby 78, 79
Nicklaus, Jack 8, 98, 118-19, 228
    1969 Ryder Cup 80, 81, 82-3
    1971 Ryder Cup 84, 85
    1973 Ryder Cup 86, 87
    1975 Ryder Cup 90, 91
    1977 Ryder Cup 95
    1979 Ryder Cup 98
    1981 Ryder Cup 103, 104
    1983 Ryder Cup 108, 109, 110
    1987 Ryder Cup 120, 121, 123
North, Andy 114, 115, 116
Oak Hill Country Club 148-53
Oakland Hills Country Club 36
Ockendon, James 14
O'Connor, Christy 88-9
    1955 Ryder Cup 61
    1957 Ryder Cup 62, 63
    1959 Ryder Cup 67
    1961 Ryder Cup 69
    1963 Ryder Cup 72, 73
    1965 Ryder Cup 74, 75
    1967 Ryder Cup 78, 79
    1969 Ryder Cup 81
    1971 Ryder Cup 84, 85
    1973 Ryder Cup 86, 87
O'Connor Jr, Christy
    1975 Ryder Cup 90

1989 Ryder Cup 127, 129
Olazábal, José María 9, 146-7
    1987 Ryder Cup 120, 121, 122, 123
    1989 Ryder Cup 126, 127, 128, 129
    1991 Ryder Cup 133, 134, 135, 136, 137
    1993 Ryder Cup 141, 142, 145
    1995 Ryder Cup 148
    1997 Ryder Cup 156, 157, 158, 159, 160, 161
    1999 Ryder Cup 164, 165, 167, 169
    2006 Ryder Cup 189, 190, 191, 192, 193
    2010 Ryder Cup 204
    2012 Ryder Cup 212, 213, 214, 215, 217, 218, 219, 221-2, 224, 225
Old Warson Country Club 84-5
O'Leary, John 90, 91
Oliver, Ed
    1947 Ryder Cup 49
    1951 Ryder Cup 54, 55
    1953 Ryder Cup 56, 57
O'Meara, Mark
    1985 Ryder Cup 114, 115, 116, 117
    1989 Ryder Cup 126, 127, 129
    1991 Ryder Cup 133, 134, 135, 136, 137
    1997 Ryder Cup 157, 158, 159, 161
    1999 Ryder Cup 167, 169
Oosterhuis, Peter 106-7
    1971 Ryder Cup 84, 85
    1973 Ryder Cup 86, 87
    1975 Ryder Cup 90, 91
    1977 Ryder Cup 94, 95
    1979 Ryder Cup 99, 100, 101
    1981 Ryder Cup 103, 104
Overton, Jeff 205, 206, 207, 208, 209
Padgham, Alf
    1933 Ryder Cup 38, 39
    1935 Ryder Cup 41
    1937 Ryder Cup 44-5
Palmer, Arnold 76-7
    1961 Ryder Cup 69
    1963 Ryder Cup 72, 73
    1965 Ryder Cup 74, 75
    1967 Ryder Cup 78, 79
    1971 Ryder Cup 84, 85
    1973 Ryder Cup 86, 87
    1975 Ryder Cup 90
    1979 Ryder Cup 99
Palmer, Johnny 51
Panton, John
    1951 Ryder Cup 54-5
    1953 Ryder Cup 57
    1961 Ryder Cup 69
Park, Brian 74
Parks, Sam 41
Parnevik, Jesper
    1997 Ryder Cup 156, 157, 158, 159, 161
    1999 Ryder Cup 165, 167, 169
    2002 Ryder Cup 174, 175, 177
Pate, Jerry 103, 104
Pate, Steve
    1991 Ryder Cup 132, 134, 135, 136, 137
    1999 Ryder Cup 166, 167, 169
Pavin, Corey
    1991 Ryder Cup 132, 133, 134, 135, 136, 137
    1993 Ryder Cup 141, 142, 143, 144, 145
    1995 Ryder Cup 149, 150, 151, 153
    2010 Ryder Cup 204, 205, 207
Peete, Calvin
    1983 Ryder Cup 108-9, 110, 111
    1985 Ryder Cup 115, 116
Perry, Alf
    1933 Ryder Cup 38, 39
    1935 Ryder Cup 40, 41
    1937 Ryder Cup 45

Perry, Kenny
    2004 Ryder Cup 181, 184, 185
    2008 Ryder Cup 196, 197, 198, 199, 200, 201
Philpot, George 26, 27
Picard, Henry
    1935 Ryder Cup 40, 41
    1937 Ryder Cup 44, 45
Pinehurst Country Club 54-5
Pinero, Manuel
    1981 Ryder Cup 103, 104
    1985 Ryder Cup 115, 116, 117
Platts, Lionel 74, 75
Plummer, Ralph 78
Pohl, Dan 121, 122, 123
Pott, Johnny
    1963 Ryder Cup 72, 73
    1967 Ryder Cup 78, 79
Poulter, Ian 226-7
    2004 Ryder Cup 182, 183, 184
    2008 Ryder Cup 197, 198, 199, 200
    2010 Ryder Cup 205, 206, 207, 208, 209
    2012 Ryder Cup 213, 214, 216, 217, 218, 219, 220, 221, 222, 223
    2014 Ryder Cup 229, 232, 233, 234, 235, 237, 239
Price, Phillip 172, 174, 176, 177
Rafferty, Ronan 126, 127, 129
Ragan, Dave 72, 73
Ransom, Henry 54, 55
Ray, Edward 12, 14, 50
    1926 competition 22
    1927 Ryder Cup 27, 28, 29
Raynor, Seth 98
Reed, Patrick
    2014 Ryder Cup 229, 230, 232, 235, 237
Rees, Dai
    1937 Ryder Cup 44, 45
    1947 Ryder Cup 48, 49
    1949 Ryder Cup 51
    1951 Ryder Cup 55
    1953 Ryder Cup 57
    1955 Ryder Cup 60, 61
    1957 Ryder Cup 62-3
    1959 Ryder Cup 67
    1961 Ryder Cup 69
    1967 Ryder Cup 78
Revolta, Johnny
    1935 Ryder Cup 40, 41
    1937 Ryder Cup 45
Richardson, Steven 133, 134, 135, 136, 137
Ridgewood Country Club 40-1
Riley, Chris 181, 182, 183, 184
Rivero, José
    1985 Ryder Cup 116
    1987 Ryder Cup 121, 122
Roberts, Loren 149, 150, 151, 153
Robson, Fred
    1926 competition 22
    1927 Ryder Cup 27, 28, 29
    1929 Ryder Cup 33
    1931 Ryder Cup 35
Robson, Ivor 229
Rocca, Costantino
    1993 Ryder Cup 141, 142, 144-5
    1995 Ryder Cup 149, 150, 151, 153
    1997 Ryder Cup 157, 158, 159, 160, 161
Rodriguez, Juan 86, 87
Rogers, Bill 103, 104
Rosburg, Bob 66, 67
Rose, Justin
    2008 Ryder Cup 197, 198, 199, 200, 201
    2012 Ryder Cup 213, 214, 216, 218, 221, 222, 223
    2014 Ryder Cup 229, 230, 232, 234, 235, 239

Ross, Donald 34, 54
Ross, Walter 12
Royal Birkdale Golf Club 74-5, 80-1
Royal Liverpool 14
Royal Lytham & St Annes Golf Club 68-9, 94-5
Rudolph, Mason 84, 85
Runyan, Paul
    1933 Ryder Cup 39
    1935 Ryder Cup 40, 41
Ryder, Joan 17
Ryder, Samuel 8, 10, 12, 16-17
    1926 competition 18-19, 22, 23
    1927 Ryder Cup 26
    1929 Ryder Cup 30-1, 33
    1931 Ryder Cup 34
    1933 Ryder Cup 39
Sandelin, Jarmo 169
Sanders, Doug 78, 79
Sarazen, Gene 42
    1927 Ryder Cup 27, 28, 29
    1929 Ryder Cup 33
    1931 Ryder Cup 35
    1933 Ryder Cup 38, 39
    1935 Ryder Cup 40, 41
    1937 Ryder Cup 44, 45
Scioto Country Club 34-5
Scott, Syd 61
Sherlock, James 14
Shute, Denny
    1931 Ryder Cup 35
    1933 Ryder Cup 38-9
    1937 Ryder Cup 45
Sikes, Dan 80, 81
Simpson, Scott 121, 122
Simpson, Webb
    2012 Ryder Cup 213, 214, 216, 218, 221, 223
Simpson, Webb
    2014 Ryder Cup 229, 232, 237
Smith, Horton
    1929 Ryder Cup 33
    1933 Ryder Cup 39
    1935 Ryder Cup 40, 41
Smyth, Des
    1979 Ryder Cup 99, 101
    1981 Ryder Cup 103, 104
Snead, J. C.
    1971 Ryder Cup 84, 85
    1973 Ryder Cup 86, 87
    1975 Ryder Cup 90, 91
    1977 Ryder Cup 95
Snead, Sam 64-5
    1937 Ryder Cup 44, 45
    1947 Ryder Cup 48, 49
    1949 Ryder Cup 51
    1951 Ryder Cup 54, 55
    1953 Ryder Cup 57
    1955 Ryder Cup 61
    1957 Ryder Cup 62
    1959 Ryder Cup 66, 67
    1961 Ryder Cup 68
    1969 Ryder Cup 80
Snedeker, Brandt
    2012 Ryder Cup 213, 214, 216, 218, 221, 223
Souchak, Mike
    1959 Ryder Cup 66, 67
    1961 Ryder Cup 69
Spieth, Jordan
    2014 Ryder Cup 229, 230, 232, 234, 235, 236, 237
Stadler, Craig
    1983 Ryder Cup 109, 110, 111
    1985 Ryder Cup 115, 116, 117
Stain, Joe 22

Stenson, Henrik
    2006 Ryder Cup 186-7, 188, 189, 191, 192, 193
    2008 Ryder Cup 197, 198, 199, 200, 201
    2014 Ryder Cup 229, 230, 232, 235, 238
Stewart, Payne
    1987 Ryder Cup 121, 122
    1989 Ryder Cup 126, 127, 129
    1991 Ryder Cup 133, 134, 135, 136, 137
    1993 Ryder Cup 142, 143, 144, 145
    1999 Ryder Cup 165, 166, 169
Still, Ken 80, 81
Stockton, Dave
    1971 Ryder Cup 84, 85
    1977 Ryder Cup 95
    1991 Ryder Cup 132, 133, 135, 136
Strange, Curtis
    1983 Ryder Cup 108, 109, 110, 111
    1985 Ryder Cup 115, 116
    1987 Ryder Cup 121, 122-3
    1989 Ryder Cup 126, 127, 128, 129
    1995 Ryder Cup 148, 149, 150, 151, 152, 153
    2002 Ryder Cup 172, 173
Stricker, Steve
    2008 Ryder Cup 197, 199, 200
    2010 Ryder Cup 205, 206, 207, 208, 209
    2012 Ryder Cup 213, 214, 215, 216, 217, 219, 221, 223-4
Sutton, Hal
    1985 Ryder Cup 114, 115, 116, 117
    1987 Ryder Cup 121, 122
    1999 Ryder Cup 165, 166, 167, 169
    2002 Ryder Cup 173, 177
    2004 Ryder Cup 181, 183, 184, 185
Taylor, John Henry 38, 39, 50
Taylor, Josh 14, 19
Taylor, Vaughn 186-7, 191
Thomas, Dave
    1959 Ryder Cup 67
    1963 Ryder Cup 72, 73
    1965 Ryder Cup 74, 75
    1967 Ryder Cup 78, 79
Thunderbird Country Club 60-1
Toms, David
    2002 Ryder Cup 173, 174, 175, 176, 177
    2004 Ryder Cup 181, 183, 184
    2006 Ryder Cup 189, 191, 192
Torrance, Sam
    1981 Ryder Cup 103, 104
    1983 Ryder Cup 109, 110, 111
    1985 Ryder Cup 114, 115, 116, 117
    1987 Ryder Cup 121, 122
    1989 Ryder Cup 126, 127, 129
    1991 Ryder Cup 133, 134, 135, 136, 137
    1993 Ryder Cup 141, 142, 144, 145
    1995 Ryder Cup 149, 150, 151, 153
    2002 Ryder Cup 172, 173, 176, 177
Townsend, Peter
    1969 Ryder Cup 80, 81
    1971 Ryder Cup 84, 85
Trent Jones, Robert 84
Trevino, Lee
    1969 Ryder Cup 80, 81
    1971 Ryder Cup 84, 85
    1973 Ryder Cup 86, 87
    1975 Ryder Cup 90, 91
    1979 Ryder Cup 99, 100, 101
    1981 Ryder Cup 103, 104
    1985 Ryder Cup 114, 115
Turnesa, Jim 57
Turnesa, Joe
    1927 Ryder Cup 27, 28, 29
    1929 Ryder Cup 33
Valderrama Golf Club 156-61

Valhalla Golf Club 196-201
Vardon, Harry 12, 14, 19, 50
Velde, Jean van de 169
Venturi, Ken 74, 75
Verplank, Scott
    2002 Ryder Cup 173, 174, 176, 177
    2006 Ryder Cup 191, 192, 193
Wadkins, Lanny
    1977 Ryder Cup 95
    1979 Ryder Cup 99, 100, 101
    1983 Ryder Cup 108, 109, 110-11
    1985 Ryder Cup 115, 116, 117
    1987 Ryder Cup 121, 122, 123
    1989 Ryder Cup 126, 127, 129
    1991 Ryder Cup 133, 134, 135, 136, 137
    1993 Ryder Cup 140, 141, 142, 143, 144, 145
    1995 Ryder Cup 150
Waites, Brian 109, 110, 111
Walker, Jimmy
    2014 Ryder Cup 229, 230, 232, 233, 235
Wall, Art
    1957 Ryder Cup 62, 63
    1959 Ryder Cup 67
    1961 Ryder Cup 69
Walton, Philip 148, 150, 151, 152, 153
Walton Heath Golf Club 102-5
Ward, Charlie
    1947 Ryder Cup 49
    1949 Ryder Cup 51
    1951 Ryder Cup 54, 55
Watrous, Al
    1927 Ryder Cup 27, 28, 29
    1929 Ryder Cup 33
Watson, Bubba
    2010 Ryder Cup 205, 206, 207, 208, 209
    2012 Ryder Cup 213, 214, 216, 218, 221, 222
    2014 Ryder Cup 228, 229, 232, 237
Watson, Tom 8, 118-19
    1977 Ryder Cup 94, 95
    1979 Ryder Cup 100
    1981 Ryder Cup 103, 104
    1983 Ryder Cup 109, 110, 111
    1985 Ryder Cup 114
    1989 Ryder Cup 126, 127, 129
    1993 Ryder Cup 140, 141, 142
    2014 Ryder Cup 228, 230, 231, 232, 233, 234, 235, 238, 239
Way, Paul
    1983 Ryder Cup 109, 110, 111
    1985 Ryder Cup 115, 116, 117
Weekley, Brent "Boo" 15, 197, 199, 200, 201
Westwood, Lee
    1997 Ryder Cup 157, 160, 161
    1999 Ryder Cup 167, 169
    2002 Ryder Cup 174
    2010 Ryder Cup 205, 206, 207
    2012 Ryder Cup 213, 214, 215, 216, 217, 221, 223
    2014 Ryder Cup 229, 230, 231, 232, 233
Weetman, Harry
    1951 Ryder Cup 55
    1953 Ryder Cup 57
    1955 Ryder Cup 61
    1957 Ryder Cup 62-3
    1959 Ryder Cup 67
    1961 Ryder Cup 69
    1963 Ryder Cup 72, 73
    1965 Ryder Cup 74
Weiskopf, Tom
    1973 Ryder Cup 86, 87
    1975 Ryder Cup 90, 91
Wentworth Golf Club 18-18, 22-3, 56-9
Westwood, Lee 202-3
    1997 Ryder Cup 158, 159

1999 Ryder Cup 165, 166
2002 Ryder Cup 173, 174, 176, 177
2004 Ryder Cup 180-1, 182, 183, 184, 185
2006 Ryder Cup 189, 190, 191, 192, 193
2008 Ryder Cup 197, 198, 199, 200
2010 Ryder Cup 208, 209
Wetterich, Brett 189, 192
Wheeler, Frank 16
Whitcombe, Charles
    1927 Ryder Cup 27, 28, 29
    1929 Ryder Cup 33
    1931 Ryder Cup 34, 35
    1933 Ryder Cup 38, 39
    1935 Ryder Cup 40-1
    1937 Ryder Cup 44, 45
    1949 Ryder Cup 51
Whitcombe, Ernest
    1926 competition 22
    1929 Ryder Cup 33
    1931 Ryder Cup 35
    1935 Ryder Cup 40-1
Whitcombe, Reg 40, 41
Will, George
    1963 Ryder Cup 72, 73
    1965 Ryder Cup 74, 75
    1967 Ryder Cup 78, 79
Wilson, Dick 90
Wilson, Oliver 198, 199, 200, 201
Wood, Craig
    1931 Ryder Cup 35
    1933 Ryder Cup 39
    1935 Ryder Cup 41
Wood, Norman 90, 91
Woods, Tiger 9, 194-5, 229, 233
    1997 Ryder Cup 157, 158, 159, 160, 161
    1999 Ryder Cup 165, 166, 167, 169
    2002 Ryder Cup 173, 174-5, 176, 177
    2004 Ryder Cup 180, 181, 182, 183, 184
    2006 Ryder Cup 188-9, 190, 191, 192-3
    2008 Ryder Cup 197
    2010 Ryder Cup 14, 204-5, 206, 207, 208, 209
    2012 Ryder Cup 213, 214, 215, 216, 217, 219, 221, 223-4
Woosnam, Ian
    1983 Ryder Cup 109, 110, 111
    1985 Ryder Cup 115, 116, 117
    1987 Ryder Cup 120, 121, 122-3
    1989 Ryder Cup 126, 127, 129
    1991 Ryder Cup 133, 134, 135, 136, 137, 138-9
    1993 Ryder Cup 141, 142, 144, 145
    1995 Ryder Cup 150, 151, 153
    1997 Ryder Cup 158, 159, 160, 161
    2006 Ryder Cup 188, 189, 193
Worcester Country Club 26-9
Worsham, Lew 49
Zoeller, "Fuzzy"
    1979 Ryder Cup 99, 100, 101
    1983 Ryder Cup 109, 110, 111
    1985 Ryder Cup 115, 116

Credits

The publishers would like to thank the following sources for their kind permission to reproduce the pictures in this book.

Action Images: /Trevor Jones/Sporting Pictures: 105, 154-155

Colorsport: 92-93, 104; /Stewart Fraser: 106-107

Corbis: /Bettmann: 28, 29, 46-47, 61, 78

Getty Images: /Allsport: 8 right; /Simon Bruty: 122, 137, 152; /David Cannon: 6, 96-97, 114, 115, 116, 124-125, 126, 132, 142, 143, 146-147, 149, 164, 166, 200, 209, 219, 221, 228, 231, 236, 240 top, 240 bottom; /Brian Cassella/Chicago Tribune/MCT: 226-227; /Central Press: 20-21; /Central Press/Hulton Archive: 33; /Timothy A. Clary/AFP: 9 right, 185 right, 197; /Chris Cole: 141, 145; /J.D. Cuban: 148; / Adrian Dennis/AFP: 173, 176, 177, 189, 206, 232; /Terry Disney/Central Press/Hulton Archive: 57; / Tony Duffy: 118-119; /Jacqueline Duvoisin/Sports Illustrated: 135; /Mike Ehrmann: 212, 220, 222, 224, 225, 235 right, 237; /Graham Finlayson/Sports Illustrated: 102; /Fox Photos: 38; /Fox Photos/Hulton Archive: 44; /Stuart Franklin: 4-5; /J. Gaiger/Topical Press Agency: 16-17; /Sam Greenwood: 199, 207; / Haynes Archive/Popperfoto: 30-31; /Jeff Haynes/AFP: 165, 167; /Harry How: 190, 191; /Hulton Archive: 26, 36-37; /Rusty Jarrett: 136; /Craig Jones: 178-179; /Ross Kinnaird: 205, 218, 241, 242-243; /Andy Lyons: 170-171, 215, 216, 223; /Ian MacNicol: 239; /Bob Martin: 103, 127; /Bob Martin/Sports Illustrated: 169; /Edward Miller/Keystone/Hulton Archive: 58-59; /Donald Miralle: 184-185; /Brian Morgan: 99, 101, 108, 112-113; /Don Morley: 70-71, 87; /Stephen Munday: 130-131, 134, 138-139, 144, 159, 202-203; /Sven Nackstrand/AFP: 188, 193; /Dennis Oulds/Central Press/Hulton Archive: 81; /Popperfoto: 35, 64-65, 86, 150, 157, 158, 160, 168; /Andrew Redington: 3, 175, 210-211, 214, 217, 229; /Tim Sloan/AFP: 198; / Jamie Squire: 156, 172, 174, 180, 183, 186-187, 192, 194-195, 208, 213, 233, 234, 235 left; /Ben Stansall/ AFP: 230, 238; /Bob Thomas: 56, 63, 68, 75, 84, 88-89, 94, 121, 123, 128, 133, 140, 163; /Tony Tomsic/ Sports Illustrated: 120; /Topical Press Agency: 42

Old Golf Images: 8 left, 9 left, 10-11, 12, 13, 14, 15, 18, 19, 22, 23, 24-25, 27, 32, 34, 39, 40, 41, 45, 50, 51, 52-53, 55, 62, 67, 69, 72, 95, 98, 100, 109, 110, 117, 129, 153, 161, 182, 196, 201, 204, 244

Press Association Images: 60, 74, 80, 82-83; /AP: 43, 48, 54, 73, 76-77, 79, 90, 91; /Elisa Amendola/ AP: 151; /Morry Gash/AP: 181; /Ross Kinnaird: 162; /S&G and Barratts: 85; /David F. Smith/AP: 66; / Kathy Willens/AP: 111

Topfoto.co.uk: 49

Every effort has been made to acknowledge correctly and contact the source and/or copyright holder of each picture and Carlton Books Limited apologises for any unintentional errors or omissions that will be corrected in future editions of this book.